Ariel and the Police

Books by Frank Lentricchia

The Gaiety of Language (1968)

Robert Frost: Modern Poetics and the Landscapes of Self (1975)

Robert Frost: A Bibliography (1976) (with Melissa Lentricchia)

After the New Criticism (1980)

Criticism and Social Change (1983)

Ariel
and
the
Police

Michel Foucault, William James, Wallace Stevens

FRANK LENTRICCHIA

THE UNIVERSITY OF WISCONSIN PRESS

Published 1988

The University of Wisconsin Press
114 North Murray Street
Madison, Wisconsin 53715

First Printing

Printed in the United States of America

Library of Congress Cataloging-in-Publication Data
Lentricchia, Frank.
Ariel and the police.
Includes index.
1. Stevens, Wallace, 1874–1955—Criticism and
interpretation. 2. Foucault, Michel—Influence.
3. James, William, 1842–1910—Influence. 4. Criticism.
I. Title.
PS3537.T4753Z6746 1988   811'.52   87-18885
ISBN 0-299-11540-2

For My Grandparents

TOMASO IACOVELLA
Sept. 2, 1882–Aug. 19, 1972

NATALINA MATTIA IACOVELLA
Dec. 25, 1887–Feb. 18, 1970

AUGUSTO LENTRICCHIA
June 10, 1892–Aug. 6, 1980

PAOLINA DICASTRO LENTRICCHIA
Nov. 12, 1892–Dec. 9, 1972

Now, Ariel, rescue me from police and all that kind of thing.

WALLACE STEVENS

Contents

Acknowledgments

My thanks to several for reading and commenting on parts of the manuscript: Jonathan Arac, Leigh DeNeef, Fred Jameson, Linda Kauffman, Lou Renza, Jane Tompkins, Robert Von Hallberg, and Susan Willis; to Myra Jehlen and Don Pease for reading the entire manuscript and for helpful reactions; and most of all to Melissa Lentricchia for reading it all many times and for many, many other things.

Portions of this book appeared in somewhat different form in *Critical Inquiry*, *Cultural Critique*, and *Raritan*.

Ariel and the Police

Anatomy of a Jar

There's a little story told by Wallace Stevens that I need to retell—actually it's an anecdote (*anekdota*, in the Greek, meaning unpublished items; more familiarly, in English, a small gossipy narrative generally of an amusing and biographical incident in the life of an important person). The anecdote I have in mind (like all anecdotes) is also a representation; in Kenneth Burke's searching phrase, a "representative anecdote."[1] So a hitherto unpublished little story, funny and biographical, apparently stands in for a bigger story, a socially pivotal and culturally pervasive biography which it illuminates—in an anecdotal flash it reveals the essence of the larger unspoken story, and in that very moment becomes exegesis of a public text; the unpublished items become published. The teller of anecdotes must presume the cultural currency of a containing biographical narrative which he draws upon for the sharp point he would give his anecdote, whose true function is political: to trigger a narrative sense of community that the evoked master biography helps to sustain by shaping. Biography so become cultural myth underwrites collective cohesion—we feel ourselves to be part of a social narrative—even as the myth gives cohesion to, as it contains, its various constituent anecdotes.

One day, when he was a little boy, George Washington chopped down a cherry tree in his father's orchard. Americans usually get the point in a hurry; the punch line need not be said. One day, my grandfather, my mother's father, at age seventy-nine, while rocking and smoking (but not inhaling) on his front porch in Utica, New York, in mid-August heat (which he refused to recognize by wearing his long johns), directed his grandson's attention (who was then about thirteen) to the man sitting on *his* front porch across the street: not rocking or smoking but huddled into himself, as if it were cold, aged eighty. Gesturing with cigarette in hand toward "this American," as he called him (in Italian he inserted between "this" and "American" an adjective best left untranslated), all the while nodding, and in a tone that I recognized only later as much crafted, he said: *La vecchiáia è carógna.* A story of biographical incident, funny if you can translate the Italian, but representative? Probably only in the mind of yours truly. You don't because through no fault of your own you probably can't get the point, though some in my family would—as would many first-generation Italian Americans, some fewer of the second generation, and fewer yet of my generation. My mother's father is dead, and those who remember him (and immigrants like him) in the right way, with necessary specificity, where do I find them? Soon this will be an anecdote for me alone because soon it will have no claim whatsoever to being what all we anecdotalists want our stories to be—a social form which instigates cultural memory: the act of narrative renewal, the reinstatement of social cohesion. Stevens' story is no more accessible than the one I just told about my grandfather. There is no Italian to trouble us in Stevens' story but its language is equally foreign and its representational power equally in peril.

So when the relation of the teller of anecdotes to a potential audience ceases altogether to be unified by a single myth, anecdotes will lose their rhetorical power. The anecdote will become (alas!) autonomous, a story for itself alone, not a literary form whose genealogy, in parable and fable, underwrites an equation of literary and social forms as forms of instruction. If anecdotes had minds of their own they'd probably say, we don't like modernist literary theories of aesthetic self-sufficiency; restore us, good reader, to the way we were. The anecdotes about George Washington are of course ceaselessly renewed— their subject (in both senses) is redeemed by the political process of American history. But who will renew my grandfather's cultural story? For whom can my grandfather's biography be important? What might it mediate? Who, anyway, makes an anecdote work—its first author or its cultural authorizer (who is rarely the first author), who by providing us with its mediations thereby both binds and activates us collectively with its cultural power?

Anecdotes would appear by their very nature to depend on a stable outside narrative, given and known, but in fact—and most dramatically in their written, high literary style—they work at critical turning points of cultural crisis when the outside narrative seems to be slipping away and its ideological energy is at lowest ebb. The anecdotalist's role (or desire) is to represent but by way of retrieval and re-creation. To tell us what we think we already know is an effect of the genial style (trick) of his rhetoric—a literary bonding proleptic, he hopes, for the social and historical bonding that he wants to resuscitate and whose absence is the trigger of his little storytelling. The anecdotalist's act of memory is generative, critical, and cautionary: his implication is always let us remember together, take it to heart, see the bigger picture. The anecdotalist is therefore necessarily a deliberately cryptic teacher; he knows that what he wants he can't achieve alone; his largest hope is to engender an engaged readership whose cohesion will lie in a common commitment to a social project and the sustaining of life therein.

So here's the little story that I promised at the beginning as it was originally told by Wallace Stevens:

Anecdote of the Jar

I placed a jar in Tennessee,
And round it was, upon a hill.
It made the slovenly wilderness
Surround that hill.

The wilderness rose up to it,
And sprawled around, no longer wild.
The jar was round upon the ground
And tall and of a port in air.

It took dominion everywhere.
The jar was gray and bare.
It did not give of bird or bush,
Like nothing else in Tennessee.

The advantage of beginning with this odd little genre of anecdotal lyric in the practice of Wallace Stevens is that we are
forced at the outset into confronting the inadequacy of the
modernist literary theory of aesthetic autonomy (inadequate
but possessed of many more than nine lives) and its corol-
lary critical stance of trying to situate and constrain all commentary within the text's formal boundaries. In its own most
deeply felt metaphor, the classic formalist reading featured in
Anglo-American New Criticism is "close" reading—a desire
for textual intimacy whose logic implies the end of reading
in self-effacement, all the while, against its logic, elaborating
itself in complex performances more complex, say its detrac-
tors, than the text being read. The American New Criticism,
whose death has been periodically announced ever since the
late 1950s, remains in force as the basis (what goes without saying) of undergraduate literary pedagogy, so that, having passed
into the realm of common sense, it has the ideological effect
in the United States of sustaining, under conditions of mass
higher education, the romantic cult of genius by dispossessing
middle-class readers of their active participation in the shaping
of a culture and a society "of and for the people." The New Criticism strips those readers of their right to think of themselves
as culturally central storytellers: an extraordinary irony for a
critical method whose initial effect was entirely democratic—
to make the reading of classics available to all, even to those
of us whose early cultural formation did not equip us to read
Shakespeare and Milton—but a predictable irony, in retrospect,
when we remember that new critical reading at the same time

defined and valued itself as secondary reading of explication. So while the New Criticism taught us to read, it simultaneously taught us how to subordinate our reading powers and humble ourselves before the "creative" authority of an ontologically superior primary writing. (The bibliographical convention of distinguishing between primary and secondary texts is here politically symptomatic.)

As a metaliterary phenomenon, anecdotal form is a representation of radical aesthetic unself-sufficiency: at the very moment of formal engagement, which cryptically crafted, riddle-like anecdotes (like this one of Wallace Stevens) force us into with all possible zeal for close reading, we are led beyond the assumptions of formalism. The anecdotal lyric is (at best) a marginal and eccentric literary form, but its eccentricity may bring all the way forward what is most typical about literary form—its resistance to formalist desire for closure: there is always something outside the text. The title of Stevens' poem and the first line make the point: "I placed a jar in Tennessee," but this is not an anecdote about a jar: it is an anecdote of *the* jar. However stylized for the purposes of anecdotal point making, however absurd if thought about through the norms of realism, the act described in the first line must nevertheless be imagined *as if* it were existentially typical. The little action of this little story begins when someone places a single object some place, but the poem asks us in its title to conceive of the particular act and the particular object placed by this particular "I" as an expressive instance of what can't be perceived and what isn't and can't be directly written about: a generic act, a generic object, a generic "I." Moreover, this is an anecdote that does not, apparently, centrally involve the human actor who places the jar and without whom presumably the jar could not be placed (since jars cannot place themselves). This is an anecdote about the jar itself, not jar placing: a fragment from the *jar's* biography. The larger narrative of which this poem is an unpublished item has to do with the jar's ideal form, its *jarness* not its *thisness*. Apparently the ideal character of the jar is the larger narrative text of which this specific jar that was placed in Tennessee is an example. In this light, the preposition in the title ("of") means not "about" but something like "belonging to," as if the jar could speak, as if the poem were really about a story that a jar might tell about itself.

But if we learn anything from Plato about ideal things we learn that there is no time in them or for them: ideal entities are part of no story. In anecdote, however, we must have narrative and the temporal dimension, and this specific anecdote of Stevens does not disappoint us: it unfolds initially as the description of an action and the effects or consequences of that action—not as the description of a jar (and not as *the consequences of a jar:* absurd phrasing for an absurd but importantly mystifying idea). The connection of jar and human subject is unavoidable in Stevens' poem (for a while); this is a poem (or so it appears in the first line) about the consequences of jar placing. The devout formalist critic can notice but not respond (as a formalist) to questions of an economic sort that begin to press upon him at this point; nothing would seem to be further from the literary texture of this poem's mode and content. Can the consequences of jars be conceived apart from the intentional human process which produces and manipulates them? Puts them, for example, on hills in Tennessee? How can any inert product of human labor ever be spoken of as having in itself consequences, as if the thing had intentions of its own? These questions are precisely questions that the poem forces us to ask because the "I" who does the initial act of placing gets lost after the first line. The human actor becomes a panoramic onlooker, a distant voice, an innocent bystander: the jar takes on, somehow, an intentional life of its own: "I placed" but "It made" and "It took" and "It did not give." The jar did it. This jar, and the character of being possessed by any jar, are necessarily implicated with human activity, yet that fact is what is shunted aside after this poem's first line. The formalist critic, forced to talk about content, and Stevens' form gives him no choice, will quickly move to the humanist's favorite sort of generalization.

Human action will be essentialized: with all specific determinants of history drained off, the activity of jar placing becomes an archetypal human act, and the anecdote/parable/fable called "Anecdote of the Jar" concerns the consequences of the type of human activity (what shall it be called?) best particularized and named by the qualities possessed by a jar, and not just any jar but the sort signaled by the modifications of grayness and bareness. This story is getting curiouser and curiouser: a human act that is like a gray, bare jar?

The act of jar placing is contextualized, almost literally—it is surrounded by wilderness—and its consequences are illuminated by the natural setting within which the act is said to take place. At the point in our formalist moment at which we notice *that*, we are tempted to step outside the aesthetic monad of the single, isolated text and step into Northrop Frye's decisively postulated closed literary universe of modes and mythoi, a synchronic totality of ever-present literary forms. We quickly translate "jar" and "wilderness" into the generative structural binary of art and nature always present to the pastoral mode, though this move from the closed, atemporal world of the isolated text to the closed, atemporal world of the autonomous literary universe will be made with a clean conscience only if the critic making that jump can ignore the word "Tennessee": a political designation, out of the lexicon of sovereignty, social order placed in the wild. Jar placing, then, is a second placing and a second ordering whose action is an echo and repetition of a politically original act of state placing? Our formalism, which couldn't help but also be a humanism, now seems poised to serve the historicist interests of American studies.

It's hard to get through our formalist moment to whatever it is that is always outside the text: the textual woods is so lovely, dark and deep. Wanting to get on with it, see the thing whole, we find it hard to get out of the first stanza. The transpositions come easily, maybe too easily: jar vs. wilderness, as art vs. nature, as culture vs. nature. But a *slovenly* nature? This eye-catching and provocative little breakdown in decorum, firmly foregrounded by the only significant metrical substitution in the poem, sends us off into etymological research (Stevens was mad for etymologies) where we find not only what we expect ("untidy especially in dress or person, largely slipshod") but, also, in close company, *sloven,* a noun in Flemish signifying a woman of low character; in adjectival form, "uncultivated, undeveloped" (in a social as well as agricultural sense). So: culture vs. nature as masculine vs. feminine? Mother Nature as a low-class slut? Is *that* somehow being said in this poem? We'd better look harder at point of view: mainly panoramic, yes, but at two crucial spots limited. In the first stanza, we see the world for a moment according to a jar, refusing to keep its proud sense of its own well-formed self to itself, smugly taking itself as the distributing point of order and sole topographical coordinate; we see wilderness forced out of itself into order: "It made the slovenly wilderness / Surround that hill"; and in the third and last stanza we experience the point of view of the wilderness in the sense that the panoramic speaker takes the side of the wilderness. An old point of controversy about this poem—is Stevens *for* art or *for* nature?—disappears when we note that he lets nature get the last word in by characterizing the autonomous jar of art, at the end of the poem, as an absence of nature. Nature: maternal, creative, pliant; the jar: a receptacle that doesn't receive and from which nothing emerges—inflexible, hard, and possessed by a classic case of womb envy. "It did not give of bird or bush, / Like nothing else in Tennessee."

Formalists must all sooner or later come to the grievous conclusion about "Anecdote of the Jar" that the aged Ezra Pound came to about his *Cantos:* it will not cohere. And things only get worse: the imposing jar is also a "port" (haven? gate? but for whom?). The original structural opposition of "jar" and "wilderness," an opposition of nouns as substances, modulates into an opposition of verbs or actions: jars "take," the wilderness "gives." Jars take power—"dominion" (supreme authority, sovereignty, absolute ownership). Who is responsible for this power? Certainly not "I"; the jar did it. No longer can we avoid the question of tone; the postulate of the literary universe will not help us now, no amount of knowledge—not even Frye's—about literary structure will help us here to hear. Structuralists, by definition, cannot attend to nonrepeatable textures of voice; structuralists, by definition, are tone-deaf. So what are we to make of the reiterated sounds of jar music, in the major key of "round"? A whole lot of "round" for such a short poem: surround, around, round (twice), ground. "Round": an insidiously invasive sound which evokes at this poem's aural level all of the big thematic points condensed in the key word of the poem: "dominion." Dominion "everywhere"— "everywhere"/"air"/"bare"—this triplet, in a poem otherwise devoid of rhyme, is unavoidable to the ear: a saturating totality, a faceless totality of authority. The jar is into every damn thing. In the world according to the jar, this aural imperialist, there is barely, just barely, one letter's worth of ground: mainly, in this world, there is "g-round." This madly incisive and potentially scary jabberwockian sense is the decisive entry to the poet's panoramic point of view, his presiding tonality: detached, above it all, neither for jars nor for nature, he writes in playful self-possession (whatever else you can say about him he's certainly not frightened of anything) this line, best read in the manner of W. C. Fields: "The jar was round upon the ground."

Northrop Frye's structuralist postulate of a literary universe of forms, always and simultaneously present to literary choice, encourages us to see Stevens' poem as a variant of traditional pastoral, and Stevens himself as on the side of nature and spontaneity (against art, culture, and systematic literariness). But the key to interpretation is not really *in* the genre that he's working with. It's in the peculiar, particular, and surprising tonal textures—in the mockery of the jar on its own aural terms ("round" being the sound which echoes the jar's essential formal property), in the individual talent over whom no tradition takes dominion. Having come to that conclusion, however, we are not much closer to answering the most pressing question of form that this poem poses: what, really, is this an anecdote of, what cautionary tale is embedded in the last line ("Like nothing else in Tennessee"), which is beginning to sound more and more like a finger-wagging warning to all us actual and would-be jar placers. If the tonal posture of this poem could not possibly be predicted, no matter how much we know about the binary oppositions of pastoral poetry, if this vocal feature seems original with this poet's handling of the genre, then maybe we need to look more deeply into this poet. And suddenly the next interpretive move virtually presents itself to us as our most enticing option yet. It seems so necessary: what is the place of "Anecdote of the Jar" within Stevens' corpus, the literary universe that inheres peculiarly in his writings taken as a totality? Not as texts written over a period of years but as texts present to one another as if they had been written all at once, in a single expressive act, bearing the poet's vision as if that vision were somehow wholly and always present to its constitutive texts, as their shaping presence.

"Anecdote of the Jar" has two contexts in Stevens' corpus. In the first, its occasion of publication, in Harriet Monroe's *Poetry*, in 1919, the poem appeared as part of an ensemble, under a title expressive of Stevens' early self-conscious decadence: "Pecksniffiana." After the original ensemble of fourteen poems was accepted, but not yet published, Stevens made several substitutions: one of them was "Anecdote of the Jar," and another he calls a "trifle" whose title, "The Indigo Glass in the Grass," will make us hear once again the aural joke "The jar was round upon the ground." In "Anecdote of the Jar" Stevens' self-deprecating decadent theory of the poem as "trifle," as his inconsequential toy (Peck's bad boy as self-ironic aesthete?) reaches through itself, in trifling play, to something more than play. The odd harmony of the Pecksniffiana ensemble consists of a blending of the tones of playfulness and dead seriousness—a blend that "Anecdote of the Jar," better than any poem in the ensemble, perfectly concentrates. In the poetic corpus as a whole, the other context or occasion, Stevens' jar poem joins several other early poems with the formal term "anecdote" as part of their title, and, then, in his middle and later years, joins a continuing and troubled meditative strain present to virtually everything that he wrote. In this context "Anecdote of the Jar" is something like a microcosm in which jars find essential kinship with various artifacts like glasses, bowls, poetic images, thought itself, even poems, and with large conceptions, in his middle and later career, of the "hero" and "major man": all various forms and effects of systematic endeavor; all the creation of structure, systems, reasons; all effects—in a word ambivalently dear to him—of "abstraction." But:

> It was when I said,
> "There is no such thing as the truth,"
> That the grapes seemed fatter.
> The fox ran out of his hole.
>
> . . . .
> It is posed and it is posed
> But in nature it merely grows.
>
> . . . .
> You must become an ignorant man again
> And see the sun again with an ignorant eye. . . .
>
> . . . .
> How clean the sun when seen in its idea,
> Washed in the remotest cleanliness of a heaven
> That has expelled us and our images. . . .[2]

That last ellipsis is not mine; it belongs most originally to Wallace Stevens: a subtle signifier of awe, what motivates the words preceding it but what can't be said in words, imaged, or conceived. The ellipsis: not words left out, but words impossible. In 1913, in the midst of modernist revolution in poetry and philosophy, Josiah Royce replayed George Santayana's attack on Whitman as a poet of barbarism by characterizing this yearning for pure perception as a sign of the modernist times: perception as a moment of consciousness utterly final, with perceiver and perceived unified in an isolated fulfillment before all community and all conversation.[3] This unspeakable moment represented by the ellipsis, this radical desire for the first perception, prior to reason, would wipe out our history and our tradition ("us and our images"): perception, the image, the attack on reason, and the interest in the primitive are all code terms for the literary and artistic modernisms whose solidarity consists in the hatred of what sociologists call modernization. Santayana's word, "barbarism," is fair as far as it goes. What it does not do justice to is the modernist's nostalgia for the barbarous, his feeling of being out of place ("You must become an ignorant man again"): his willingness to suspend social relations, not because he's antisocial but because the society he finds himself in seems to have designs upon his health.

Jars are metonyms of modernization: they get in the way, they mediate. Jars are like bowls: cold, a cold porcelain, low and round . . . a bowl brilliant in its clarity. The day becomes a bowl of white, the world becomes a world of white.[4] Jars and bowls have centers because they are the products of rationalists, those fanciers of square hats. We want so much more than that; the imperfect is our paradise:

> It was when the trees were leafless first in November
> And their blackness became apparent, that one first
> Knew the eccentric to be the base of design.[5]

The "eccentric," or uncentered, as subversive foundation of "design" understood as intention without prior conception, purpose, plan, project, scheme, plot: intention somehow unintended. The eccentric, or uncentered, as also the subversive foundation of "design" understood as structure (shape, pattern) without classic structurality—structure somehow unstructured yet still structured. The eccentric is the base of *design*. Design, from the Latin *designare*, and *signare* from *signum* (a mark or sign): eccentric signs would be signs unplotted, surprising. Eccentric design would resolve the greatest of antinomies because it would be both necessary and spontaneous; a form of determination, yet free. Jars—they're not that kind of design, and what's more they seem to have designs upon power. They take dominion, they can even make something as unmanageable as a wilderness shape up, imitate their structural roundedness. A jar can make a wilderness surround itself; a jar can make the very ground into its mirror. Jars are humorless narcissists who think they are ungrounded. And they are involved in a secret, undercover narrative (a "plot"): What is it?

To move, as I just have, from the single poem as closed, isolate, verbal system, a world unto itself, to the poem as microcosmic fragment of a poetic corpus, is to move, in a sense, not at all: for the corpus so conceived, as a synchronic whole, is likewise closed and isolate. And to invoke an agent called "the poet" as creator of a corpus is to invoke a subject who always contained and expressed it all, so that those temporal distinctions of career ("early," "middle," and "late") are truly gratuitous—they make no difference. Not even "career," in this interpretive context, makes much sense since the term suggests a determinate act of will to shape a life, to set an ordered narrative in motion and thereby bring your life into control (into art) by making it a story. To so read either the single poem or the corpus, as I have, is to read *for* (look for, read on behalf of, from the perspective of) self-sufficient system. To invoke "the poet" in this context is not to invoke a human being who needs to be differentiated by categories of, say, class, or gender, or race (or all three) and who would need to be historically located; it is to invoke an agent whose function is to trigger a verbal agency which, once triggered, mysteriously operates itself as a rule-bound machine. In either instance, single poem or corpus, the verbal system must be treated as if it were its own magnificent cause of being. "The poet" so invoked as an originator is a necessary fiction (we have to invoke an individual at some point), yet at some other level he must be real ("Wallace Stevens" after all is the name of a person who was born, went to Harvard, liked his mother better than his father, married, worked for an insurance company and loved it, often took vacations to Florida alone, listened to the Saturday afternoon broadcasts from the Metropolitan Opera House, did not get divorced, made a lot of money, died of cancer, and maybe converted on his deathbed if you want to believe the nuns who attended him at the end, which I do.) Wallace Stevens, "the poet," is not subject to those modifications. For devout critics of system—all structuralists by deed if not by name—he is a verbal operator who functions in an ideal space.

But to pose the question about narratives, secret or otherwise, as I have throughout, is to move to history, or at least to be poised (or seem to be poised) at the brink of concerted historical reading. Even the devoutest formalist critic cheats; history makes them do it. I'm not devout; I've cheated two or three times to this point, I'm not quite sure how many, contaminating formal purity by mentioning Tennessee and American studies, and it could have been worse. I held back mentioning that Tennessee is an englishing of a Cherokee place name—a Cherokee village named Tanasi. And no use getting too sentimental about Indians and the wilderness. It was here first, apparently, I mean the wilderness, then the Indians, who "our forefathers" (whose forefathers?) slaughtered. Tennessee eventually took dominion over Tanasi, but the Indians did a little political placing of their own; they engaged frequently in their own territorial wars with considerable intensity. They set their cultures in the wilderness first; then we placed ours over theirs: we supplanted them, plowed them under. Jar placing, then, is a third-order placing? A metonymic representation of a repetitive action of domination, hard to separate from the course of American history?

I also brought in Josiah Royce and what he thought of modernism—he didn't like it but he knew what it was—and I wrote down dates, 1913, when Royce published the statements I alluded to, and 1919, when Stevens published "Anecdote of the Jar." Nineteen-nineteen becomes a readable fact for interpretation within the historical horizon of avant-garde modernist upheaval; that is the poem's immediate cultural context; its date of publication makes that context surround the poem. "Tennessee" is more difficult. It is surely a term for interpretation but one that resists formalist reading, though not altogether if we can count, as "reading," formalist forgetting ("jarring") of its ground, a covering of the ground not unlike the way Tennessee covers up Tanasi. "Tennessee" looks like a determinate historical and political term in Stevens' poem, looks like an unambiguous invitation to do the work of historicizing this poem, but probably "gap" is better than "term." What are the limits of the historical horizon within which we would situate "Tennessee"? How far back does it go? To the Cherokee Indians? How far forward? Maybe all the way to Vietnam.

In its immediate literary culture Stevens' critique of artifice joins the general critique, at the center of the imagist movement and polemically (and entrepreneurially) urged in the criticism of Ezra Pound, of what was passing for "literature." It was a critique not of literature *tout court* but of official poetic practice in the 1890s and early years of this century, when those who would become the chief modernists were growing up and beginning to read what was being honored as "contemporary" poetry—an exercise, or so it seemed to Pound, Frost, and others, in ever-increasing poetic vagueness inversely proportioned to the ever-increasing particularity (often of a harsh sort) in the language of realist fiction; frightened literariness, withdrawal into genteel hermitage. As Frost tirelessly pointed out, it was a language that never was, except in books: real people, at any rate—Frost meant those not born to high cultural privilege— don't talk *that* way. In this light, poetic modernism is round 2 of English romanticism, especially in its Wordsworthian phase. Pound's revisions of Yeats's early poems are in the mode of Wordsworth's legendary attack on Thomas Gray in the preface to *Lyrical Ballads*, as is Stevens' late meditation in *Notes toward a Supreme Fiction*, when he evokes and then one-ups Wordsworth's attack on Gray's use of archaic language. Stevens writes, "the sun must bear no name," not even the name "sun," which is just as artificial as "Phoebus"—the mythological object of Wordsworth's literary and social-revolutionary scorn. The sun must simply be, let be, "in the difficulty of what it is to be." Words are like jars: Shelley thought the truth to be imageless;[6] Stevens, immoralist of modernist lyric, appeared to think it altogether silent.

Wordsworth's critique of Gray is part of the larger romantic injunction: to "strip the evil of familiarity" from the world.[7] Not to make it strange but to see the strangeness there: a radically realist epistemological project replayed in the theoretical premises of imagism by Pound and T. E. Hulme. ("Could reality come into direct contact with sense and consciousness, art would be useless," Hulme wrote, "or rather we should all be artists."[8] Or as Pound urged the project of the image: "Direct treatment of the 'thing,' whether subjective or objective."[9]) A radically realist project, epistemologically, and an ethical and political project as well. Wordsworth's attack, like Frost's later on mannered language, is also an attack on the manners (social and poetic) of a class. Wordsworth argues, on behalf of a newly emergent class (of which Frost may be the great American modernist representative), that the poetry of privilege speaks nothing like the language spoken by real men in a state of nature, who work farms, or the language of the new urban worker sunk into "savage torpor" by the self-alienating nature of his labor. The poetry of privilege—Frost is especially strong on this point—does not *speak;* it has no aural referent in the various worlds of communication (not even in the world of the privileged). Stevens, who had none of Frost's vocal sentiments, makes critical allusion to the issue by surrounding the pompous and empty "port" (comportment, carriage, syntax) of jar-speak ("of a port in air") with plain-speaking syntax ("I placed a jar in Tennessee"). A new poetry would presumably clear our consciousness—"wash" it "clean" of artifice and a contaminating social discourse and bring us into contact with (help us to see again, re-cognize) a social outside, a "ground" ruled and exploited by the class represented by Gray, the social outside now seen in an act of sympathy which a new poetry would encourage. The social and socialist implications of Wordsworth's theory of the poet (an instigator of radical community, he "binds together by passion and knowledge the vast empire of human society, as it is spread over the whole earth"; he does "not write for poets alone, but for men"),[10] these implications were drawn out by Shelley: "The great secret of morals is love; or a going out of our own nature, and an identification of ourselves with [a] person not our own. A man, to be greatly good, must imagine intensely and comprehensively; he must put himself in the place of another and of many others."[11] As a figure for the poetry opposed (not for the same reasons and on behalf of different goals) by Wordsworth, Frost, and Pound, the jar shows kinship with the letter that kills (jars do not "give of bird or bush"). Jars are representations not of the spirit of love but of the spirit of abstraction. In the romantic lexicon, from Wordsworth to Stevens, "artifice" and "abstraction" are synonyms and key coded words in a political anecdote of struggle.

Stevens' is an American jar, plain, bare, and gray, not Thomas Gray-like and not richly worked and elaborated, like Keats's Grecian urn, but something of a commentary on Keats's most famous ode and on Keats himself: commentary not in anxiety and competitiveness but in self-definition and political critique very close to home. This is a jar that provokes in Stevens no Keatsian desire for the death of identification and therefore no Keatsian pulling back from self-extinguishment, no Keatsian shock of awareness that the urn's life is dead life, no need to say "cold pastoral." And Stevens' jar is not tempting for another reason. It represents nothing like Keats's double-edged Western cultural heritage maybe worth being embarrassed by because maybe (for Keats) worth recuperating, sustaining, being engaged with. Nor is Stevens replaying Henry James's criticism of American culture as too thin to support really "fine" writing. Stevens' biographical formation is close to that of Keats, but its American ground kept him from wishing to die out of his unprivileged class into the class of a precapitalist landed aristocracy (there is no American memory for this) which bears the burden of tradition. Keats's desire to die, reread from Stevens' perspective, is a desire for social death and rebirth: to become not a sod or a nightingale but a gentleman.

Stevens' poem, in this double focus of literary and social history, is an American poem which at once works as a metapoem, an anecdote of the wider cultural story of romantic and early-modernist poetics, an antipoetics urging a literature against official literature, and a critical evaluation of the wider story. The literary criticism which Stevens called "Anecdote of the Jar" is a criticism not of Grecian urns and Thomas Gray's poetry but of plain old democratic American jars which he insists we see as figuring a work of oppression that cannot be explained in classic European terms of class relations (in classic Marxist terms). Wordsworth and Keats had the griefs and consolations of English society at a moment of decisive social change—they might have said: "The jar is them." Stevens, who has some of Wordsworth's and Frost's feeling for ordinary people, who celebrated ignorance in his poems as the pure access to the real, who once said of himself, in self-congratulation, that he had been working like an immigrant Italian,[12] who never wanted to write in the language of real men and, like Shelley, never did, has no sentimentality for democratic myths. He forces us to say: "The jar is us."

Had Wallace Stevens lived through our Vietnam period he might have had the right answer to the question posed by Norman Mailer in 1967: *Why Are We in Vietnam?* Had he forgotten what he knew, long before our military intervention in Southeast Asia, he would have been (had he lived so long) reminded by Michael Herr who at the end of his book *Dispatches* (1970) wrote: "Vietnam Vietnam Vietnam, we've all been there." Herr maybe in part knew what he knew because he had read Stevens, who taught him about where we've all been, all along: "Once it was all locked in place, Khe Sanh became like the planted jar in Wallace Stevens' poem. It took dominion everywhere."[13] Herr's perversely perfect mixed metaphor of the "planted jar," if it might have struck Stevens as an incisive reading of his poem, might also have awakened in him an obscure memory of one of the powerful philosophical presences of his Harvard days, William James, writing out of the bitterness of his political awakening, writing on 1 March 1899 in the *Boston Transcript* against our first imperial incursion in the Orient: "We are destroying down to the root every germ of a healthy national life in these unfortunate people. . . . We must sow our ideals, plant our order, impose our God."[14] James might have ended his letter: "The Philippines the Philippines the Philippines, we've all been there."

The hypothetical "ifs" and subjunctive "mights" which fairly pepper my preceding paragraph may represent something like the lure of bad-faith political criticism: the desire for objective laws of historical force to offer themselves to the reader who then need only record them as the true causes of texts like "Anecdote of the Jar" and *Dispatches*. James and Stevens, of course, did not read Herr; Herr did read Stevens, but I see no reason to think that he read James. Herr, Stevens, and James can be constellated as a single discursive body only because I've read them in a certain way; I name the constellation, I give it a shape: "can be constellated," a deluded construction; its passivity obscures what goes on in the act of interpretation. So my hypotheticals and subjunctives may be taken in another way, as an indication of where we always stand in the interpretive act: not on the realist's terra firma but in active ideological contest to shape our culture's sense of history. I offer Herr, Stevens, and James (in that order, reading backward, which is always the way reading takes place: through our cultural formation) as three voices from a tradition of American anti-imperialist writing (a unified cultural practice) that cuts through the boundaries of philosophy, poetry, and journalism, a discourse of political criticism.

Stevens' poem is an anecdote of that political story, but to reach for American anti-imperialism and isolationism in the first two decades of this century, when he was coming of age as a writer, as the political cause of his poem is absurd, yet no more absurd perhaps than to reach for objective laws of historical influence. In either instance what is longed for is direct reflection of political reality in a literary text, a vulgar form of historicism, periodically practiced in Marxist circles (though hardly limited to those), in which the "time" of the literary text is treated as one and the same with political "time," as if the episode in the Philippines gave rise to the poem. The varieties of vulgar formalism are more useful; they at least put the stress where it belongs, on the strange differences; it is easier to believe in literary causalities of literary texts, as if literature were self-originating. For the text in question, these causalities might be: Stevens' verbal play, the generic history of pastoral, the inner imperatives of Stevens' unfolding corpus, the literary-historical forces of romanticism, the first surge of modernist literary polemic, manifesto, and experiment (the ethical imperative of imagism). As an "effect" of such "causes," "Anecdote of the Jar" partakes of the time of literature whose integrity seems impervious to "outside" pressures. But it isn't: cultural practices are neither autonomous nor homogeneous. With all differences respected, they sometimes are made to stand in unity by acts of reading, acts of re-telling or cultural constellating like Herr's remembering of Stevens in Vietnam, like my remembering of Herr's and James's anti-imperialist efforts; like my placing of Stevens as a writer "between" James and Herr and "between" our first intervention in Cuba, 21 April 1898, and our second intervention in Cuba, 21 April 1961. The storyteller's most powerful effect comes when he convinces us that what is particular, integrated, and different in a cultural practice (like the writing of rarefied high-modernist poetry) is part of a cultural plot that makes coherent sense of all cultural practices as a totality: not a totality that is there, waiting for us to acknowledge its presence, but a totality fashioned when the storyteller convinces us to see it his way.

It would have been possible to speak, as I have not yet spoken, of the intersection of literary causes and Stevens' personal social history: his literary self-consciousness as a middle-class American male who faced economic imperatives that his aristocratic European and English predecessors did not have to face.

It would have been possible to link his sexual pun on "slovenly nature" and his phallic parody of the jar—it may look like a port but nothing enters, it receives nothing—with his sexual self-consciousness, the suspicion which his father encouraged that real men don't write poems. Those are in fact the sorts of possibilities that I pursue in the third section of this book, "Writing after Hours," in an effort to redeem the personal subject of Wallace Stevens for history by thinking about his poems as literary actions. In the course of pursuing that effort I write small critiques of new historicism, neopragmatism, and essentialist feminism, but I've written critically at no one isolable place on literary Marxism because I intend the book as a whole to be a dialogue with Marxism precisely on the issue of the personal subject which it dismisses by calling a bourgeois illusion.[15] Like other contemporary styles of criticism, Marxism has a way of jarring the subject out of its historical orbit: either by ignoring it or by merging it much too soon with a social text—obliterating the subject by making it immediately typical. Contemporary literary Marxism is a representation of the broad range of contemporary critical theory whose origins in France and the United States constitute the triumph of structuralism over Sartre's desire to turn Marxist thought to actual individuals acting in history. Sartre's *Search for a Method*, the road not taken in contemporary theory, was simply routed by the voracious Abstractionism put into vogue by Lévi-Strauss and Frye—and still with us. Literary Marxists, like other contemporary theorists, will have virtually nothing to do with biography—impatient for the secret plot, they get there too quickly. I think we most believe in plots when they are hard to see; and a conspiracy that includes James, Foucault, and Stevens had better be hard to see.

Contemporary styles of literary theory and practice resemble nothing so much as Don De Lillo's funny anecdotal personification (in *Ratner's Star*) of a terrible fear not really separable from the modernist dream. Consider De Lillo's "Supreme Abstract Commander": one Chester Greylag Dent, "unaffiliated and stateless," who lives in a nuclear-powered submarine, thirty-five thousand feet under the sea ("just idling there in the dark and cold . . . the quietest place on earth") attended by a eunuch who talks of an international cartel interested in "abstract economic power" and named ACRONYM (a "combination of letters formed to represent the idea of a combination of letters"); who is so old as to verge on transparency; who has been awarded a Nobel Prize in literature for his books on mathematics and logic, "handblocked in a style best described as undiscourageably diffuse"; who says in response to the question, What do you do? "I think of myself as the Supreme Abstract Commander. That's what I do"; who considers us mortals "not as a collection of races and nationalities but as a group that shows the same taxonomic classification, that of Earth-planet extant"; who never laughs but instead, when moved to such spontaneous expression, says, "Hilarious," or "Extremely mirth-provoking"—Chester Greylag Dent, who believes that the reason that he has been referred to "more than a few times as the greatest man in the world" has to do with "the life choice I've made. To suspend myself in the ocean zone of perpetual darkness. To inhabit an environment composed almost solely of tiny sightless feeble-minded creatures palpitating in the ooze"; who when asked about his shawls says he buys them from "this man in Sausalito."[16]

When he wants to, De Lillo can evoke the horrors of abstraction, not impotently removed, but actively engaged in a deadly work of the sort which Herr describes in the work of MACV (an acronym representing Military Assistance Command, Vietnam), or in the cartographic work of reinscribing Vietnam as a military arena "which made for clear communication, at least among members of the Mission and the many components of . . . the fabulous MACV." And "fabulous" is just right: of a fable, not Vietnamese, generating and imposing a fable not Vietnamese: "Since most of the journalism from the war was framed in that language [MACV, I Corps, II Corps, DMZ] it would be as impossible to know what Vietnam looked like from reading most newspaper stories as it would be to know how it smelled." Like Stevens' and like De Lillo's, Herr's writing is a counterdiscourse, working to undermine discourses of abstraction and domination—Supreme Abstract Commanders, whether they are called jars, the ruling class, Khe Sanh, or MACV, or imperialism. These counterdiscourses imply (rarely state) their deepest alternative values in desires for particularity; in the way it looked and smelled; in little scraps of dialogue about "this man in Sausalito." For life in the small things, "birds and bushes," which ought to be but are not invulnerable to imperial imposition.[17]

The object of De Lillo's unmasking humor is captured in other stories which are not funny, told with great penetration by William James and Michel Foucault in reaction to their nightmare of system and discipline: the horrific accompaniments of what sociologists call modernization. Foucault's disciplinary society and James's systematic life are the outcomes of a historical process and are twin accounts insofar as they take the price of modernity to be the loss of self-determination in the normalizing actions of institutional life that James, long before Foucault, excoriated for "branding, licensing and degree-giving, authorizing and appointing, and in general regulating and administering by system the lives of human beings."[18] James, writing before the paranoid age of surveillance and computer information banks, had his hopes: "I am against all bigness and greatness in all their forms, and with the invisible molecular forces that work from individual to individual, stealing in through the crannies of the world like so many soft rootlets, or like the capillary oozing of water, and yet rending the hardest monuments of man's pride, if you give them time."[19] James believed that somehow the Supreme Abstract Commanders would lose and that history would finally come around to putting the individual on top. In this light, contemporary styles of literary theory, including Marxism, are part of the problem, not—as in their self-description—part of the solution; cultural effects of the technology of modernization, literary normalizations of individuality via the impositions of structure, myth, textuality, essentialized gender and class relations, the mode of production. They are expressions of system and discipline, not their critique: destructions of the subject.

Foucault is not sanguine about the survival of the individual. Discipline insidiously invades the ground of individuality in order to master it. Discipline takes us all through the gate of modernization, into safe port, where our individuality is studied so much the better to be controlled. Foucault's antidote is writing: not as a space for the preservation of identity and the assertion of voice, but as a labyrinth into which he can escape, to "lose myself," and, there, in the labyrinth, never have to be a self (a self is a dangerous thing to be)—write yourself off, as it were, "write in order to have no face." Give no target to discipline: "Do not ask who I am and do not ask me to remain the same: leave it to our bureaucrats and our police to see that our papers are in order. At least spare us their morality when we write."[20] If for James "individuality" translates into a philosophical positive—a given of liberalism—a holdout in freedom and the site of the personal and of "full ideality,"[21] then for Foucault undisciplined individuality may be precisely the unintended effect of a system which would produce individuality as an object of its knowledge and power (the disciplinary appropriation of biography), but which instead, and ironically, inside its safe, normalized subject, instigates the move to the underground where a deviant selfhood may nurture sullen counterschemes of resistance and revolution.

Stevens inhabits the world of James and Foucault; he is wary of system and surveillance and of the police in all their contemporary and protean guises. But Prospero-like he called upon his Ariel and Ariel rarely failed to respond, sometimes bearing unexpected gifts. After the jars, glasses, bowls, designs of various sorts, and images, after the (male) hero and (male) major man—all of them "must be abstract"—comes the fat girl. Who is she? No "central man" who, "cold and numbered," "sums us up," no canonical men ("men but artificial men"), "admired by all men"—those major men, they may be seated in cafés, but we will never see them. Instead we will see the "dish of country cheese / And a pineapple on the table." If we're lucky, we'll hear someone—could it possibly be the major man?—talk about "this man in Sausalito" who makes beautiful shawls. Coming late, after all his anecdotal portraits, so allegorical in intent,[22] the fat girl seems real: not a literary device, not what anyone wants her to be—she's a fulfillment that can be wished for, as Stevens wishes for her in some of the most moving of his lyric lines, but what his writing itself cannot grant.

In the key verbs of "Anecdote of the Jar," the fat girl gives but she cannot be taken. Refusing to show herself in anecdotal lyric, she awaits, instead, the purer romantic lyricist in his mood of praise. In "Anecdote of the Jar" Stevens tells a story whose most cryptically encoded lesson is the necessity of forsaking action, and the genre of action—storytelling—in favor of aesthesis, praise's ultimate awestruck medium. (Conjure if you can your grandparents' cultural difference.) Stevens' story against story represents a longing for lyric itself and its imperative: a politics of lyricism which in James, Stevens, Herr, and Foucault amounts to a directive not to set molecular individuals into social system, not even into literary systems of narrative; not to reencode Vietnam in the coordinates of American imperial cartography. To find the fat girl is not to impose—it is to find a "moving contour," unfixed and incomplete because alive, and moving because we are moved. She appears:

> Fat girl, terrestrial, my summer, my night,
> How is it I find you in difference, see you there
> In a moving contour, a change not quite completed? . . .
> Bent over work, anxious, content, alone,
> You remain the more than natural figure. You
> Become the soft-footed phantom. . . .[23]

Michel Foucault's Fantasy for Humanists

Is it surprising that prisons resemble factories, schools, barracks, hospitals, which all resemble prisons?

MICHEL FOUCAULT, *Discipline and Punish*

All materialist concepts contain an accusation and an imperative.

HERBERT MARCUSE, *Negations*

. . . I quote Marx without saying so, without quotation marks, and because people are incapable of recognizing Marx's texts, I am thought to be someone who doesn't quote Marx. When a physicist writes a work of physics, does he feel it necessary to quote Newton and Einstein? He uses them but he doesn't need the quotation marks, the footnote and the eulogistic comment to prove how completely faithful he is being to the master's thought. And because other physicists know what Einstein did, what he discovered and proved, they can recognize him in what the physicist writes. It is impossible at the present time to write history without using a whole range of concepts directly or indirectly linked to Marx's thought and situating oneself within a horizon of thought which has been defined and described by Marx. One might even wonder what difference there could ultimately be between being a historian and being a Marxist.

MICHEL FOUCAULT, *Power/Knowledge*

W*here does* Michel Foucault stand on the question of Marx? In one of my epigraphs, in which he appears resolutely to set himself within the horizon of a Marxist theory of history, Foucault declares himself a Marxist, not by choice or intention—categories for which he has no use—but by historical inevitability. He is situated (the passive form is necessary here) within a discursive practice founded by Marx. In the essay "What Is an Author?" Foucault says that the "distinctive contribution" of Marx and Freud is "that they produced not only their own work, but the possibility and the rules of formation of other texts." And what this means is not what intellectual historians generally mean when they speak of the "influence" or "tradition" of the "major" writer. Foucault has in mind not merely the notion that Marx and Freud made it possible that a "certain number of analogies" could be adopted in future texts—made possible historical relations of continuity and repetition—"but, as importantly, they also made possible a certain number of differences. They cleared a space for the introduction of elements other than their own, which, nevertheless, remain within the field of discourse they initiated." To place Foucault with Marx in a relationship marked by difference, discord, and strife, as well as (and at the same time) by analogy, homage, and continuity—in other words, to relate Marx and Foucault as father and son—might make problematic in the extreme Foucault's declaration of place (and peace) within the Marxist horizon.[1]

Not that we need a genealogical theory of author and authority to sense the trouble. In numerous places in *Power/ Knowledge* Foucault takes pains to spell out his contempt for the French Communist party; also, and more seriously, he there works out in some theoretical detail a frontal assault on Marx himself and the main lines of Marxist tradition. Foucault's critique is focused, moreover, on classical Marxist concepts: ideology, alienation, exploitation, class struggle, the decisive role of the economic, and, tied to these, behind these, an implied theory of power as a sort of private property. Can Foucault, can anyone call himself or herself a Marxist and not affirm these concepts in something like their classical elaboration? Does Foucault's attack on these cherished terms in the Marxist lexicon prove, as chief figures on the left seem to think today, that Foucault is not only anti-Marx but also, at bottom, a secret affiliate of a paranoid theory of a power so perfectly coercive, so insidiously ingrained at the capillary levels of the social body, that resistance and social change are but figments of fantasy with no possibility of realization? In spite of his own work in French prisons, does Foucault's theory of power, and his account of the emergence of modern society, constitute, however unwittingly, a testament of despair?

I doubt, for one thing, that we have sufficient evidence to settle such questions. For another, I am not sure what would constitute sufficient evidence. In light of contemporary theories of structure and discourse, *écriture*, *différance*, archive, episteme, discursive formation, discursive practice, and the unconscious, I doubt that what Foucault himself in the open, and with full intention, has had to say against Marx can be decisive. Against those who have already made up their minds in the negative (I allude mainly to the left), and against Foucault's own hostile statements, I quote one of Foucault's wicked ironic gems: "so many authors who know or do not know one another, criticize one another, . . . pillage one another, meet without knowing it and obstinately intersect their unique discourses in a web of which they are not the masters, of which they cannot see the whole, and of whose breadth they have a very inadequate idea."[2]

With that sobering (and I think convincing) theory of discourse before us, I want to set aside the question of intention and move directly to as careful an examination as I can manage of *Discipline and Punish*, grounded in Foucault's assertion that his and (by extension) my own discourse on the subjects of history and power are situated within a Marxist horizon, are radically constrained by Marx's own practice. I want to read one of the decisive works of intellect produced in our century in roughly Marxist terms, but not because I wish to venerate Marx's writings as sacred texts, or to bring Foucault to the bar of Marxist justice. Though I find Marx's writings powerfully sympathetic on almost every issue, I find them at times also heterogeneous to the point of confusion, often insufficiently worked through at the theoretical level, and (but how could this be otherwise?) in need of the work done on them, to them, and for them by the major twentieth-century Western Marxists. I am confessing, I suppose, that I cannot myself conduct such a reading in any other terms and that I cannot myself avoid the ambivalence felt by those who work (in two senses) "after" Marx. That Foucault thinks we cannot avoid working within the horizon of Marx gives me some consolation. On the other hand, the complexity of his genealogical theory of "authorial" relations—more specifically, of his and (necessarily) our relationship to Marx as authoritative founder of a discursive practice—pretty much assures that my reading will in some ways reinscribe the problems as well as provide an advance upon them.

I

The depth of theoretical heterogeneity in *Discipline and Punish* may be sensed in its opening chapter, "The Body of the Condemned." It is not hard to see what Foucault has in mind in an introductory sort of way. In effect, the plan of the book, his narrative of the emergence of modern society as a whole (his macrocosm), is previewed from what will be his consistent microcosmic perspective: changing penal styles. Beginning roughly with the early seventeenth century and running through to the later nineteenth century, Foucault shows us how styles of punishment shift slowly—without rupture, and always bearing traces of older styles—from a juridical mode, with the question of guilt and innocence as sole object of investigation and the body of the criminal as a focus of punishment, into what must be called an epistemological mode, with knowledge of the offender as the new object and the disciplined control of individuals (power over individuals) the ultimate value of such knowledge. Hence, in the initial chapter, Foucault's major examples: the spectacular public torture and execution of Damiens the regicide (1757), a brutalization of the body to the nth degree; and, only eighty years later, Leon Faucher's rules for the "House for young prisoners in Paris," what Foucault calls a "time-table" whose interest (a devious word) is in the "soul" created by the knowledge available to modern society—juridical, medical, psychological, and (much later) the various sciences of man practiced in the academy. This movement from body to soul is not a dramatic leap to a wholly new human subject. The shift in penal styles signifies no epistemic cataclysm (as in the structuralism of *The Order of Things*) but a strategic maneuver to protect the concentrated political apparatus of the old regime whose focus was the body, by transforming it into the somewhat hidden, wholly dispersed authority characteristic of our penal regime, a powerful, interlocking, massively embracing network of experts ("wardens, doctors, chaplains, psychiatrists, psychologists, educationalists") whose amalgamated epistemic force saturates modern society from top to bottom. No more dangerous exposure, in open spectacles of torture and execution, of the authority which governs and punishes.[3]

The soul is not produced, in the new style, for its own sake; knowledge is never "disinterested." The soul is produced only in order so much the better to get back at the body, not to deliver upon it the horrifying tortures of the old regime, but to discipline and coerce it for one purpose: in order to utilize it. The post-Christian soul is not, of course, in this view, theological substance, but the creation, instrument, and effect of what Foucault calls a "political anatomy." In a scathing allusion he tells us that the soul has become, for our disciplined society, "the prison of the body"—the medium of operation for coercive force. So the "slackening of the hold on the body," which is marked by the disappearance of public execution in its spectacular, theatricalized form, is a misleading appearance in the history of punishment. For the new penal regime which even now we recognize in its liberal claims for humanity—correction, reclamation, cure—the body remains useful as an intermediary, an instrument through which to deprive the bourgeois subject of capitalism of that liberty which it regards as a right and property. There is, then, in modern society a disciplinary process, with twin objectives, which aims at the body in order to invest in the control of consciousness ("soul"); and which aims at "soul" in a central effort to dominate and thereby appropriate the forces of the body. That, very schematically, is the narrative previewed in the first chapter of *Discipline and Punish*. And that narrative, more or less, constitutes the discernible historical intention of Foucault.[4]

Foucault's narrative is fleshed out with details so gripping that an alternative portrait (*grosso modo*) of contemporary society is difficult to imagine. At the level of dramatic historical portraiture Foucault has few peers. Having said that, it may seem almost ungratefully beside the point to raise the always abstract question of the theoretical determinations of Foucault's vivid achievement. But I want to argue that, far from being beside the point, it is precisely *that* point that Foucault's text raises on almost any page. To get down to cases: one recurrent problem in *Discipline and Punish*, as in his earlier books, is his account of change and transition. What *really* caused the transformation from the old to the new regime of penal styles? One of Foucault's answers, and it is virtually the first thing that he has to say about the issue, is distinctly outside the Marxist horizon within which he locates his writing; it is metaphysical by way of anthropology and, in the contemporary scene, recalls the obsessions of René Girard: "The public execution is now seen as a hearth in which violence bursts again into flame. . . . Punishment, then, will become the most hidden part of the penal process."[5] Or again:

> physical confrontation between the sovereign and the condemned man must end; this hand-to-hand fight between the vengeance of the prince and the contained anger of the people, through the mediation

of the victim and the executioner, must be concluded. . . . it was revolting. . . . it was shameful. It was, in any case, dangerous in that it provided a support for a confrontation between the violence of the king and the violence of the people. It was as if the sovereign power did not see, in this emulation of atrocity, a challenge that it itself threw down and which might one day be taken up: accustomed as it was to "seeing blood flow," the people soon learnt that "it could be revenged only with blood."[6]

In this account, violence is a dormant but inherent human disposition that can only be awakened and goaded into mimetic expression by the example of garish and gory public torture and execution. The violence of the prince—so overt, so focused, and, this is the chief point, so *accessible*—must be extinguished, not because it is revolting and shameful (Foucault cites the moralism of Enlightenment reformers only to reveal its hypocrisy) but because it was dangerous; because it might incite a counterviolence, a revolt that could not help but be directed at the heads of the sovereign's representatives. The sovereign's power, pointed and palpably there, almost as if it were a thing that could be touched (and confiscated and reversed in its effects), this power to do violence and oppression was dangerous only because it could be seized by the oppressed in an open revolutionary encounter that it unintentionally encouraged. That is why power must be hidden and dispersed: so that the violent potential of human beings will remain *in potentia*.

Foucault's text, at this point, forces this conclusion upon us: the power that does violence to our bodies and our minds must be hidden and dispersed because we are instinctually violent creatures who are prone to the expression of a will to dominate. The violence of the powers that be must be masked and dispersed in order that the authority in place may not be displaced by the currents of a universal violence circulating through us all, exploiters and exploited alike. That reading of power is not only totalizing and metaphysical, it is also cynical: "Wait until *we* get in, you bastards!" In this version of Nietzsche there can be no justice—only the desire to dominate. Such a politics of will, innocent as it is of class conflict and other historical categories—wherever such a politics is grounded, it is not grounded *there*—must be situated beyond Marx, probably in a concept of human nature. Nietzsche, as Heidegger observed, was the last metaphysician, and we can add, when arguing in this vein, Foucault is his faithful son.

Yet even within his opening chapter he gives us other interpretations of change. Perhaps one way to historicize the tension that I am trying to describe in Foucault's thought is to say that his intellectual paternity is shared by two hostile fathers—Marx and Nietzsche—and that the most lurid of family romances is played out when he attempts to kill off one with the club of the other. Foucault quickly reinscribes Marx into *Discipline and Punish* in ways more subtle and true to the spirit of his texts than the many reinscriptions done explicitly in the name of Marxism. Thus Foucault will openly accept the thesis of the Marxist historians Rusche and Kirchheimer (in *Punishment and Social Structures*, 1939)—he calls theirs a "great work"— that from the point of view of epochal analysis, as opposed to up-close, detailed analysis of the interiors of social formations, the "different systems of punishment" must be related (as effect to cause) to "systems of production within which they operate." Foucault credits such recognizably Marxist analysis as a point of "essential reference."[7] (His relationship to Marx at this point is not either-or, as it tends to be in his generalizations about power in *Power/Knowledge* or in the self-conscious theoretical passages in *Discipline and Punish*.) From this definitive Marxist axiom Foucault moves directly to a subtler Marxist point which he proceeds to enrich in a way that seems to me not only consistent with Marx's thought but also its necessary theoretical expansion within the context of a later, more thoroughly disciplined capitalist formation. The structural principle of classical capitalist economic practice, as Marx theorized it, can be located in that moment of exchange when labor becomes a commodity (a founding as well as a synchronic gesture), in which exchange value constitutes as its only possible ground an "abstract labor power" rising freely from the ashes of highly determinate, highly individuated acts of work. Foucault completes this insight by insisting that "abstract labor power," despite its ideal character, is itself grounded in the body: not in the sensuous, personal, individuated body (a locus of specific talents) on which Marx would ground use value, but in something like (my term, not Foucault's) an "abstract body"—the conforming, straitjacketed, generalized physical capacity to do work required by the genius of capitalism. It is this body, as Foucault writes, that is

> directly involved in a political field; power relations have an immediate hold upon it; they invest it, mark it, train it, torture it, force it to carry out tasks, to perform ceremonies, to emit signs. This political investment of the body is bound up, in accordance with complex reciprocal relations, with its economic use; it is largely as a force of production that the body is invested with relations of power and domination; but, on the other hand, *its constitution as labor power is possible only if it is caught up in a system of subjection . . . the body becomes a useful force only if it is both a productive body and a subjected body.* (Emphasis mine)[8]

The body, in this view of it, functions simultaneously within what traditional Marxism, in its key metaphoric spatialization of social structure, called superstructure and base. Not merely an essential part of any society's productive forces, the body, by inhabiting both superstructural (political) and base (economic) levels, becomes a means for calling into question the conventional one-way determinism of the superstructure-base model of history and society. Moreover, the body does not somehow operate in two realms, as if such operation were inherent to its mode of functioning. The body's economic and political potential is simply captured by a single force (discipline and its numerous mechanisms) which, as it submits the body to "subjection," makes it a useful and docile economic and political "subject." The body, then, is made to function in the economic and in the political spheres by a power, itself neither economic nor political, which shows no respect for the compartmentalizing metaphors of superstructure and base. Foucault's revision of this classic metaphor of Marxism, at this stage in his argument, moves not in the direction of Antonio Gramsci (a direction too suspiciously idealistic for Foucault) but in the direction of a more and perhaps too thoroughgoing materialist theory of culture and society. I can imagine an argument, and in some part I intend to unfold it, that Foucault does for the theory of discipline in the twentieth century what Marx did for the theory of capital in the nineteenth, and that these two theories, far from being antagonistic, are necessary components within a fully articulated theory of historical materialism.

But Foucault moves directly from this passage on discipline, not to an acknowledgment of kinship, but to this criticism of Marx: "this power is exercised rather than possessed; it is not the 'privilege,' acquired or preserved, of a dominant class, but the overall effect of its strategic positions—an effect that is manifested and sometimes extended by the position of those who are dominated."[9] Foucault believes that the weakest point of Marxism is its position on power: its theory of power as essentially static and negative, repressive, conspiratorially "owned" by the ruling class (as if power and the means of production were identical), a "thing" that can be "possessed." Whether or not that reading of the concept of power in Marxism is the fairest that might be managed, it is certainly a possible reading. It is, moreover, a reading that can be linked to the major rhetorical passages in Marx in which the seizing, by revolutionaries, of the means of production is equivalent to seizing power. For Foucault power is relational, not substantial—it is produced by relations of domination; it is an effect of domination, not the cause of domination. Power is always exercised, and its effects are manifested in the position of those who are dominated. It doesn't "prohibit" or "deny" the dominated as much as it invests them, even as the dominated, unstrategically positioned as they are in the struggle against power produced by domination, "resist the grip it has on them."[10] All social relations are simply power-saturated. Therefore, far from being negative and repressive, power is positive and productive—just what the capitalist economic machine needed. Foucault concludes this self-conscious reflection on power with a remark that is echoed in many of his later writings. Since power is not a property, since its effects must be attributed to "maneuvers, tactics, techniques," since one can decipher in power "a network of relations, constantly in tension, in activity, rather than a privilege that one might possess," then it would appear to follow that relations of power are never "univocal," that they "define innumerable points of confrontation, focuses of instability, each of which has its own risks of conflicts, of struggles, and of an at least temporary inversion of power relations."[11] Foucault's revision of the repression thesis that we generally attach to Marx and Freud seems ultimately useful, then, because power, ever present to any and all social relations, may be the basis for something like perpetual microrevolution ("a network of relations, constantly in tension . . . innumerable points of confrontation"). Reversals at the microlevel are always very much in a state of active possibility, because there structural change itself may be no dream, and there, at the microlevel, the dominated, now more robustly endowed by Foucault's positive view of power, seem more realistically placed to break their chains and to emerge. That, at least, is a possible reading of Foucault on power through the first chapter of *Discipline and Punish*.[12]

2

To ignore the highly figurative discourse through which Foucault's representation of the story of modern society's emergence is given to us is to miss one of the most compelling revelations of the theoretical reach and complexity of *Discipline and Punish*. It is to miss the political figures that theory makes in this text. In his second chapter, "The Spectacle of the Scaffold," Foucault moves from a description of the bloody details of public executions to an explanation of torture old-style. For "explanation" we will need to think "representation," for that term, especially in its literary heritage, speaks more accurately to the activity of Foucault's interpretation than does the neutral-sounding but epistemologically deceptive term "explanation." Foucault's "explanation" involves the deployment of a presiding metaphor of theatricality and ritual in which, and through which, his representation of punishment in the old regime is projected. Foucault's metaphor is constitutive of his reading of penal history, of the penal authority desired by royal authority and the status quo, and how that desire was thwarted by the repressed and insulted. His metaphor of theatricality constitutes our understanding of transition, change, and transformation: not as "events" which are located "after" the old regime, or "between" the "old" and the "new," but—and this is the strength of Foucault's strategy of representation in *Discipline and Punish*—as forces already embedded within the "old."

The scaffold is a theater for punishment whose major object is not the enactment of punishment itself but the reception of punishment in pure terror. The principal instrument of terror, in this theater of terror, is deliberately excessive, "spectacular" violence. Torture: no expression of lawless rage, but an "act of maintaining life in pain," a correlation of specific corporal effects with the gravity of the crime, an act whose true object is the minds of those watching. In the theater of terror, the sovereign is a kind of playwright, the scaffold is his stage, the condemned and the executioner (with his chief assistants) are his actors, and those watching are his audience. In the theater of terror the sovereign-playwright stages a drama that is allegorical and didactic—rhetorical through and through. In an eerie echo of Kafka's "In the Penal Colony," Foucault writes of how the body of the condemned was turned into a kind of text: "in him, on him, the sentence had to be legible for all."[13] At one level, this penal text has a purely juridical function: it says, this is the guilty man, this his crime, and these are the physical consequences which must be visited upon the perpetrator of such an act. At another, somewhat more ambiguous level, the text is avidly read (Foucault speaks of the "insatiable curiosity that drove the spectators to the scaffold") for its moral and theological signification.[14] If the putatively guilty man, for example, endures his suffering with dignity, perhaps his suffering in the afterlife will be by that much alleviated. On the other hand, perhaps resignation is a sign of the despair of hell. If the condemned man dies quickly, perhaps that is a kind of proof that he is in fact innocent and that God does not wish him to suffer any further pain; if he screams, struggles, blasphemes, and dies slowly, perhaps this is an image of the abandonment of eternal damnation. In all of these readings, the text is transformed into a complicated sign of crime, innocence, and destiny. As Foucault summarizes it: "There is, therefore, an ambiguity in this suffering that may signify equally well the truth of the crime or the error of the judges, the goodness or evil of the criminal, the coincidence or the divergence between the judgment of men and that of God."[15] The text is not, of course, in itself theologically ambiguous, but is made so by the play of theological reception. Since the audience is the true subject of punishment, it demonstrates in the range of its responses that the effects of punishment cannot themselves be controlled by the mechanisms of torture, by those who run the mechanism, or by the sovereign behind it all. The desire of the playwright to produce a single meaning with a single effect is frustrated. The true subject of punishment is not quite subjugated.

Public execution serves in part a juridical function, in part a religious function, but most of all it needs to be understood in its third register (already implied in the others) as "political ritual." "It belongs, even in minor cases, to the ceremonies by which power is manifested," for besides "its immediate victim, the crime attacks the sovereign."[16] So public execution had to do not so much with the reestablishment of justice as with the activation of power. The sovereign represents the sort of power "for which disobedience was an act of hostility, the first sign of rebellion, which is not in principle different from civil war."[17] Public execution is therefore a brutalization intended to terrorize an audience of potential rebels with the message of absolute power. On the scaffold what is performed is the political allegory of restoration:

> however hasty and everyday, [punishment in the old regime] belongs to a whole series of great rituals in which power is eclipsed and restored (coronation, entry of the king into a conquered city, the submission of rebellious subjects); over and above the crime that has placed the sovereign in contempt, it deploys before all eyes an invincible force. Its aim is not so much to re-establish a balance as to bring into play, at its extreme point, the dissymmetry between the subject who has dared to violate the law and the all-powerful sovereign who displays his strength.[18]

In the theater of terror what is produced, or so the sovereign-playwright desires, is a single message: I can pursue without fear a policy of terror because my force is invincible: dissymmetrical, unbalanced, excessive, and—you must never forget this—*irreversible.* All acts of hostility, disobedience, rebellion, and revolution directed against me and my regime can have only a momentary success. Such acts of insurrection, in the end, are futile because the structure of our power relation is impervious to your actions.

But if the sovereign-playwright could not control the theological response of his audience, neither could he coerce his audience into a single, politically necessary response of abject fear and resignation. In the rhetorical principle of its functioning, the theater of terror would produce the very effect that it had most intended to repress. If penal "theater" is to have real social force, then the theater of public torture will require most of all an audience; but what is discovered is that the audience's power to resist cannot be utterly subdued, and the reason would appear to be (Foucault does not make this point explicitly) that its response cannot utterly be manipulated. Foucault argues that the role of "the people" at the "scene of terror" was "an ambiguous one." The audience "drawn to the spectacle intended to terrorize it could express its rejection of the punitive power and sometimes revolt." When in the theater of terror the sovereign's rhetoric fails, when not only does it fail but its intention is reversed, then that theater no longer has a reason for being. There will be change—history will be made, as it were, from below: "If the crowd gathered around the scaffold, it was not simply to witness the sufferings of the condemned man or to excite the anger of the executioner: it was also to hear an individual who had nothing to lose curse the judges, the laws, the government and religion." Foucault draws out the irony: "The public execution allowed the luxury of these momentary saturnalia. . . ."[19]

From didactic theater of terror to saturnalian orgy, from repression to the return of the repressed—the carnival inversion of rules, authority, customs, class relations: in a word, the transformation of the social structure. The criminal as social hero, as revolutionary. We are witnessing through Foucault's metaphors of theater and ritual the description of not two penal styles, but one. One style or mechanism of punishment ("the spectacle of the scaffold") produced two effects simultaneously. Let me call them the repression effect and the revolutionary effect. The fear was that the revolutionary effect (which we may see as the effect of an effect: the repression effect being its cause) would take hold. And the central effort of the reformers of the eighteenth and nineteenth centuries is directed precisely to that fear. They "were not to forget that, in the last resort, the execution did not, in fact, frighten people. One of their first cries was to demand their abolition."[20] The liberal reformers, in this interpretation, work toward a better mode of repression out of a political fear of what was produced by the ambiguous rituals of public torture. I quote Foucault now at some length, in a passage of considerable richness which summarizes the crisis of punishment in the old regime while, at the same time, offering an attractive if somewhat problematic interpretation of that crisis:

> It was evident that the great spectacle of punishment ran the risk of being rejected by the very people to whom it was addressed. In fact,

the terror of the public execution created centers of illegality: on execution days, insults or stones were thrown at the executioner, the guards and the soldiers; attempts were made to seize the condemned man, either to save him or to kill him more surely; fights broke out, and there was no better prey for thieves than the curious throng around the scaffold. . . . But above all—and this was why these disadvantages became a political danger—the people never felt closer to those who paid the penalty than in those rituals intended to show the horror of the crime and the invincibility of power; never did the people feel more threatened, like them, by a legal violence exercised without moderation or restraint. The solidarity of a whole section of the population with those we would call petty offenders— vagrants, false beggars, the indigent poor, pickpockets, receivers [of] and dealers in stolen goods—was constantly expressed. . . . And it was the breaking up of this solidarity that was becoming the aim of penal and police repression. Yet out of the ceremony of the public execution, out of that uncertain festival in which violence was instantaneously reversible, it was this solidarity that was likely to emerge with redoubled strength.[21]

Foucault's reading of the intention of public execution is consistent with his developing analysis. Penal and police repression produced an unintended ironic effect. Aimed secretly at all noncriminals who might be potentially subversive of political stability, such repression created a response which doubled back on the playwright's representatives. This theater of terror must therefore be abolished because it cannot preserve the status quo. Other means of punishment must be located, and Foucault's ensuing narrative tells the story of how such means took shape and eventually became the indispensable instruments of the disciplinary society's governing institution. Yet something is left out of this account of change and transition. Note the floating reference (twice made) to "the people." Who are these people? They are what is termed a "whole section of the population," but which section? And why do they feel "solidarity" with a wide range of petty offenders? The social, political, and, one assumes, the economic condition of solidarity, or potential solidarity, preexisted the theater of terror, was what the theater of terror was concerned to break up but instead merely galvanized. What one wants from Foucault, at this point, is precisely the sort of historical detail which he, among contemporary theorists, has shown himself to be the exemplary master of. And yet what we get is not richly contextualizing detail but surprisingly vague and even sentimental gestures about "the people" and a "whole section of the population" which tends to side with criminals. And more even than the detail which would identify these actors in this drama of princely terror and its reversal, we want additional theory about how this condition for a resisting solidarity came into being.

Foucault's refusal either to specify the historical setting of "the people," their precise political and economic status and relations, or to contextualize their function as a class (or classes) within a larger historical narrative of relations of exploitation (I do not say that he should limit himself to economic relations of exploitation), makes the concept of "the people" an unhistorical reference to a kind of social being stubbornly resistant to modification by the ministrations of human praxis. In other words, "the people" appears to refer to a permanent kind of underclass, permanently angry and resistant, who in the seventeenth and eighteenth centuries came down on the side of the criminals not so much because such alignment gave them a specific point of resistance to repressive authority (it did give them that) but mainly because the rituals of public execution permitted, unwittingly, a therapeutic expression of rebellion, an orgy of linguistic lawlessness (curses, blasphemy, etc.) whose main function, according to Foucault, was the release of furiously pent up emotions.

Foucault's metaphoric formation of such rebellion as "saturnalian" is crucial then in two ways. It speaks to an urge for transformation and liberation while, at the same time, it roots that urge in a ritual whose very periodicity (and rituals are nothing if not periodic) attests to the invulnerability of an authoritative social structure which permits, produces, and contains such rituals. The saturnalian ritual that Foucault describes will be recurrent because it can make nothing happen—that is why he calls it "momentary." It can force no real changes in society and that is why it is needed: to provide periodic relief from an unalterable condition. What the metaphor of saturnalian ritual—I am speaking not of what happened but of what Foucault thinks happened—really celebrates is the occasional overflow of an energy that will always be hopelessly "outside." Strictly speaking, useless and asocial, but safely so because such energy, however subversive in its expression, can never, by virtue of its status within ritual, have integral oppositional effects on the long-range prospects of society. As a metaphoric perspective on the disruptive moments in the old penal system, saturnalian revelry signifies Foucault's recurrent lyricism of marginality, a lyricism of the criminal, the outcast, the madman, the homosexual, the freak: a lyricism of that figure who roams the edges of society as the other of that society's perfected identity (reason, health, sanity, normality, etc.). The metaphor of saturnalian revelry presumes a social structure founded on exclusion by a kingly power that is repressive and negative. Precisely the sort of power that Foucault's text is dedicated to debunking.

Foucault's metaphors call critical attention to themselves because they are engaged in a serious conflict with the larger narrative pattern of *Discipline and Punish*. The theater of terror created more than the relatively harmless saturnalian ritual as its necessary backlash. The interpretation of the penal reformers points to a dangerous situation: the saturnalian responses were read by them as signs of a deeper, more ominous rebellious energy, one that would not be calmed by the palliative of a licentious holiday. Public executions had to be phased out because they might galvanize a collective will and trigger a response that could not be contained. So the very historical narrative that Foucault unfolds constitutes a negative judgment on his key metaphors of theater and saturnalian ritual; these metaphors, that narrative tells us, somewhat trivialize the real drama of social forces at work in his history, the real counterpower that was unleashed at the public execution, and the real power in dominance that responded in the move to what was called a humane system of punishment.

Foucault completes the first section of his text, "Torture," by showing how a hegemonic mechanism of the old regime, the production of a discourse of criminality—the gallows "speeches" published in broadsheets, pamphlets, almanacs, and adventure stories—produced effects contrary to the intention of such literature. There can be no doubt about what this literature was supposed to do: it was supposed to be a denunciation, delivered by the criminal himself, of crime, the criminal life, and all manner of "deviant" behavior. Such traditional morality, when represented as the repenting last words of a condemned man, was supposed to have the effect of ideological control, and that, no doubt, was why those broadsheets and almanacs were allowed to be printed and circulated. But Foucault's analysis uncovers the contrary powers of resistance and domination: "Against the laws, against the rich, the powerful, the magistrates, the constabulary or the watch, against taxes and their collectors," the criminal "appeared to have waged a struggle with which one all too easily identified. The proclamation of these crimes blew up to epic proportions the tiny struggle that passed unperceived in everyday life." The indomitability of the criminal, Foucault says, is a claim to "greatness: by not giving in under torture, he gave proof of a strength that no power had succeeded in bending. . . . Black hero or reconciled criminal, defender of the true right or an indomitable force, the criminal of the broadsheets . . . brought with him, beneath the apparent morality of the example not to be followed, a whole memory of struggles and confrontations."[22]

How shall we understand this indomitability of the charismatic criminal? Shall we think of it, on the analogy of Foucault's discourse on reason and its other, as a force of incorrigible irrationality, an irrepressible impulse to contrariety, a mode of being human that not only is excluded by reasonable society (which negates it in the discourse of reason) but excludes itself in its will to be outside, to be beyond the pale? And, likewise, this "strength that no power had succeeded in bending"—what is that? Where does it come from? Why is it contrary to the powers that be? Why can't it be bent or dominated? A recent complaint about Foucault is that in *Discipline and Punish* he turns power into a metaphysical force. It needs to be noted that counterpower, resistance to domination, seems equally metaphysical in its transcendence of history, so that what Foucault has created, in his examination of punishment in the old regime, is another allegorical drama of opposites, a Manichean theology of God and the Devil as power and counterpower, or is it the other way around? And how are we to decide which is the power of good, which of evil? Does it depend only on our point of view? Where we happen to be situated within economic and political authority? Is it that easy and that cynical?

In any event Foucault is wrong. His reading of resistant power as impervious metaphysical force is belied by the history which he narrates. The strength of resistance *was* bent. The literature of the gallows *was* reappropriated. The literature of crime, so avidly read by the lower classes—it "formed part of their basic reading"—this literature which was received by the exploited as the cry of the exploited; this literature, which seemed to be a fitting expression of a "ceremony that inadequately channeled the power relations it sought to ritualize"; this literature, which activated a critical memory, had to be suppressed through an act of appropriation which would transform crime into fine art, the "work of only exceptional natures, because it reveals the monstrousness of the strong and the powerful, because villainy is yet another mode of privilege." Crime is rewritten, then, from De Quincey to Baudelaire as an expression of romantic genius: the "exclusive privilege of those who are really great." In this appropriation of the literature of crime Foucault evokes what is always buried beneath his prose and on occasion comes to the surface—an image of class conflict: "The literature of crime transforms to another class the spectacle that had surrounded the criminal. Meanwhile the newspapers took over the task of recounting the grey, unheroic details of everyday crime and punishment. The split was complete; the people was robbed of its old pride in its crimes; the great murders had become the quiet game of the well behaved." No more epic magnification of those tiny resistances that studded the texture of everyday life. Crush the critical memory of struggle and confrontation.[23]

3

In the second part of *Discipline and Punish*, "Punishment," Foucault moves his history to the later eighteenth century and a slashing sardonic analysis of the enlightened penal reformers. He will show us that the task of the reformers is not to abolish penal theater but to make it work by finding a mode of punishment and repression that would not produce the disordering consequences that the theater of terror inadvertently introduced into society: the "hand-to-hand fight between the vengeance of the prince and the contained anger of the people, through mediation of the victim and the executioner, must be concluded."[24] Penal style would need to change from spectacle to another kind of theater, one that could "adjust the mechanisms of power that frame the everyday life of individuals." And not only frame everyday life but sink into it. The trouble with the old penal style was that it represented a "bad economy of power." Consequently, the litany of the reformers of "too much power" was directed against inefficiency and crudity, not injustice. And not, of course, against an inefficiency that was merely wasteful, but against one that made power vulnerable. "The true objective of the reform movement . . . was . . . to set up a new 'economy' of the power to punish, to assure its better distribution, so that it should [not] be . . . too concentrated at certain privileged points," so that it might be "more regular, more effective, more constant and more detailed in its effects." The power that concentrated itself "at certain privileged points" was simply asking for resistance and attack.[25]

It is perhaps in his detailed descriptions of the changing

spaces of tolerated illegalities (always part of the political and economic life of any society) that Foucault gives us his socially and politically most riveting and believable account of the historical change marked by the shift from the ancien régime to the bourgeois form of capitalist society. We are no longer asked, in this section of his argument, to accept a thesis about the enduring ontology of violence and the necessarily conspiratorial response to violence by the reformers who wanted it hidden, so that repressive mechanisms could do their work without exciting counteraction. Rather, we are asked to understand that historical change is grounded on the economic requirements of capitalism and an emerging bourgeoisie. What was tolerated in the old social system as an illegality of rights—a space of tolerance in which those in the lower regions could with a certain impunity engage in activities of smuggling and looting— became, in the new formation, intolerable: "The illegality of rights, which often meant the survival of the most deprived, tended, with the new status of property, to become an illegality of property. It then had to be punished." More specifically yet: "The way in which wealth tended to be invested, on a much larger scale than ever before, in commodities and machines, presupposed a systematic, armed intolerance of illegality." The economy of illegalities was therefore restructured in the development of capitalist society—an illegality of property was separated from the illegality of rights, and this distinction represents nothing less than a class opposition, because the illegality of property, which is most accessible to the lower classes (the violent transfer of ownership), and the illegality of rights (like fraud and tax evasion), crimes of business, were then expressed and differentiated through a "specialization of the legal circuits." Illegalities of property were dealt with in the ordinary criminal courts and with punishments appropriate for "criminals." But what we would now call white collar crime demanded "special legal institutions applied with transactions, accommodations, and reduced fines." Foucault concludes acidly: "The bourgeoisie reserved to itself the fruitful domain of the illegality of rights."[26]

Foucault's description of the move from the old penal regime to the new is a mirror, then, of a larger social transition: from the "vengeance of the sovereign to the defense of society," from sovereignty to "public power," from subject to system—the economy of the power to punish becomes "restructured with the development of capitalist society."[27] In the new context punishment must no longer be an art of torture, slowly and skillfully meted out, but an art of effects. So punishment will remain rhetorical; what will soon change is its medium: "The example [of the criminal] is no longer a ritual that manifests; it is a sign that serves as an obstacle," and the new pain of punishment is not the actual sensation of pain "but the idea of pain, displeasure, inconvenience—the 'pain' of the idea of 'pain.'"[28] Though the old regime also made use of an art of representation—the body that functioned as an allegorical sign—in the old regime representation was tied too closely to the brute referent. It worked in a too immediate, too existential sort of theater; that was both its fearful strength and its political weakness. The new regime must work toward a greater liberation of representation from its putative object: "Punishment has to make use not of the body, but of representation. Or rather, if it does make use of the body, it is not so much as subject of a pain as the object of a representation. . . . what must be maximized is the representation of the penalty, not its corporal reality."[29] The need of the reformers is to appropriate minds, and the best way to accomplish that is to inscribe mind, as if it were a naked writing tablet—"the 'mind' as a surface for the inscription of power, with semiology as its tool; the submission of bodies through the control of ideas; the analysis of representations as a principle in a politics of bodies that was much more effective than the ritual anatomy of torture and execution."[30] What we are moving toward, in Foucault's analysis, is a more sophisticated rhetorical theater; we are on the way to the disciplined society and a nightmare political state in which the power to control and to manipulate ideas is not located in a few ideological state apparatuses (the Marxism of Althusser) but is more pervasively disseminated and more minutely effective because such power traverses body and consciousness, the body through consciousness, and vice versa.

Foucault's chief and wonderfully lucid example of the new power of a system of representation freed from its corporal effect is drawn from Beccaria's *Traité des délits et des peines* (1764). Beccaria had proposed that perpetual slavery replace the death penalty for two reasons: first, because it was more humane ("the pain of slavery, for the condemned man, is divided into as many portions as he has moments to live; it is an infinitely divisible penalty," a Zeno's paradox of penalty); second—this is what counts—for those who see and contemplate slaves (the "audience" of punishment), a very different, a very fiendish phenomenology of time is activated. For those who "represent" slaves to themselves, "the pains they bear are concentrated into a single idea; all the moments of slavery are contracted into a representation that then becomes more terrifying than the idea of death. It is the economically ideal punishment: it is minimal for him who undergoes it (and who, reduced to slavery, cannot repeat his crime) and it is maximal for him who represents it to himself." The always lyrical reformist rhetoric of humanization and leniency is the basis of a power more calculatedly deployed, a power whose object is the "mind or rather a play of representations and signs circulating discreetly but necessarily in the minds of all." This, then, is "Generalized Punishment" (the title of the first chapter of part 2 in *Discipline and Punish*)—a necessary step toward the iron rule of discipline and surveillance.[31]

In "The Gentle Way in Punishment," the poker-faced title of the second chapter of part 2, Foucault demonstrates that the visionary goal of the reformers is tied to a technology of representation whose purpose (and now I appeal to the Marxist phase of Roland Barthes) is to cloak history in the guise of nature in order to carry out in secret the varied works of ideological abuse. The first job of such a technology, an art of associated images, is to forge "stable connections that defy time: it is a matter of establishing the representation of pairs of opposing values." The representation of these paired images of crime and punishment will function (this is the hope) within the minds of all potential lawbreakers as "obstacle-signs." (The reformers had really very little interest in the criminal himself.) The major condition of ideological life for this kind of sign, as for all others, is the appearance of its unarbitrariness. The ratio must seem reversible if it is to be powerful: crime is to punishment (act is to response) as sign is to referent, and vice versa. As Foucault puts it: "by assuming the form of a natural sequence, punishment does not appear as the arbitrary effect of a human power." The human power that punishes is hidden. A highly specified series of "proper" punishments, linked "naturally" with the crimes that give birth to them, in the form of the signified and signifier, occupy consciousness (as the legal code) and will define the occupied consciousness (military metaphor intended) as a juridical subject who will activate the entire constraining legal code at every mention and with every thought of crime. The legal code so internalized becomes not the occasion for but a condition of bourgeois experience: "In the penalty, rather than seeing the presence of the sovereign, one will need to read the laws themselves." In such a world, crime would simply not be worth it.[32]

The shift in penal styles that Foucault describes is accompanied by a shift in his master metaphor of theater. It is not a change from theatricality to something else, but a change to a different sort of theatricality; to theater more assiduously, more effectively didactic; to theater as school, or as book to be read for its instructions. Above all children must be brought to this school in order that they may learn their lessons in civics. This pedagogical intent of reform is clothed in the mechanisms of representation; in this way penal theater may become (or so the reformers desired) more skillfully hegemonic. The Enlightenment ideal of everyday life (Foucault calls it "the punitive city") is therefore dominated by an image of theater, for everyday life must be thoroughly penetrated by numerous penal theaters.

The punitive city, that dark surreal dream of law and order, is not located at a single point (the scaffold) as in the bad old days; penal theater is now everywhere, and there is never not an audience for its productions since the prime condition of enlightened social being is always to be in the theater of punishment as subject or audience or administrator. In the quiet domestic dramas of the punitive city, so different from the big spectacles of public torture, in this theater for bourgeois families (rated PG) children will be taught something about their correct relationship to political authority, through the mediation of their relationship with parental authority, for the privileged interpreters of domestic theater are fathers and mothers.

Foucault's rendering of the ideal punitive city deserves to be quoted at length:

> At the crossroads, in the gardens, at the side of roads being repaired or bridges built, in workshops open to all, in the depths of mines that may be visited, will be hundreds of tiny theaters of punishment. Each crime will have its law; each criminal his punishment. It will be a visible punishment, a punishment that tells all, that explains, justifies itself, convicts: placards, different colored caps bearing inscriptions, posters, symbols, texts read or printed, tirelessly repeat the code. Scenery, perspective, optical effects, *trompe-l'œil* sometimes magnify the scene, making it more fearful than it is, but also clearer. From where the public is sitting, it is possible to believe in the existence of certain cruelties which, in fact, do not take place. But the essential point, in all these real or magnified severities, is that they should all, according to a strict economy, teach a lesson: that each punishment should be a fable. And that, in counterpoint with all the direct examples of virtue, one may at each moment encounter, as a living spectacle, the misfortunes of vice. Around each of these moral representations, school children will gather with their masters and adults will learn what lesson to teach their offspring. The great terrifying ritual of the public execution gives way, day after day, street after street, to this serious theater, with its multifarious and persuasive scenes. And popular memory will reproduce in rumor the austere discourse of the law.[33]

The change from old to new theater seems complete but for one telling exception which constitutes nothing less than a powerful trace of recollection—the sort of representation that is inseparable from the very process of history-as-genealogy that Foucault is concerned to get at. It is an interesting moment in Foucault's text because what is revealed is a theory of historical movement as a kind of intertextuality far removed from the ruptures and discontinuities in historical time portrayed in *The Order of Things* and *Madness and Civilization*. The exception that I am referring to concerns what was imagined by the reformers as the most terrible of crimes (parricide, of course) and its punishment. When Vermeil tried to imagine its proper punishment, he came up with, in Foucault's words, "something equivalent, in the new penal system, to what regicide had been in the old."[34] The new and old meet in the punishment of the parricide and the regicide, because what both systems were punishing, within different political contexts, was an expression—potentially representative of collective desire—of naked aggression against a principle, male and patriarchal, of absolute, repressive authority. Suspended in an iron cage high above the public square, blind, naked, and subjected to the rigors of all seasons, the parricide, like the regicide, will represent, in his agony, a reprise of terroristic theater, a return of the old regime in the emerging bourgeois imagination.

The reformers were devotees of theater: they opposed imprisonment because it did not permit the leading actor to be seen, did not permit the leading actor to take part in the theatrics of penal representation. Imprisonment could have no effect: no audience, no reception, no effect. Yet the punitive city was never realized. In the midst of reformist passion against imprisonment as the universal penalty, imprisonment quickly became the universal penalty: "The scaffold, where the body of the tortured criminal had been exposed to the ritually manifested force of the sovereign, and the punitive theater in which the representation of punishment was permanently available to the social body, were replaced by a great enclosed, complex and hierarchized structure that was integrated into the very body of the state apparatus."[35] How could this have happened? How could a penalty associated with arbitrary royal powers, and with all the abuses of royalty, so quickly become the most generalized form of punishment within a social system so opposed, and not in superficial ways, to the ancien régime? As he makes his transition to the nineteenth century and his deepest interests, the disciplined society, Foucault raises just those questions. On his way to providing answers, he works in detail through earlier carceral models (the Rasphius of Amsterdam, the *maison de force* at Ghent, the various English types, the Walnut Street model in Philadelphia). But let me move directly to his key theoretical conclusion: "The most important thing was that this control and transformation of behavior was accompanied—both as a condition and as a consequence—by the knowledge of individuals."[36] Imprisonment as expression of a desire to control in order to know: the carceral system, an expression of the will to knowledge, moves us beyond penal theatrics. What was needed most in the nineteenth-century society of Europe and the United States was not the stunning display of regal spectacles of torture, nor even the placid, domesticating didacticism of a sober theater of representation shaped for family consumption. What was needed most were training centers for capitalism.

Prisons, military barracks—these become the crucial metaphors, as Foucault's analysis develops, of all the central modern institutions of constraint, control, and coercion (factories, schools, hospitals are highest on his list) where a "whole corpus of individualizing knowledge was being organized." Not generalized knowledge of groups, but particularized knowledge of individuals was both instrument and product of coercion. The great political value of prisons is that they function as the apparatus of such knowledge, for there better than any place else what can be studied is the "potentiality of danger that lies hidden in an individual and which is manifested in his observed everyday conduct." Is Foucault reverting here again to our presumed residual capacity for violence? Probably not: more perhaps to a residual human capacity for resistance, but resistance to what? At this point in the text the answer that Foucault implies is that of the anarchist—resistance to authority. (Though whether Foucault is an anarchist of the individualist or socialist type is never clear.) "What one is trying to restore in this technique of correction is not so much the juridical subject, who is caught up in the fundamental interests of the social pact, but the obedient subject, the individual subjected to habits, rules, orders, to an authority that is exercised continually around him and upon him, and which he must allow to function automatically in him." So this freedom-loving "individual," who rebels against any and all authorities, will be forced into obedience through techniques of coercion that exclude all theatricality. For the mistake made by styles of punishment and repression organized as theater is that the thing that they most need in order to achieve their rhetorical purposes—namely, an audience—is the very thing (this reservoir of discontent and potential dissent, subversion, rejection) that poses the greatest danger to the authority in place. Because penal theater generates its own subversive contradiction, the task of our society, a task mostly completed according to Foucault, is to eliminate the audience for punishment. Coercion will exclude spectacle and its audience: in our age, the age of punishment, no "third party" will "disturb" the exercise of "total power."[37]

So there, at the end of the eighteenth century, three penal styles, three options for punishment converge with the emergence of modern society: that of monarchical law, that of the reforming jurists, and that of the (quickly universalized) project for a prison institution. As his transition to the analysis of "Discipline" and "Prison" (parts 3 and 4 of the text) Foucault gives us a summary that looks forward as well as backward: the ritual "mark" of monarchy inscribed in the flesh of the criminal; the "obstacle-sign" of the reforming jurists circulating freely, saturating the minds of all with its reactivation of the penal code; finally, the "trace" of coercion in the form of obedient behavior and habits in individuals who must, at all times, be watched in order to be controlled. The question, then, "is the following: how is it that, in the end, it was the third [of these options] that was adopted?"[38] That question preoccupies Foucault in the last half of his text.

4

The dream of discipline is the dream of penal theater without audience: the extermination of all resistance through total occupation of the space of resistance. The opening sentences of the first chapter of "Discipline" ("Docile Bodies") are oddly reminiscent of the opening sentences of the book: something is being done to the body; this time, however, not a brutalization unto death but a coercion (shaping, training) that will produce a useful and obedient individual. In the seventeenth century, the soldier was a noble, natural man; now, in the later eighteenth century, he is *made;* the new soldier will be the prototype of good pupils, good patients, good workers. In whatever its forms in the old regime, punishment as rhetorical theater, with its emphasis on communication, on reaching *minds,* was overly idealistic in its conception of the human subject. The disciplined society of the nineteenth and twentieth centuries, on the other hand, is rooted in a "materialist reduction of the soul and a general theory of dressage"—it discovers the body as "object and target of power." The prison will become the microcosm of all our institutions.[39]

Like those of horses, the bodies of humans must be made to perform; they need to be "broken." As a mode of training, *dressage* implies an "uninterrupted, constant coercion, supervising the process of the activity rather than its result and it is exercised according to a codification that partitions as closely as possible time, space, movement. These methods, which made possible the meticulous control of the operations of the body, which assured the constant subjection of its forces and imposed upon them a relation of docility-utility, might be called 'disciplines.' Many disciplinary methods had long been in existence—in monasteries, armies, workshops. But in the course of the seventeenth and eighteenth centuries the disciplines became general formulas of domination."[40] Discipline, then, serves two purposes: by making the body docile it controls its forces, both to keep them from politically dangerous expression and to make them economically useful. The obedient subject is the useful subject which capitalism above all requires, but it cannot have use without obedience. Capitalism always knows that, and that is why it is the genius of discipline. Though Foucault tends not to use Marxist categories explicitly, at this point he seems to employ them in all but name, as, for example, in the following passage: "Discipline increases the forces of the body (in economic terms of utility) and diminishes these same forces (in political terms of obedience). In short, it dissociates power from the body; on the one hand, it turns it into an 'aptitude,' a 'capacity,' which it seeks to increase; on the other hand, it reverses the course of energy, the power that might result from it, and turns it into a relation of strict subjection. If economic exploitation separates the force and the product of labor, let us say that disciplinary coercion establishes in the body the constricting link between an increased aptitude and an increased domination."[41] Even though Foucault places the twin phenomena of alienation and reification in a subordinate clause, with a somewhat demeaning hypothesis implied ("If economic exploitation separates the force and the product of labor. . . ."), his theory of disciplinary coercion is not a contradiction but a necessary extension of Marx. Capitalist exploitation creates abstract labor power; discipline tames that force lest it become collectively insurrectionary.

Not only does Foucault's theory of discipline give us a powerful description of the corporal technology of alienation and reification, but in doing so it implies another revision of the base/superstructure model which in its conventional conception has debilitated Marxism. Where, in other words, shall we locate discipline or dressage? From Foucault's analysis I would conclude that discipline occupies the shared space of economics and ideology, a space that effects real integration of base and superstructure, so that we cannot, on the basis of a theory of discipline, speak of determination as a one-way street. Let me put the point in another way: discipline works within the economic base, on bodies, and though it would not qualify as a "force of production" in the traditional Marxist analysis of that concept (it seems too involved in the forming of docile political consciousness to qualify), it is discipline which assures an efficient level of productivity. From the other side, and with the Marxist analysis of ideological state apparatuses in mind, the practice of discipline would apparently not find a place in the domains of Gramsci and Althusser: it is too much involved with materiality (the body and its operations within the workshop, school, army, and so on), and not enough involved in the refashioning of potentially resistant minds, in the creation of unthinking consent to ruling-class power, values, and ideas. And yet discipline is profoundly involved in achieving the classic goal of exploitative hegemonic rule: it produces political subjugation in the form of agreement, and without having to utilize the violent methods of military and police repression. Therefore, to the question "where and what is discipline?" I answer: it functions organically for Foucault throughout the social formation, from base to superstructure, as economic and hegemonic force, as a thorough materialization of hegemonic process. The theory of discipline is not anti-Marx. It is ultra-Marx, and that is both its strength and its weakness.

As a "political investment of the body," a "microphysics of power," a "political anatomy of detail," discipline—this malevolent, cunning monster that "turns everything to account"—has a long and complicated history.[42] It is no sudden discovery of the capitalist mode of production. And to say this is not to underestimate the strength of capitalism, but only to underscore its flexibility and ingenuity—its cultural catholicism, its shrewd sense of the past, and, most of all, its infinitely self-interested uses of the past. If Marx gives us the theory of pure capitalism, then Foucault, on discipline, gives us the theory of practical capitalism whose essential category is *detail*. Detail, which "had long been a category of theology and asceticism"—

"in the sight of God, no immensity is greater than a detail, nor is anything so small that it was not willed by one of his individual wishes"—detail becomes crucial for the practice of discipline, not because, as in its theological conception, it bears traces of otherwise hidden intentions, but because it provides a hold for power. In the school, the barracks, the hospital, and the workshop, a huge will to supervision joins a minutely attentive fussiness for detail to produce a "laicized content, an economic or technical rationality for the mystical calculus of the infinitesimal and the infinite."[43] Disciplinary theory and strategy appropriate asceticism and in turn will be appropriated by an emergent capitalism. The fruit of such appropriation, though Foucault does not mention it, is Taylorism, that fiendish mastery of detail provided by one of capitalism's darkest angels of asceticism in the early years of the twentieth century. The phenomenon of Taylorism completes the portrait of discipline's long historical duration; its persistence grounded not in truth but in a power that produces truth as detailed knowledge of individuals in their everyday activities, in a will to knowledge that endures from the medieval monastery to the factories of industrial capitalism because it is the chief weapon of domination and exploitation of class by class, group by group. All of this Foucault does not quite say. He gives us the historical material, and an invaluable analysis of that material, but he refuses—deliberately, I think—to forge connections with a more clearly defined perspective from the left. I want to come back to this gap in Foucault's text, and, more specifically, to the issue of Taylorism. But first, more detail.

Discipline is first of all an "art of distribution" of individuals in space. Discipline requires *enclosure.* But the enclosed space of schools, barracks, hospitals, and (most strikingly) factories is not space merely enclosed. The architecture of enclosure that Foucault analyzes is no monolith of containment, as were the structures he studied in *Histoire de la folie.* For example, in the factory, the "aim is to devise the maximum advantage and to neutralize the inconveniences (thefts, interruptions of work, disturbances, and 'cabals'), as the forces of production become more concentrated; [and] to protect materials and tools and to master the labor force."[44] But how is such an aim to be accomplished? Certainly not by permitting the free interaction of individuals within homogeneously enclosed space. Along with gross enclosure there must be a series of distributed, detailed, smaller enclosures placed within the larger structure—a factory with walls like a monastery or walled town, a veritable fortress, within the fortress a principle of *partitioning,* or *elementary location,* which, when functioning optimally, ensures that each individual be placed in his own cell. Foucault's description of this procedure is eloquent: "Each individual has his own place; and each place is individual. Avoid distribution in groups; break up collective dispositions. . . . One must eliminate the effects of imprecise distributions, the uncontrolled disappearance of individuals, their diffuse circulation, their unusable and dangerous coagulation; it was a tactic of anti-desertion, anti-vagabondage, anti-concentration. . . . It was a procedure . . . aimed at knowing, mastering, and using. Discipline organizes an analytical space."[45] In conclusion: the purpose of the disciplinary partitioning of space is "to break dangerous communications, but also to create a useful space."[46]

Partitioning promotes the twin aims of disciplinary capitalism, and after Foucault it is hardly possible to characterize capitalism without the term *discipline* and the rich meanings that he has endowed it with. Individuals are dangerous; Foucault is silent about the reasons for this. Collectives, the circulation of individuals, coagulations are even more dangerous. Again, he chooses not to contextualize this danger. What he calls the technique of "anti-desertion, anti-vagabondage, anti-concentration" was and is directed against more than petty theft in the workshop and other small manifestations of disobedience. Coagulations, he more convincingly suggests, are economically unusable. They inhibit efficient production. Concentration of the forces of production in big industry is an immense advantage for wealthy exploiters of labor, but it is also dangerous because it may provide the staging area for a kind of disobedience that would do more than take home a few of the company's screwdrivers and paintbrushes. I am referring to a level of disobedience that becomes insurrectionary and that would promote a reversal of the power relation at that most sensitive of all crossings: at the very economic site of exploitation. Discipline promotes the efficiency that capitalism dreams of, and, at the same time, dissolves the sort of consciousness that would turn workers into enemies. At this point I want to revise a little my sense of Foucault's relationship to Marx by saying that he provides not only an extension of Marx's thought. More important, after *Discipline and Punish*, in a certain sense the economic theory of Marx and the theory of discipline of Foucault stand in symbiotic relation. One of our responses to Foucault's repeated criticism of Marx and Marxism must be: Marx never existed and Foucault is his only son. And that explains why Foucault could write the following: "At the emergence of large-scale industry, one finds, beneath the division of the production process, the individualizing fragmentation of labor power; the distribution of the disciplinary space often assured both."[47]

Space is the great constitutive category of Foucauldian discipline. (Yet it is also, in a much different terminology, and under the aegis of concepts like objectification, reification, and commodification—all of which, finally, are products of a certain spatialization—a powerful constitutive category of the Marxist critique of capitalism in its Lukácian form.) In a commanding summary of the disciplinary conception of space, Foucault writes: "The first of the great operations of discipline is . . . the constitution of '*tableaux vivants*,' which transform the confused, useless or dangerous multitudes into ordered multiplicities."[48] If discipline can transform the monolithic enclosure of excluded space (*Histoire de la folie*) into partitioned, minutely analyzed space, thereby making dangerous multitudes useful and safe at the same time, then it can also do something similar for that most stubbornly subjective of human categories, time itself. Foucault's description of discipline's awesome assault on time becomes, in so many words, a comment on phenomenology's prized category and its romantic reservation of time against space. In the light of discipline, the chief humanist gesture of phenomenology seems merely sentimental. Disciplinary capitalism's assault on time appropriates temporality for the utterly manipulated world of analytic space, and in that moment of appropriation Foucault's antihumanist vision of history comes to a climax.

For its usable past, discipline reaches back into the monastic communities, taking over the rigorous life regulated by the timetable for the new rigors of the industrial period. The "new disciplines," as Foucault puts it, "had no difficulty in taking up their place in the old forms."[49] (Or, as Kenneth Burke once characterized the great stamina of elements in the medieval system, the continuity of medieval and capitalist formations is grounded in "morphological parallels.")[50] "The principle that underlay the time-table in its traditional form was essentially negative; it was the principle of non-idleness: it was forbidden to waste time, which was counted by God and paid for by man—a moral offense and an economic dishonesty. Discipline, on the other hand, arranges a positive economy; it poses the principle of a theoretically ever-growing use of time: exhaustion rather than use; it is a question of extracting, from time, ever more available moments and, from each moment, ever more useful forces."[51] In order to exhaust time for utility, and to appropriate its every available moment, time must be utterly seriated—with each moment of each activity broken off from all others and, thus isolated (and spatialized), then quantified, and only *then* brought back together with all other moments likewise submitted to discipline's analytic gaze. Discipline says to the idealists: the whole is nothing but the sum of its parts. All temporal dispersions will be integrated in a mathematically defined series. Disciplinary capitalism will defy the dreams of Wordsworth, Bergson, and Poulet, whose sense of an organic temporality is either mere fantasy or, depending on our place in the struggle, a fundamental criticism, a cry from the heart against capitalism's transformation of human existence. Time thus mediated and invested by power is (like disciplined space) not only time made useful, but time made safe. In the mystical and ascetic mode, the ordering of time was a key step in the conquest of salvation; gradually, in the history of the West, disciplined time would come to assure the earthly paradise of the industrial capitalists. In his portrait of the body "capitalized" in space and time, Foucault gives us a vivid account of the technical process through which capitalism extracted abstract labor power and value (in Marx's sense) from human beings. One of Foucault's consistent (but unnamed) targets in twentieth-century Marxism, Georg Lukács, fully anticipated Foucault's point about the disciplinary spatialization of time:

> Thus time sheds its qualitative, variable, flowing nature; it freezes into an exactly delimited, quantifiable continuum filled with quantifiable "things" (the reified, mechanically objectified "performance" of the worker, wholly separated from his total human personality): in short, it becomes space. In this environment where time is transformed into abstract, exactly measurable, physical space, an environment at once the cause and effect of the scientifically fragmented and specialized production of the object of labor, the subjects of labor must likewise be rationally fragmented.[52]

Now we need to add to Lukács' and Foucault's highly theoretical discourse on discipline and reification the practically oriented study of Harry Braverman in *Labor and Monopoly Capital: The Degradation of Work in the Twentieth Century*. Specifically, we have to address Braverman's analysis of Frederick Taylor and the phenomenon known as Taylorism. If Taylorism is no longer much mentioned as a theory of labor control and productivity today, Braverman argues, that is because "it is no longer the property of a faction, since its fundamental teachings have become the bedrock of all work design." Like Foucault's discipline, Taylorism is a theory concerned with the maximizing of productivity and poses itself as "an answer to the specific problem of how best to control alienated labor."

Foucault's need to avoid Marxist discourse does not permit him the jargon "alienated labor," but he will speak of "dangerous" laborers. Braverman and other Marxists argue that laborers are dangerous *because* they are alienated from the product of labor (as an object against a subject), from the means and place of production (owned and controlled by others), and from their very selves (fragmented into a "public" working life and a "private" leisure-time existence). Marxism would provide a rationale for that danger as well as a rationale for the need of capitalism (in Foucault's words) to break up the concentration and coagulation of individuals. Marxism would provide an explanation for capitalism's fear of any and all collectives, with the exception of the collective of its own ruling forces. Braverman's Marxism would locate Taylorism, the long history that preceded it, and what followed from it, as a "classic instance of the manner in which the antagonistic relations of production express themselves in the workplace." As the theory of scientific management, and with its chief weapon, the study of time and motion, Taylorism is a logically necessary expression of the disciplinary society.[53]

Braverman's analysis shows what Foucault will not show: the stripping of power (as knowledge) from the worker and its appropriation by management. Braverman stresses the economic basis of the investment of power in time and space: "the essential element is the systematic pre-planning and pre-calculation of all elements of the labor process, which now no longer exists as a process in the imagination of the worker but only as a process in the imagination of a special management staff. Thus if the first principle is the gathering and development of knowledge of labor processes, and the second is the concentration of this knowledge as the exclusive province of management—together with its essential converse, the abuse of such knowledge among the workers—then the third is the *use of this monopoly over knowledge to control each step of the labor process and its mode of production.*"[54] Braverman's analysis is very close, especially in the italicized section, to the spirit of Foucault's argument, but in a crucial sense it is also very far, because for

Braverman power is not, in the end, "anonymous," as Foucault says it is.

Let me come at this problem of power and the economic site of its application from another angle. While in one sense Foucault's analysis (from the inside, so to speak) of power and its relations to the means and forces of production moves toward Marx, that is not his desire. For Foucault the economic relation of power has no special status among the various power relations, and it is one of his crucial contributions as a social theorist to have brought into the light (as Marxists for the most part have not) other sorts of power relations. But his refusal to totalize the economic relation, admirable as that is, may be itself grounded in a grander totalization, a metaphysics of power. (The more sympathetic reading of Foucault would affirm that his criticism of the Marxist totalization is grounded in a keenly analytical sense of the variegated, multiple relations of power in contemporary society, most of them—at least at the surface—not economic.) If power is always productive, as he says it is, then one wants to know what is *produced* in the general domination of women, or homosexuals, or blacks, or Palestinians, or children. But he does not pursue that question and instead emphasizes in his theoretical reflections not the productive character of power, which I am convinced would take him ever more deeply into economics, but rather its anonymous quality—a pursuit which takes him away from history and society and into carceral fantasies. As he puts it in a well-known and intriguingly tautological passage, power is "organized as a multiple, automatic and anonymous power; for although surveillance rests on individuals, its functioning is that of a network of relations from top to bottom, but also to a certain extent from bottom to top and laterally; this network 'holds' the whole together and traverses it in its entirety with effects of power that derive from one another: supervision perpetually supervised."[55] This power, which is "not possessed as a thing, or transferred as a property . . . functions like a piece of machinery. . . . it is the apparatus as a whole that produces 'power.' . . . it is everywhere and always alert since by its very principle it leaves no zone of shade and constantly supervises the very individuals who are entrusted with the task of supervising."[56]

That is his definition of "relational power," or is it really a definition of paranoid metaphysics whose root metaphor totalizes society as a manipulative machine with consciousness, an all-penetrating gaze "everywhere and always alert"?[57] In another section of the text, on Bentham's Panopticon, he says that the model of supervision favored by panopticism permits the supervision and criticism of the workshop manager, the foreman, the prison governor, and the physician in charge of the hospital. If it were the managers of the world who stood most to gain by wielding power, then Foucault's point would be a telling one. To be sure: managers of all types are themselves supervised, but who would really want to argue that disciplinary mechanisms work for the interests of management? Foucault's point that managers are themselves managed should have suggested to him that the disciplinary mechanism works ultimately for the interests of those who do not work: those outside the mechanism. It may be that one cannot stand outside power, but one can, if one is so privileged, stand outside specific mechanisms of discipline.

When Foucault argues that power is not possessed as a thing or transferred as a "property" he is at the same time arguing against Marx that power is not controlled by any group or any class. In his social theory power tends to occupy the "anonymous" place which classical treatises in metaphysics reserved for substance: without location, identity, or boundaries, it is everywhere and nowhere at the same time. If it functions as a "network of relations from top to bottom," thereby giving the appearance of an elite privilege, Foucault is quick to tell us that it also, to a certain extent, operates from bottom to top—an idea which has perhaps not yet been entertained by the exploited in our society. To say that power moves from bottom to top is to promote the misleading understanding that anyone at any time can grab a piece of the action. To put it as Foucault puts it is to suggest that power has no predominant direction, no predominant point of departure, no predominant point of terminus. Like the God of theism, it is ubiquitous; unlike God it has no intention.

Power leaves "no zone of shade"; it cannot be escaped. And since power is without identity, is located nowhere in particular, since in some sense we all have it—it traverses us all—it is not a thing to be resisted but a force to be used. But for what purpose? If we are "always already" in power, and if power "sustains itself by its own mechanism," and if no one is in control of the mechanism, then what is the point? [58] Foucault's theory of power, because it gives power to anyone, everywhere, at all times, and to no one, nowhere, no time, provides a means of resistance but no real goal for resistance. The numerous, non-totalizable relations that Foucault sees at work in the jungle of contemporary society—his analysis tends to project an image of an unceasing guerrilla warfare of all against all—these relations are grounded on a power that rivals the imperviousness of some Eastern metaphysical force that ensnares us all ("I am the slayer and the slain"). In this version the economic relation of exploitation seems insignificant ("I am the exploiter and the exploited"). And what is for me most troublesome of all: this generalization of power, while pretty much ignoring the role of classes, while making resistance ever-possible and ever-meaningless, promotes a view of the dominated that is starkly at odds with the vision of society that Foucault himself energetically polemicized for almost thirty years. The horrors of domination are his great theme, but the theory of a power accessible to all refocuses our attention from the suffering of the exploited to their putative strength. If that is one of the effects of his theory of power, if his theory of power has that kind of rhetorical power, then the theory requires reconsideration. Does Foucault's theory of power betray the hard-faced ruthlessness that some partisans of Nietzsche are pleased to advertise, or does it (and this would be another reading of Nietzsche) express the cold fury of those who see our relations governed without the guidance of any ideals of community or justice? In other words: is Foucault's discourse on power an angry description of our society, or is it an ideal?

5

Because he leaves no shaded zone, no free space for real alternatives to take form, Foucault's vision of power, despite its provisions for reversals of direction, courts a monolithic determinism. His response to the disciplinary appropriation of the worker's space and time is delivered with controlled fury, but it is a fury that cannot be satisfied because he leaves no room (no space, no time) not thoroughly dominated by disciplinary capitalism and its various mechanisms. His theory of power courts determinism, and determinism courts despair: the roots of both lie in what I can only call his supermaterialism, which needs to be distinguished from historical materialism. For Foucault, the control of the worker's space and time, through the detailed manipulation of the worker's body, is the same thing as the control of the worker's mind. Consciousness is reduced to body. It is the purpose of disciplinary capitalism to produce mindlessness, to create in our factories and other institutions, compliant zombies. Foucault is right about that. And his major concepts, furthermore, are materialist in the sense defined by Herbert Marcuse: they contain at once an accusation and an imperative, as well as an explanation. But the curiosity of Foucault's materialist concepts is that there is no alternative space out of which he can propel the changes implied by his accusation. His theory of discipline cannot explain why he himself is not a mindless zombie, how he himself can mount a criticism of the system.

Antonio Gramsci's rendering of that discipline which takes the form of Taylorism is more compelling because it provides just the ground that Foucault needs—a space of resistance that is no mere reflex of the anonymous power that saturates us all. Reflecting upon the mechanization of work that Taylor's techniques helped to bring about, and the prospects for dehumanization that Taylorism would seem to have brought to frightful realization, Gramsci is ever the dialectician—if nothing in Western history is wasted, if discipline can appropriate the past, then discipline's proper historical enemy, Marxism, should be seen in somewhat similar but crucially different perspective. Gramsci will appropriate even discipline:

> it is done and it is not the spiritual death of man. Once the process of adaptation has been completed, what really happens is that the brain of the worker, far from being mummified, reaches a state of complete freedom. The only thing that is completely mechanicised is the physical gesture; the memory of the trade, reduced to simple gestures repeated at an intense rhythm, "nestles" in the muscular and nervous centers and leaves the brain free and unencumbered for other occupations. One can walk without having to think about all the movements needed in order to move, in perfect synchronization, all the parts of the body, in the specific way that is necessary for walking. The same thing happens and will go on happening in industry with the basic gestures of the trade. One walks automatically, and at the same time thinks about whatever one chooses. American industrialists have understood all too well this dialectic inherent in the new industrial methods. They have understood that "trained gorilla" is just a phrase, that "unfortunately" the worker remains a man and even that during his work he thinks more, or at least has greater opportunities for thinking, once he has overcome the crisis of adaptation without being eliminated: and not only does the worker think, but the fact that he gets no immediate satisfaction from his work and realizes that they are trying to reduce him to a trained gorilla, can lead him into a train of thought that is far from conformist.[59]

In the enthusiasm of his sublation of Taylorism, Gramsci (or so it seems to me) somewhat overstates the case for freedom and understates the degree to which disciplinary capitalism has in fact created trained gorillas, or mummies who neither think nor feel. Foucault's tough-mindedness on that point is realistic and necessary: no program for social change can afford to ignore his portrait of human degradation. But Gramsci's overall point casts considerable critical light on Foucault's vision of the disciplined society. By refusing the supermaterialist reduction of mind to body, Gramsci directs us to a ground of resistance, a critical consciousness developing at the very economic site of a would-be monolithic discipline. Not everyone will be comfortable with the social content of Gramsci's critical consciousness: especially in the United States, Marxophobia remains a powerful force. But whatever else one might say about the critical consciousness theorized by Gramsci, one could never say that its major interest was to grab a piece of the power for the sheer fun of sticking it to the rulers. The social content born of a critical consciousness is not cynical in the fashionable Nietzschean style: it aims to generate a replacement in social structure, in values, and to encourage, and help to engender, a new life. It aims to do these things in opposition to the structure, the values, the way of life it finds revealed to itself, represented in brutal detail in the very institutions whose effort is to wipe out the possibility of criticism.

The closely related issues of potential collective oppositional praxis, cooperative labor in factories, and systematic coercion all surface in rather stark form in *Discipline and Punish* when Foucault quotes from chapter 13, volume 1, of *Capital*. Here Marx reminds us that capitalist production truly begins only when capital can employ a labor force large enough to produce relatively large quantities of products. On the basis of that fact Marx makes the following points: (1) The cooperative labor of a large number of workers generates a productive power greater than the mere sum of the productive power of the individual laborers involved. (2) Therefore, "the capitalist mode of production is a historically necessary condition for the transformation of the labor process into a social process." (3) When labor becomes cooperative and collective in this sense it requires supervision, directing, and "discipline," all of which is provided by that special kind of wage laborer, the manager, the foreman, the overseer "who command[s] during the labor process in the name of capital. The work of supervision," Marx writes, "becomes their established and exclusive function." (4) Because the capitalist needs to pay the individual laborer only the value of his individual abstract labor power (and really only a part of that), and because cooperative or collective labor produces more than the sum of its individual laborers, then in addition to the surplus value of individual labor appropriated for his projects, the capitalist appropriates the entire amount of value produced by the collective power of labor. As Marx puts it with characteristic irony: "Because this power costs capital nothing, while on the other hand it is not developed by the worker until his labor itself belongs to capital, it appears as a power which capital possesses by nature—a productive power inherent in capital." (5) Despite all of the above, and in this very process of exploitation, what is brought onto the historical stage of human labor for the first time (for different reasons neither the tribal nor the slave modes of cooperation can qualify: hence the historical necessity of capitalism) is a truly social process of labor on the scale of a world-historical phenomenon. In this way, capitalism, in that ironic move of history for which Marx (like Hegel) has such a keen eye, helps the worker to break the "fetters of his individuality" (forged in different ways in tribal, slave, and feudal systems) and to develop class consciousness as an international worker, and, finally, to develop the "capabilities of the species." (I note in passing that Althusser's thesis of an antihumanist Marx, who developed after the "break" marked by *The German Ideology*, will have difficulty coming to terms with this passage from deep in the first volume of *Capital*. Its echoes of the romantic humanism of the manuscripts of 1844 are powerful, and they are central to the entire argument of *Capital*.) (6) In the process of creating cooperation in labor for the purpose of achieving the "greatest possible exploitation of labor power," the capitalist necessarily creates a collective "resistance to the domination of capital" which will require precisely the elaborate disciplinary mechanisms that Foucault analyzes. Capitalism, in one sense, will have to break up concentrations and coagulations, but, in another sense, it must create such coagulations and the means to control their political potential while wringing from them maximum economic

Michel Foucault's Fantasy for Humanists   73

advantage. At this level, I find Marx's argument historically more persuasive than Foucault's. Resistant concentrations or collectives are not ahistorical ontological entities which ruling power must control through torture, punishment, the law, or discipline: they are themselves productions of history, within a specific socio-economic formation; they are the structural contradiction which capitalism cannot help but generate. Here is Marx's Foucauldian conclusion with a difference: "The control exercised by the capitalist is not only a special function arising from the nature of the social labor process, but it is at the same time a function of the exploitation of a social labor process, and is consequently conditioned by the unavoidable antagonism between the exploiter and the raw material of his exploitation."[60]

Foucault, who cannot be accused of wishing to ignore politics and history, ignores at least half of Marx's analysis. Foucault sees no contradiction: obsessively fixed on one theme (monolithically treated), he can see only an unbroken, ever-burgeoning development of disciplinary capitalism headed, apparently without significant opposition, to a carceral dystopia of manipulation. The only piece of Marx's analysis in which he shows interest is that part having to do with the necessity for capitalism to compose and to discipline an efficient productive "machine." Foucault says "machine," not "force of laborers" or "workers," thereby granting, I think, what Marx and Gramsci do not grant: that disciplinary capitalism actually did cause the death of the human spirit.[61] Foucault's refusal to grant that capitalism can create its contradiction in the form of a collective labor process and that workers thus collectivized will resist domination by their exploiters, his refusal to recognize capitalism's necessary *agon*, sometimes plunges his analysis into hopelessness. The most pressing question must be, I suppose, why does Foucault ignore the redemptive possibilities of the cooperation created by the capitalist mode of production? A difficult question, but one which Foucault helps to answer. The first passage that he quotes from *Capital* has to do with how cooperation generates more productive power than the mere sum of the individuals involved, and he clearly is taken by Marx's military metaphor, deployed to explain the true character of the supervision of such large forces of workers. But he stops short, by just one sentence, of reproducing Marx's remarks about how the "individual" sheds his "fetters" and develops the capacities of his "species." What he leaves so conspicuously out points directly to what may be his most cherished (if generally unannounced) principle—that of the sanctity of the individual in his or her isolate freedom. In the truncation of the passage from Marx we see surfacing the instincts of the anarchist: the *fetters* of individuality? Marx, Foucault says in all but words, has surely gotten things turned upside down: for if history is the process of shedding individuality, then history is the nightmare from which we must awake.

6

What appears to trouble Foucault most is the extraordinary success of the disciplinary society in pursuing to a degree almost unimaginable the detailed segmentation of concentrations and coagulations, so as to isolate and reveal each individual in individuating particularity. The disciplinary mode of penal style and its quick institutional generalization in the nineteenth century forged an overarching social structure which would ensure efficient economic exploitation of labor as well as political stability. The achievement of these twin goals rested (and rests) on the exercise of discipline which presupposes "a mechanism that coerces by means of observation; an apparatus in which the techniques that make it possible to see induce effects of power, and in which, conversely, the means of coercion make those on whom they are applied clearly visible."[62] Within enclosed and segmented space visibility becomes a trap. The much to be desired but apparently just about hopeless contrary here and there implied by *Discipline and Punish* would be a social space that permits privacy, hiddenness, invisibility, freedom from coercion. Even freedom from power itself: though that is a pastoral dream which Foucault's theory of power would not allow.

The most impressive model that Foucault generates through the latter half of *Discipline and Punish* is the educational one, for there in the schools, more openly than in other institutions, and especially in the hoary ceremony of examination, the "superimposition of the power relations and knowledge relations assumes . . . all its visible brilliance." Examinations are the technical expression of a will to "normalize" in order to coerce into conformity and also of a deadly hold on individuality. Discipline (now to be understood in both senses), and the normalizing judgment that is indigenous to it, produce both "norm" and "difference," for what is "specific to the disciplinary penalty is non-observance, that which does not measure up to the rule, that departs from it." Discipline cannot tolerate gaps. It cannot produce *standardization*, however, in the schools, in the hospitals, and in the factories unless it first produces the norm through which differences can be recognized, evaluated, and reduced. What capitalism requires in the industrial process is standardization of the product: the ultimate fruit of the capitalist use of cooperative labor. But in order to achieve such standardization it must first standardize workers.[63]

Yet alongside this normalization (or Taylorization) the need remains to keep the powerful gaze of disciplinary knowledge fixed on the individual so that "all the shading of individual differences" will come to light. At one level, discipline must create conformity; at another level, and at the same time, discipline must keep track of individuals, develop an efficient information bank so that, ideally, everyone at all times is everywhere visible, known, and controlled. The academic examination enables the teacher, "while transmitting his knowledge, to transform his pupils into a whole field of knowledge." What is going on overtly in the classroom is not what is really going on, and on this issue of hermeneutic suspicion, Foucault adds a new dimension to the traditional Marxist analysis of education.[64]

But neither in Althusser's analysis of the ideological educational apparatus is what is overtly going on what is *really* going on. Althusser shows how the hegemonic process, aimed always at the minds of those to be manipulated, works its ideological will while hiding itself within "objective" subject matter, the knowledge that the teacher transmits. Here, I think, Foucault's general impatience with the idealism of Gramsci's and Althusser's treatments of ideology pays off richly (though it could hardly have damaged his main point had he been willing to add the ideological function of educationalists to their disciplinary function). Deliberately subordinating the teacher's ideological function, Foucault shows us how the teacher "learns" from his students. Students present the teacher with a "whole field of knowledge"—an opportunity to learn who they are and, by so doing, to objectify their individuality. The disciplinary gaze that produces such knowledge through the examination simultaneously produces a positive power over individuals—not a power that represses them, but one that produces students as a domain of objects to be known and used. The lesson that disciplinary society in its capitalist form would teach to monarchical rule is simply that a negating and censoring power is dangerous because it doesn't work very well. It leaves individuals in the shade, on their own recognizance, free to circulate, hidden from the gaze that controls. This, then, is Foucault's greatest fear; this is the horror of discipline: "For a long time ordinary individuality—the everyday individuality of everybody—remained below the threshold of description. . . . The disciplinary methods reversed this relation, lowered the threshold of describable individuality and made of this description a means of control and a method of domination." Individuality known is individuality defused. At this point in his history of punishment, it is important to remind ourselves just how far from the main line of humanist intellectuals in the West (especially modern literary intellectuals) is Foucault in his conception of knowledge. Never dispassionate and disinterested, knowledge is always useful, an expression of a will to dominate, and Foucault's glory as a philosopher-social theorist is to display such knowledge *in action*.[65]

And now, having sufficiently prepared his theoretical and historical entrance (and with an uncanny sense for the theatrics of his own unfolding text), Foucault introduces his archfiend, Jeremy Bentham, the dark counterrevolutionary of *Discipline and Punish* who envisioned the scheme of the Panopticon, the architectural realization of discipline's dream of the perfectly governed society. Once more—how typical a maneuver it is in this book—Foucault takes us back into the seventeenth century, this time in order to root discipline in a double, contradictory, political dream of the plague. One of the dreams takes on literary expression: revolutionary, collectivistic, antihierarchical, what is imagined is a festival of "suspended laws, lifted prohibitions, the frenzy of passing time, bodies mingling together without respect, individuals unmasked, abandoning their statutory identity and the figure under which they had been recognized."[66] We encounter again in *Discipline and Punish* an image for which Foucault has the most passionate affection, an image at the heart of his kind of socialism: that of the saturnalia. The other dream of the plague is an exact reversal of saturnalian revelry:

> not the collective festival, but strict divisions; not laws transgressed, but the penetration of regulation into even the smallest details of everyday life through the mediation of the complete hierarchy that assured the capillary functioning of power; not masks that were put on and taken off, but the assignment to each individual of his "true" name, his "true" place, his "true" body, his "true" disease. . . . Behind the disciplinary mechanism can be read the haunting memory of "contagions," of the plague, of rebellion, crimes, vagabondage, desertions, people who appear and disappear, live and die in disorder.[67]

The disciplined society would take its cues from this second dream, of course, and not from dream alone but from the actual details of plague-time governance: space, segmented and frozen; inspection functioning ceaselessly; and surveillance based on a system of permanent registration.

The resolution of this double dream of the plague in favor of discipline represents about half of Foucault's characterization of the genealogy of modern society. The other half lies in the resolution of another, related double dream, that of power. This too is a political dream: first of a negative power that would give rise to rituals of exclusion, to a "massive, binary division between one set of people and another." For those who do the excluding, this is the dream of purification, of a perfect because pure community. The chief example of a politics of negation for Foucault lies in the response to leprosy and the formation of what he calls the great Confinement—and it was his task in *Histoire de la folie* to write a special kind of history of negating power. The second dream is not of a purified utopia, with all undesirables cast into a roiling, confused "outside"; in the second dream there is no "inside" of purity, no "outside" of filth and madness: there is simply the dystopia of totalization, the perfectly governed city. "The leper and his separation; the plague and its segmentation. The first is marked; the second analyzed and distributed." But consider this: "Generally speaking, all the authorities exercising individual control function according to a double mode; that of binary division and branding (mad/sane; dangerous/harmless; normal/abnormal); and that of coercive assignment, of differential distribution (who he is; where he must be; how he is to be characterized; how he is to be recognized; how a constant surveillance is to be exercised over him in an individual way, etc.)." So the nineteenth century, which saw the full flowering of disciplinary society, receives the uninterrupted impact of two epistemic formations, that of a classical power that excludes, and that of an emerging capitalist power that produces. And Bentham's Panopticon provides the architectural figure of this double power.[68]

Even in translation the deadly cold of Foucault's description of Bentham's Panopticon is preserved:

> at the periphery, an annular building; at the center, a tower; this tower is pierced with wide windows that open onto the inner side of the ring; the peripheric building is divided into cells, each of

which extends the whole width of the building; they have two windows, one on the inside, corresponding to the windows of the tower; the other, on the outside, allows the light to cross the cell from one end to the other. All that is needed, then, is to place a supervisor in a central tower and to shut up in each cell a madman, a patient, a condemned man, a worker or a schoolboy. By the effect of backlighting, one can observe from the tower, standing out precisely against the light, the small captive shadows in the cells of the periphery. They are like so many cages, so many small theaters, in which each actor is alone, perfectly individualized and constantly visible.[69]

The core group of our institutions derives its main structural features from Bentham's scheme. That visionary architecture of discipline, in providing for the invisibility of the supervisor, guarantees order; from the other side, the total and constant visibility of the madman, patient, student, or worker constitutes a perfect trap and something like a rational ground of paranoia. Foucault's description carries over the bankrupt metaphor of theater, as if to indicate that the disciplinary society, looking over its shoulder, as it were, and feeling the residual force of an earlier formation, decided to preserve the theatrical style of punishment, in homage to the past, but only after asserting its own originality by imposing a shocking modification on the classical style. This will be theater without audience, except for the audience of the directors, producers, and playwrights; each actor will perform in isolation on the stage, as if in audition without end, while being watched from the dark by those in judgment of the performance. As the totally visible object, who can return no gaze of his own, the actor-citizen in our disciplinary society is transformed into an object of knowledge/power.

The effects of such transformation are suitably horrific: the individual becomes an "object of information, never a subject in communication"; the convicts cannot plot collective escape, or new crimes, or influence one another for the worse; with patients there will be no danger of contagion; the mad will not be able to commit violence upon one another; students will not copy, make noise, talk to one another, or waste time; and workers will not be distracted into slowdowns, nor will they steal, create disorders, or enter into coalitions. Those "compact, swarming, howling masses that were to be found in places of confinement" are avoided; the "crowd, a compact mass, a locus of multiple exchanges, individualities merging together, a collective effect, is abolished and replaced by a collection of separated individualities." The individuality produced by the disciplinary society stands in dramatic contrast to the romantic, free, Dionysian individual evoked in various places in *Discipline and Punish*. The collective merge, communication and community, are periodically evoked by Foucault as powerful though elegiac counterforces to discipline. The dream of perfect anarchy and the dream of socialism are alike nightmares for the powers that rule Foucault's history. The antidote is this: never a subject in communication, never a subject in community. Disciplinary society banishes the "outside." Disciplinary society speaks: What we cast into the swarming confusion of the outside may come back to haunt us. Therefore let us use everything. Especially deviancy must be saved; it must be our chief "institutional product." Let us leave the lyricism of marginality, an unwitting affirmation of the center, the mainstream, the status quo, to the newest literary critics. That will keep their minds off subjects of substance. Permit them to enjoy the liberty of literature and the pleasures of disinterested knowledge. Let them never know that "the power to punish is not essentially different from that of curing and educating."[70]

One great strength of the Panopticon is that its uses are so easily transferable. A marvelous machine of coercion, it can be put to work in any institution. The conclusion that Foucault's history moves inexorably toward is this: panoptical technology has been fully appropriated. Our social system, from gross structure to capillary level, is nothing but a carceral system. A second virtue of panoptical technique is that it creates a self-supervising mechanism: the "incompetent physician who has allowed contagion to spread, the incompetent prison governor or workshop manager will be the first victims of an epidemic or revolt." Moreover, an inspector, arriving unexpectedly, will be able quickly to judge the functioning of the entire mechanism—the supervisor supervised, ad infinitum. Of course managers, supervisors, directors, chairmen, and deans can be watched, but they direct only in the name of something else, and, repeatedly, Foucault refuses to credit that something else. Though mainly convincing about the intention and functioning of the disciplinary mechanism, he has resisted the obvious: disciplinary machines do not operate on behalf of management. Though the perfect realization of a panoptical vision would certainly produce the individual as pure object of information, never a subject in communication, Foucault has not produced convincing evidence that Bentham's demonic ideal is our only social reality. Foucault's idea that the power of panoptical structures is "supervised by society as a whole" is an echo of the most repressive of all myths of Western capitalism—the myth of bourgeois democracy that the largely unsupervised most desire to promulgate because it keeps *them* in the shade.[71]

But when Foucault moves away from quasi-metaphysical notions of power, self-operating disciplinary mechanisms, and subjects reduced utterly to the perfectly manipulable matter desired by ruling class intellectuals like Frederick Taylor, his analysis becomes focused, luminous, and more credible, as, for example, when he argues that the needs of industrial capitalism required the ransacking of history, from medieval monasteries to Jeremy Bentham—required the appropriation of all disciplinary technique. As the means of production become more complex and more costly, efficiency must be maximized or profits will disappear. And when he argues that apparatuses of production—not only economic apparatuses but those that produce knowledge in schools, health in hospitals, and destructive force in armies—all require a disciplinary mechanism to govern the means of production, and that this governance will ensure the capitalist formation, he makes the kind of sense generally ascribed to Marxist rationality. Certainly the left should not be disturbed by his summation of disciplinary power as counter-revolutionary: "it must neutralize the effects of counter-power that spring from the forces of [organized multiplicities] and which form a resistance to the power that wishes to dominate it—agitations, revolts, spontaneous organizations, coalitions, anything that may establish horizontal conjunctions."[72]

Discipline and Punish teaches that there are no fat and sassy winners, but at times it contains a message contradictory to the frequent anti-Marx diatribes of Foucault's interviews, a message which I read this way: No horizontal conjunction must be permitted; no community rooted in a nonhierarchical principle of cohesion can be tolerated, because it would threaten and maybe subvert the society in place which is rooted in a vertical principle of order. The disciplines must constantly make use of procedures of partitioning and verticality because the disciplines are representations of a vertical order of power; power does have some locations of concentration; it is in some sense a privilege of the economically elite; there are those who don't enjoy its force. Moreover, those vertical orders of power are not limited to capitalism's bourgeois democratic form, as Foucault argues: "Political anatomy can be operated in the most diverse political regimes, apparatuses, or institutions." Verticality, the contrary of horizontal conjunction, implies the domination of the many by the few.[73]

7

The prison must be the microcosm of a perfect society in which individuals are isolated in their moral existence, but in which they come together in a strict hierarchical framework, with no lateral relation, communication being possible only in a vertical direction.

MICHEL FOUCAULT, *Discipline and Punish*

As the "concentrated and austere figure of all the disciplines," a "microcosm" of a dystopic world which Foucault describes as a "carceral continuum," the prison stands as a counterrevolutionary image for a society that manages human relations so that collective revolt against the structure of verticality, on behalf of a social structure based on the lateral or the horizontal community, is more than prohibited and discouraged: it is impossible. Unlike Orwell, Foucault does not offer the carceral society as a dystopia. It is real, it is where we live and work. As *fact*, the prison is the place where individuals are deprived of their liberty; as a *focus of power* it is the place where individuals may be studied and transformed; as *figure* it stands (in an especially vivid manner) for the various ways that our central institutions all contribute to the totalization of the carceral whole. Foucault more and more in his last years spoke out against the totalizing tendency of Marxism to reduce too quickly to the economic principle of the mode of production. But the carceral continuum is nothing if not the product of a totalizing theory of society.[74]

The concluding pages of *Discipline and Punish* raise a single question repeatedly: What specifically are prisons for? Foucault gives us several answers. First of all, prisons function as capitalist training centers in which asocial individuals are made docile through forced labor: the economic form of penal labor is itself empty, but it constitutes a power relation, a "schema of individual submission and of adjustment to a production apparatus" which, it is hoped, will socialize the criminal into capitalist norms of behavior. It doesn't much work; there are better uses for prisons than transforming thieves into acquiescent workers. The chief among such uses is the transformation of the criminal, who is defined generally by his act—he "offends" in this way or that—into the "delinquent," who "is to be distinguished from the offender by the fact that it is not so much his act as his life that is relevant in characterizing him." Through a detailed psychobiographical investigation, the delinquent is created as that sort of human being who exists "before the crime and even outside it"—delinquency as a mode of existence, a complex of social and psychological factors which, whatever their sources (the disciplined society is not much interested in origins), characterize a definable way of life—the sort of person who "tends" to commit crimes. Foucault's strength in these concluding chapters lies in his blunt connection of the fabricated soul of the delinquent with a particular class.[75]

Justice and the law tend to serve the interests of class—that is traditional Marxism. Foucault complements and enriches his unavoidable "Marxist horizon" on this issue in his argument that prisons are, in a sense, meant to fail in the effort of rehabilitation; they mean to produce not so much criminals as a kind of criminal class, a group that will be looked upon, and that will (tragically) look upon itself, as constituted by that kind of person—persons who are just *that way*. These people are never to the manner born: corporation presidents who engage in price fixing are not delinquents; political leaders who order the bombing of civilians are criminals mainly in the opinion of those bombed; the sons and daughters of the wealthy who are arrested for possession of drugs or, say, attempt to assassinate the president rarely earn the distinction of delinquency. The delinquent group is always a subgroup within a class (how shall we characterize that class in the late-twentieth-century United States?) comprising all those who always find themselves at serious economic disadvantage (though their take-home pay may officially put them above the poverty level), and whose criminal acts are expressions of "character," not responses to a social order. All of this is well known, or should be well known.

"Law and justice do not hesitate to proclaim their necessary class dissymmetry."[76] The reasoning that Foucault adds to classical Marxist thought is something like the following: if the prison can produce a lower-class criminality upon which we can fix our attention as legally defined criminality, then the criminality of ruling interests (which few recognize as criminality: it is within the law) may operate outside the lights of justice, "in the shade," as Foucault puts it. The acts of delinquents, as we all by now know, are politically and economically rather harmless. Who, really, is harmed by so-called delinquent criminality? Overwhelmingly those who occupy the same neighborhoods as the delinquents. And this is all to the good of ruling interests. For one thing, so well-defined and enclosed, the class of criminals can be socially contained. For another thing, since this criminal class is virtually recruited from the ranks of the poor, delinquency is pretty much self-reflexive. The ruled terrorize the ruled, and the carceral society produces this effect quite coldly and openly. Crime is the work of the poor. Let that be known to all. In this way potential collectivization and radical action are forestalled, disadvantaged pit themselves against disadvantaged, and constant internal warfare is encouraged among groups ranging from lower to middle classes. And from this follows the ultimate hegemonic effect. The constantly frustrated and insulted of our society invest in the system ever more deeply. The way out is the way up: leave the ranks of the exploited; join the ranks of the exploiters.

If *Discipline and Punish* is in some ways, against Foucault's intention, the originating work in a strange new tradition of neo-Marxism—Marx being Foucault's unconscious as historian —it is also the most thoroughgoing argument that I have read against Marx's, and Marxism's, hope for radical social change: the most persuasive, if depressing, statement yet published, from radical quarters, on the apparently endless stamina, the perfect flexibility, and the bottomless cunning of capitalism to sustain itself. After Foucault, those who utter—ah, with what desire!—the phrase "late capitalism" run the strong risk of proving themselves theoreticians for Pollyanna.

Foucault's Legacy—A New Historicism?

Literature is "not a mere play of imagination," nor is it "a solitary caprice of a heated brain."[77] With those polemical bullets fired off in the opening sentences of his *History of English Literature* (1863), Hippolyte Taine published one of the inaugural works of old literary historicism in the atmosphere of science's positivistic heyday. "Play"/"imagination"/"solitary"/"caprice" —the syntactical proximity of these and related terms in Taine's discourse refashions them into elements of a rhetorical equation in which they operate as figures of a free, autonomous, isolated, single text and as polemical deflations of a perspective (call it idealist, romantic, formalist, humanist) which irresponsibly portrays the author of the literary text as an originary agent—the exemplary instance of the self that is supposed to be prior to society, precisely the sort of self that might create autonomous literature. Historicism, old and new, is always reactive against a prior idealism—an ever-recurring "German Ideology" which produces the historicist's need to slay by satirically sending up ever-recurring young Hegelians. And one enduring achievement of Taine's introduction to his literary history is precisely the creation of a satirical historicist rhetoric, a debunker's style shared by old and new historicists alike.

Historicism, old and new, would replace the originary self of idealism with its prime antihumanist assumption that all cultural and social phenomena, especially selves, like all natural phenomena, are to be understood as effects produced by imperious agents of causality (cultural traditions, institutions, race, ethnicity, relations of gender, economic and physical environments, dispositions of power). In its earlier scientific phase, historicism tends to be deterministic in the hard sense—it casts determining forces as abstract, monolithic, and oppressively exterior to human activity and it suffers no guilt that I can discern for doing so. In its newer phases, historicism rejects the metaphysics of determinism while cunningly retaining (not without discomfort) a complicated commitment to the principle of causality, for without causal explanation there is no historicism, old or new. Raymond Williams has written that "A Marxism without some concept of determination is in effect worthless. A Marxism with many of the concepts of determination it now has is quite radically disabled."[78] Substitute historicism for Marxism and perhaps Stephen Greenblatt for Raymond Williams, and you have a description of the theoretical quandary within which some recent historically minded literary critics, with strong and problematical relations to Michel

Foucault, and who tend to specialize in the English Renaissance, now find themselves.

In addition to the basic principle of causality, Taine's old historicism includes the following points. Taken all together they constitute the generative incoherence of his legacy: (1) A rejection of Enlightenment philosophy and historiography which marks the origin of modern historicism: in other words, there is no human nature and therefore no subject which can be its free expression. (2) The assumption (following from the first point) that history is no "flow" of continuity (like a stream) but a series of discontinuous spaces (like geological strata) contiguous with each other; the space within which the historical interpreter stands is one of those relative spaces. And from this point epistemological mayhem would appear to follow. Accordingly, the question, In what sense, if any, can a historian know his or her object of study? marks the self-consciousness of the newest of new historians, it is their badge of hermeneutical sophistication, what they accuse old historicists of lacking. But Taine has more awareness of this limitation placed upon his work by his key assumptions than he is ever credited for,[79] while new historicists tend to be allowed, mainly by themselves, more credit than is necessary for a presumed insight of contemporary critical theory which in practice produces (by intention, I think) an often disarming, if ritualistic, gesture about the problematic (that is the jargon term) nature of historical study and the need to be "self-conscious" lest we delude ourselves and others into believing that objective historical understanding is possible. (3) A commitment to continuity. Though the relation of different historical spaces appears to be a disrelation of discontinuity, within any given historical space all cultural phenomena bear a relation to one another of strong resemblance because they are thought to be the "expression" of a "cause" or "center," an "essence" never itself visible but which nevertheless makes all else visible. And the degree to which a historicist commits to this theory that a social formation can be interpreted by a principle of "expressive causality," to a theory that any given cultural phenomenon is a synecdoche which makes it possible to produce an "essential section" of the formation (a miniature, a quintessence), and that differences in expressive forms are accidental and decorative—so not to be pursued—then to that degree will a historicist be committing to determinism in its boldest sense.[80] In Taine this full commitment to determinism reveals strange bedfellows by overruling differences between the mechanical (physical) causality of positivism and the expressive (spiritual) causality of Hegelian character, both of which he freely draws upon.

Point 4, the last point, and a subversion of all the others: a humanist impulse. The antihumanist drift of historicism from Marx and Taine to Foucault and his American followers turns—virtually without warning—wholly humanistic and individualistic when the historicist in question is a literary one (as in, say, the cases of Taine and Greenblatt), or when, as global theorist, the historicist in question turns his attention to literary and aesthetic matters in the course of his global theorizing (as in, say, the cases of Marx and Foucault). The literary historicist (old and new) grants literature precisely what historicist theory (especially new-historicist theory, with its emphasis on the constitutive presence of the historical reader) is not supposed to grant to any distinct cultural form: the very power which formalist theory claims for literature, the unique privilege of putting us into authentic contact with the real thing through the medium of the "great writer" and his canonical texts. Thus Taine: "a great poem, a fine novel, the confessions of a superior man, are more instructive than a heap of historians with their histories. I would give fifty volumes of charters and a hundred volumes of state papers for the memoirs of Cellini, the epistles of St. Paul, the table-talk of Luther, or the comedies of Aristophanes. In this consists the importance of literary works: they are instructive because they are beautiful. . . . a grand literature . . . resembles that admirable apparatus of extraordinary sensibility, by which physicians disentangle and measure the most recondite and delicate changes of a body."[81] Now Greenblatt: "The literary text remains the central object of my attention in this study . . . because . . . great art is an extraordinarily sensitive register of the complex struggles and harmonies of culture. . . . So from the thousands [of writers available] we seize upon a handful of arresting figures who seem to contain within themselves much of what we need, who both reward intense, individual attention and promise access to larger cultural patterns."[82] So in the end, science is most compelling to Taine not in its systematic and impersonal guise but as the activity of a great man, an individual of "extraordinary sensibility"—and this exemplary scientist is his metaphor of the literary penetration of history; a metaphor which survives intact in Greenblatt's "handful of arresting figures," compelling concrete universals who write those "extraordinarily sensitive" registers of cultural conflict and harmony.

In a useful summary of old and new, and the differences between them (he notes no continuity), Greenblatt, now perhaps the leading voice of American new literary historicists, argues that mainstream literary history "tends to be monological"—he means (in Bakhtinian allusion) to say that it is "concerned with discovering a single political vision, usually identical to that said to be held by the entire literate class or indeed the entire population." This single vision is represented by mainstream historicists as what was really and solely there, as historical fact—not the product in the period under scrutiny of "a particular social group in conflict with other groups," not, surely, the product of the historian's own ideological formation. Against this (Taine-like) view of the expressive unity of culture, and against this serene notion of representation (historical interpretation may confidently represent the past at two removes because what it represents, literature, in turn perfectly represents its society, but only at a hair's breadth of barely one remove)— against this, Greenblatt asserts the new self-questioning historicist who views literary works "as fields of force, places of dissension and shifting interests, occasions for the jostling of orthodox and subversive impulses." So for a new historicist literature is no cool reflection on a "background" of stable and unified historical fact. It is at once part of the "fact" itself and what gives shape to what we know as the fact. The mainstream historicist must therefore practice a triple repression: first, of his own active participation in the creation of the history he thinks he objectively mirrors; second, of the interest-ridden complicity of the literature that he studies in the shaping of what we are given as history; third, of the political conflict of dominant and subaltern social groups which presumably constitutes literature's true shape and content. In short, he covers up struggle with monologue.[83]

A strong feature of new-historicist rhetoric and substance is on display in the typical beginnings of Greenblatt's essays, where he would violate the traditional literary sensibility with lengthy citations of bizarre, apparently off-center materials: an account, roughly contemporary with Shakespeare—thickly, arcanely detailed—of a social practice (say, exorcism) far removed from the high literary practice of the Renaissance. With that gambit Greenblatt would shock his traditional reader into the awareness that here, at last, is no literary business as usual. Greenblatt's beginnings seem to promise what, in theory, new historicism, so hermeneutically savvy, isn't supposed to promise—direct access to history's gritty ground-level texture. In that very moment, while doing that sort of rhetorical work in the arena of contemporary critical maneuvering, Greenblatt initiates his reader to a central new-historicist perspective on culture that recalls the debt of new historicism not only to Foucault but also to the *Annales* school and Geertz's functional anthropology—a strange mix of voices ultimately dominated by Foucauldian tone: the feeling, usually just evoked, almost never argued through, that all social life is organized and controlled down to its oddest and smallest details.

Old historicists are politically innocent—issues of ideology and class conflict rarely touch their literary work. Greenblatt more or less tells us that they needed to open their Marx. New historicists not only have reopened their Marx; they have embraced Michel Foucault (the deeper theoretical influence on their work), and the effect of this (I think, uncritical) acceptance is traced everywhere in new historicism in the coded term "power." The odd theoretical identity of new historicism is constituted by its unlikely marriage of Marx and Foucault, with Foucault as dominant partner.[84] Greenblatt describes his intention as an attempt to "achieve a concrete apprehension of the consequences for human expression—for the 'I'—of a specific form of power, power at once localized in particular institutions—the court, the church, the colonial administration, the patriarchal family—and diffused in ideological structures of meaning, characteristic modes of expression, recurrent narrative patterns."[85] In the context of the specific analyses he produces in his landmark book, *Renaissance Self-Fashioning* (1980), Greenblatt's statement on power in his introduction rings with all the paranoid resonances sounded in Foucault's account of the death of the "I" in *Discipline and Punish*. The liberal disposition (Greenblatt's and ours) to read "self-fashioning" as free, expressive self-making is repeatedly and wickedly subverted in *Renaissance Self-Fashioning*. Greenblatt's title announces to liberal optimists (we see this with hindsight) Foucault's depressing message, and his description of power endorses Foucault's theory of power, preserving not only the master's repeated insistence on the concrete institutional character of power, its palpability, as it were, but also his glide into a conception of a power that is elusively and literally undefinable—not finitely anchored but diffused from nowhere to everywhere, and saturating all social relations to the point that all conflicts and "jostlings" among social groups become a mere show of political dissension, a prearranged theater of struggle set upon the substratum of a monolithic agency which produces "opposition" as one of its delusive political effects. Greenblatt's account of the "I," like Foucault's, will dramatize its entrapment in a totalitarian narrative coincidental with the emergence of the modern world as dystopian fruition.

To summon the specter of totalitarianism is to summon determinism once again, not in Taine's positivistic manner but in the political style of *1984*.[86] New historicists are officially on record as critics both of determinism and its sentimental alternative (Greenblatt says that "Renaissance English theater in general functioned neither as a simple extension of constituted religious or political authority nor as a counterchurch or subversive assault upon that authority").[87] Moreover, new historicists typically strike more than pro forma attitudes on the issue; Greenblatt is capable of spectacular acrobatic efforts in the analysis of the relationship of literary texts and history in order to avoid determinist schemas of understanding. But the new historicism nevertheless does have a concept of determination; and far from making it worthless, this concept— which just might be the typically anxious expression of post-Watergate American humanist intellectuals—makes new historicism what it is.

Toward the end of a highly detailed and fascinating essay on the relations among theater, the practice of exorcism, and religious and political authority in the Renaissance in France and England—his most recent study of the relations of literature to its contexts—Greenblatt pulls back from his empirical work for a pause of theoretical reflection that may not refresh. He persuades us that English theater is not a reflex of constituted political authority, but in the process of making that point against old-historicist determinism, he may have instituted a profounder version of it. Consider these remarks:

1. It is no accident, I think, that one of Harsnett's tasks as Bishop [of London] Bancroft's assistant was to license plays for publication: this licensing is an element in the fashioning of social categories—the process of demarcation—that confers upon the public theater the cultural meaning that Harsnett wishes to exploit. The official church dismantles and cedes to the players the powerful mechanisms of an unwanted and dangerous charisma: in return, the players confirm the charge that those mechanisms are theater and hence illusory. . . . They therefore do the state some service.

2. Elizabethan theater does not simply reflect the official policy

toward the demoniac; it is in part constituted by it and it contributes in its turn to the concrete shaping of the spiritual and political discourse upon which it drew.[88]

With those statements that sit at the heart of his theoretical reflections Greenblatt affirms both ends of the spectrum of Marxist literary criticism, from the legendary vulgarity of reflectionist modes (and the artist as pawn and lackey) to the sophistication of the culturally sensitive Western (modernist-bent) Marxism (which grants literature formative power). Elizabethan theater shapes political discourse and at the same time is constituted by an official policy, which is executed by villainous agents whom Greenblatt can name (Bancroft, Harsnett), who exploit the theater by granting it a little freedom in return for which the players "do the state some service." But there is always something else in Greenblatt—the Foucauldian transposition of an apparent Marxist perspective. He tells us that in order to grasp the pattern of the relations of artistic and other social practices "we must be particularly sensitive to similitudes for in the Renaissance similitudes are the most well-travelled pathways of exchange, the great trade route along which cultural power is circulated." There are various social practices, like those of theater and exorcism (whose similitude is said to be "coercive"), there are—to cite *Renaissance Self-Fashioning* again—institutions, like those of the patriarchal family, church, and colonial administration, and there are characteristic modes of expression, from everyday communication to high literary narrative. The ground of grounds for understanding these practices and institutions is either "similitude" itself—the great Renaissance idea—or cultural power which is indistinguishable from political power and which "circulates" (Greenblatt's master trope for the action of power). In the first instance Greenblatt retrieves Taine and Lovejoy: similitude is the invisible expressive center, a "world view" which functions as the principle of making sense of all things, causing (in this particular instance) all things to be visible and coherent in a relation of similarity. In the second instance he summons up

Foucault by suggesting that the ground of all practice—cultural and political power—is not itself either an "idea" or a practice: "circulating" power—the master agency located in, and motivated by, no specific agent—fashions and demarcates all social categories, causes all relations of similitude and enhances and flows through all practices and human agents, is not itself a subject but sweeps up all subjects, even Bishop Bancroft and his personal operative, his intellectual, Harsnett.[89]

Bancroft and Harsnett are triggering or channeling agents only, nothing more. Not free agents. The anonymous power for which they are the medium has the obvious advantage that conspiratorial versions of history in the name of Marx do not have. The "circulating" activity of this power in all social and cultural spaces gives new and shocking meaning to the notion that nothing is outside politics. But the curious (or is it the predictable?) thing about this concept of a power that coerces all practices is that it gives rise in Foucault and (as we'll see) in Greenblatt to the desire to get outside politics—strange new-historicist desire!—and it has no way of explaining (with its but casual interests in class and economics) why some distinctively not marginal types enjoy staying inside, not only feel powerful but act accordingly.

Greenblatt's recuperation, under the mask of power, of Hegelian expressive unity of culture (a monological vision), is one but not the most interesting theoretical anomaly of new historicism. The most interesting anomaly is generated by Foucault's insistence that historians cannot objectively represent the past because they cannot know and therefore put distance between themselves and the circumstances which produced and disciplined them as social beings enmeshed in the practice of a historical *discipline.* At one level a lurking Hegelianism subverts the Foucauldian new-historicist desire to move beyond mainstream historicist practice and guarantees, in advance, the unity of the culture under historical question. At another, deeper level, mainstream historicist desire, under the very mask of its new-historicist negation, resurfaces in Greenblatt's modest statement of limitation. Greenblatt gives voice to Foucault's project of introducing the forbidden concepts of rupture and discontinuity as antidotes to traditional reliance on the grand humanist assumptions of the narrative unity of history; then (in the same breath) he puts Foucault's theoretical program at bay when he speaks of the "impossibility of fully reconstructing and reentering the culture of the sixteenth century, of leaving behind one's own situation: it is everywhere evident in this book that the questions I ask of my material and indeed the very nature of this material are shaped by the questions I ask of myself. I do not shrink from these impurities—they are the price and perhaps the virtue of this approach—but I have tried to compensate for the indeterminacy and incompleteness they generate by constantly returning to particular lives and particular situations." This apology for his limitation as a historian (it is an unwanted echo of an earlier one made by Taine) remarks ruefully on the price of new historicism—we can't help but note the implication in Greenblatt's tone that objectivity, determinacy, and completeness in historical interpretation are values reluctantly being bid elegiac farewell—yet oddly this apology shifts into a subtle claim to virtue. What is called an "impurity" is embraced as the enabling weapon of a new historicism. Forbidden traditional desires for objectivity and a unified narrative of past and present are replaced by open deployment of self-concerns; the supposed discontinuity of present and past (a Foucauldian axiom) is mapped as a continuous narrative whose source and end is "myself."[90]

The question then is, when Greenblatt says "myself," who exactly is he talking about? When he says that he seizes upon a "handful of arresting figures who seem to contain within themselves much of what we need," just who is the "we" in "need" and what is the nature of this need? Greenblatt's "myself" is representative, it finds its home in "we," and "we" is nothing other than the community of disappointed liberal middle-class literary intellectuals—and how many of us really stand outside this class?—whose basic need is to believe in the autonomy of self-fashioning and who find this need dramatized in certain standard writers of the sixteenth century, who find, therefore, the Renaissance to be peculiarly modern, a theme of traditional Renaissance theory with this twist: this need for autonomy is thought to be set up and stimulated in the emerging bourgeois world and then wholly and cruelly denied. New historicism is another expression of the bitter and well-grounded first-world suspicion that modern history is the betrayal of liberalism. The Renaissance turns out to be "modern" not only in a sense not intended by Jacob Burckhardt but in one which would have horrified his liberal confidence: the Renaissance is *our* culture because it is the origin of our disciplinary society. That, I take it, is the final, if unintended, significance of Greenblatt's re-mark that we study the Renaissance "by analogy to ourselves." The personal story that he tells in the epilogue of his book functions as a cautionary tale of the archetypal political awak-ening of liberal man to the realities of power. His advice is to imaginatively interiorize the dream of self-fashioning because only by so doing will we keep ourselves from being swept away in history's narrative of repression, in the inevitable movement to the carceral nightmare as the daylight world of everyday life. Greenblatt tells us at the end that the human subject which he (and we) wanted to be autonomous and believed to be so "begins to seem remarkably unfree, the ideological product of the relations of power in a particular society."[91]

The truly revealing (ideological) pages of *Renaissance Self-Fashioning* are those on Marlowe, the creator of "heroes who fashion themselves not in loving submission to an absolute authority but in self-conscious opposition." And yet (a typical new-historicist "yet") each of these rebel heroes is "not the exception to but"—like the Jew of Malta—"the true represen-tation of his society." ("What wind drives you thus into *Malta* road?" "The wind that bloweth all the world besides, / Desire of gold.") Greenblatt at this point brings his Marx to bear, with two quotations from *On the Jewish Question*: (1) "Judaism is a universal *anti-social* element of the *present time*"; (2) in the world of capital the marketplace is everywhere, and all things—including all human beings—are turned "into *alienable*, saleable objects, in thrall to egoistic need and huckstering." Barabas, Greenblatt argues winningly, is "simply *brought into being* by the Christian society around him," and he expresses this society in a literal sense, since he gives voice to the dominant culture by constructing his speech out of its materials, speech "virtually composed of hard little aphorisms, cynical adages, worldly maxims, all the neatly packaged nastiness of his society," its "compressed ideological wealth," "the money of the mind." Greenblatt follows out his logic: "As the essence of proverbs is their anonymity, the effect of their recurrent use by Barabas is to render him more and more typical, to *de-individualize* him."[92]

The rebellious, oppositional subject, where has he gone? He has disappeared, his identity effaced by the society structured (in Greenblatt's Foucauldian code) by "disciplinary paradigms" which produce what we desire and fear, including the modes of social opposition that in the end merely confirm the original paradigms from which the rebel never departs. Greenblatt closes this portion of his analysis with further support from Marx, this time the most famous passage in *The Eighteenth Brumaire of Louis Bonaparte*: "Men make their own history, but they do not make it just as they please; they do not make it under circumstances chosen by themselves, but under circumstances directly found, given and transmitted from the past. The tradition of the dead generations weighs like a nightmare on the minds of the living. And just when they seem engaged in revolutionizing themselves and things, in creating something entirely new, precisely in such epochs of revolutionary crisis they anxiously conjure up the spirits of the past." Greenblatt moves on to other plays, *Tamburlaine* most importantly, but only in order to enhance the basic point—that radicalism is a representation of orthodoxy in its most politically cunning form and that all struggle against a dominant ideology is in vain.[93]

Marx, theorist of social change and revolution, now reread on Foucauldian ground and converted into a forerunner of Foucault, becomes a servant of the councils of cynicism, a theorist of repetition. But even if you've read no Marx at all you see, in the very passages that Greenblatt deploys to make his political point, that Marx is saying something else. The Jew is not a "universal phenomenon," to cite Greenblatt's curtailment of Marx, but a "universal *anti-social* element." And he is a "universal *anti-social* element" not for all time but for the "*present time*," the time of capital and Christianity which he represents. What is historically specific in Marx is metaphysically general and eternally oppressive in Greenblatt and Foucault. What is always clear in Marx—the antisocial is the undesirable condition of society, Marx imagines alternatives—is rarely clear in Greenblatt and Foucault. Likewise, in *The Eighteenth Brumaire*, in that famous passage, Marx was in effect writing a preface to his reading of a specific (failed) effort of class struggle in France to make revolutionary change. He was not saying (as Greenblatt implies) something general about revolutionary praxis—that it is impossible, that acts of social change are really repetitions in disguise of the past—he was saying that we are marked indelibly by the past and that in revolutionary crises (this, I suppose, is his general point) the desire for rupture, what Marx carefully phrases as the "entirely new," is a guarantee that the past will be conjured up. The past survives as residual culture in the present, but survival is not synonymous with repetition. In *The Eighteenth Brumaire* Marx was not writing a preface to Faulkner. Yet it is precisely the "entirely new," the negation of history (strange new-historicist negation!), that Greenblatt and Foucault set up as the proof of authentic opposition, and failing to find *that* feel licensed to say that oppositional activity is a rebel's delusion cagily incited by the powers that be.

Where does this leave Greenblatt? In a political and psychological posture which he, like Foucault, can't really stomach. His alternative, strongly implied by the title of his chapter on Marlowe, "Marlowe and the Will to Absolute Play," is rigorously aesthetic (strange new-historicist alternative!) and a strong echo of Foucault's preference for so-called marginal figures of anarchy. "Marlowe's heroes," Greenblatt concludes, "nevertheless manifest a theatrical energy that distinguishes their words as well as their actions from the surrounding society. If the audience's perception of radical difference gives way to a perception of subversive identity, that too in its turn gives way: in the *excessive* quality of Marlowe's heroes, in their histrionic extremism, lies that which distinguishes their self-fashioning acts from the society around them." The inevitable question—so what?—is answered by Greenblatt with a directness usually absent from Foucault's prose: "The will to play," he says, "flaunts society's cherished orthodoxies, embraces what the culture finds loathsome or frightening, transforms the serious into the joke and then unsettles the category of the joke by taking it seriously, courts self-destruction in the interest of the anarchic discharge of its energy. This is play on the brink of an abyss, *absolute* play." Surely what Greenblatt is describing as the aesthetic moment of absolute theatricality is a moment of freedom from dominant, determining ideology and power which presumably can't be escaped except in such moments of aesthetic extremity. This is a literary politics of freedom whose echoes of Nietzsche and his joyful deconstructionist progeny do not disguise its affiliation with the mainline tradition of aesthetic humanism, a politics much favored by many of our colleagues in literary study, who take not a little pleasure from describing themselves as powerless. This is a literary politics that does not and never has answered the question: So what? [94]

The central commitment of historicists, old and new, is to the self as product of forces over which we exercise no control—the self as effect, not origin: that commitment makes historicists what they are. The central, unacknowledged, and perhaps unacknowledgeable desire of historicism—it is not part of their officially stated position on the self—is to avoid the consequences of that central commitment, to find a space of freedom and so free us from a world in which we are forced to become what we do not wish to become. There is a self-subversive tug in historicist discourse—a need to ensure that there is always something left over, a need to say what historicists are prohibited from saying and which they do not ever quite say: that there is a secret recess of consciousness as yet unmanipulated, some hiding place where we do not feel ourselves to be utterly just entities who have been enabled by vast, impersonal systems. There, in that special place, we know we are because we feel ourselves to be discontented; in that reflective space we make the judgment that no system enables—that we are unhappy. And we locate our unhappiness precisely in those systems that have produced and enabled us as selves. So the Foucauldian new-historicist account in its entirety—both what it believes to be the truth and what speaks through and undoes that belief—is the best if unwitting account of new historicism and its political quandary that I know. Hating a world that we never made, wanting to transform it, we settle for a holiday from reality, a safely sealed space reserved for the expression of aesthetic anarchy, a long weekend that defuses the radical implications of our unhappiness.

The lesson Greenblatt seems eager to impart in the personal anecdote he relates at the end of his book is that we must not abandon self-fashioning even if selfhood is to be conceived as a theatrical fiction—for to give up "is to die." He admits to an "overwhelming need to sustain the illusion that I am the principal maker of my own identity." So we sustain the dream of free selfhood in our disappointed liberal collective imagination, we sustain it there and cherish it there, because we know, or think we know, that we cannot touch the structure of power that denies us such freedom everyplace else. That such knowledge, if that is what it is (I prefer calling it a paranoid fantasy, one especially characteristic of the recent literary mind), is necessary to the sustaining of a totalitarian culture (or, as I prefer to say, to the sustaining, in ostensibly democratic contexts, of the illusion of totalitarianism): none of this seems ever to give Greenblatt, Foucault, or other new historicists pause. New historicism in its strong Foucauldian vein is an important because representative story of the American academic intellectual in the contemporary moment of literary theory, a moment which we had presumed to be a definitive break with the business as usual of literary study.

CHAPTER 2

The Return of William James

*W*illiam James is on his way back: under the banner of a "new pragmatism," and what they are calling "against theory," he may be on the verge of recapturing the imagination of the American literary humanist from its fascination with the French intellectual scene, even though the canons of social responsibility say that James is not responsible, that he lacks something in genuine seriousness. The return of James is all the more surprising in the light of our preoccupation with theory because what the canonical standards of seriousness declare that James lacks is nothing other than the proper sense of theory, which George Santayana, his younger colleague and competitor at Harvard, defined in its traditional Arnoldian setting when he wrote that theoretical consciousness is "a steady contemplation of all things in their order and worth. . . . No one can reach it who has not enlarged his mind and tamed his heart. A philosopher who attains it is, for the moment, a poet; and a poet who turns his practice and passionate imagination on the order of all things, or on anything in light of the whole, is for that moment a philosopher."[1] If the very sound and rhythm of Santayana's phrasing make us a little uncomfortable that's because James or James-like attitudes have already carried the day against traditional theory and the theorizing posture. What is a little rankling about Santayana's writing is not the traditional idea of the theorist, per se, which he describes, but his unruffled performance of that idea, his commanding vocal assumption of the referential object of his sentences: such authority seems to us epistemologically self-deluded—no one can know *that*—and politically scary. The political force of James's writing is directed against the politics of that kind of voice from on high: Santayana (European, urbane, aristocratic, Catholic, and so cool) can tell us what a theorist is because he is the theorist of theorists. He can observe the moment of the intersection of the disciplines of philosophy and poetry because he knows the difference (being neither philosopher nor poet and above both). And he knows the order of things with such confidence that he can speak the declarative sentence from its ur-space, ex cathedra: "No one can reach it . . . ," says Santayana, who has already reached it: "it" being the theoretical consciousness for which Santayana, Pope of Theory, establishes the conditions of attainment.

What Santayana says openly is what traditional theorists generally only imply when they define their activity as theorists: that to think theoretically is to concern yourself with "wholes," to think beyond the parochialisms of the schools, and to achieve some ultimate humanity of inclusive broad-mindedness by rising above the particular involvements of passionate commitment. Becoming nobody, no place, no time, we achieve the theorist's ideal, which Santayana's phrasing reminds us is the very ideal of reason as it has been traditionally conceived in the West since the Greeks. In this serene, epistemologically and morally secure space, beyond ideology, one has knowledge of the real order and value of all things. Early-modern philosophical commentators on this view of theory—those for it and those against—called it "absolute," as in "absolute idealism" (they were thinking mainly of Hegel); recent Marxists and anti-Marxists alike (thinking of Lukács in his Hegelian mode) say "totalizing." And more recently (after Richard Rorty, a Jamesian of sorts) the tendency is to say "foundational"—Rorty, when he uses that word, is thinking of all of philosophy with the exception of a few names: a different Hegel, Dewey, Wittgenstein, Heidegger, himself. James's coded synonyms for both theory and traditional philosophy are "reason" and "rational," close cousins to his pejorative of pejoratives—"abstract."

My central point will be this: independently of Marx, and as the founding gesture of his work, James in effect accepts the most famous of Marx's theses on Feuerbach—that philosophy should be trying to change, not interpret, the world—but James out-Marxes Marx by saying that all the interpretive efforts of philosophy are always simultaneously efforts to work upon and work over things as they are. All intellectuals play social roles, whether they like it or not, James believed, because interpretation is always a form of intervention, a factor in social change or in social conservation. The recurring double point of James's pragmatism is that all theory is practice (situated intellectual involvement with real local effects) and that all practices are not equally worthy. If all thought is a mode of action, a tool, not a representation—an instrument for doing work—then the key consequence forced upon us by this philosophy of consequences would not be the recognition (James's banal and potentially dangerous starting point) that there is nothing but practice. The key consequence of Jamesian pragmatism would be the urgent directive that we attend to the different consequences of different practices, for only in their different consequences can we know and evaluate such practices as different epistemological and political alternatives. No difference in consequences, no difference in practice. No difference in consequences, no difference in belief.

"Belief"—which is what a pragmatist prefers to "theory"—boils down to a "set of rules" for the action of changing-by-interpreting the world's various texts, verbal and otherwise.[2] Belief shapes our interpretive conduct—a redundancy: all conduct is interpretive—and conduct is the sole significance and real content of belief. It is a strong implication of what James believes about "belief" that the rules synonymous with belief are open to reflection and revision. Whether the set of rules which constitutes belief is knowable in advance of the conduct it shapes, or whether such rules are extrapolated from conduct, after the fact, the ethical and political imperative embodied in pragmatism tells us that we must evaluate the consequences of belief—action in the world—by evaluating the conduct-structuring rules of belief, and, in doing that, become responsive to and maybe responsible for the future of a belief (the conduct and consequences that belief will produce): not from some transcendental standpoint in "theory" but from within a situation that is both primal and recurrent, the situation of emergency.[3] We are lost in the woods, we need to find our way home, but we have no map. Then we see a path, choose to believe (maybe because of what we take to be irrefutable olfactory evidence) that it is a cowpath which if followed will lead us to the safety of the farmhouse. Surfacing here in James's representative anecdote of cognitive emergency, which is at the same time an existential emergency, is the temporal character of belief. As tools for getting done the various works of liberation, beliefs are instruments of desire; they are born locally in crisis and have local consequences only. When they do not lead us out of the cognitive woods, we revise them—still in the woods, still in crisis, we remeasure our context—for other beliefs that might work. If it is the case that the triggering emergency (or the occasion for belief), the actual work of belief, and the consequences (or future) of belief are always bound to local contexts, then it is also the case that all efforts to escape temporal and geographic locality are expressions of a passion that is the traditional theoretical impulse par excellence. The desire to move to theory according to James is the desire to move over the arena of work to a place where all possible situations of work can be surveyed in a single glance, gathered up, and mastered. The site of theory turns out to be the totalitarian site of imposition where all local situations are coerced into conformity, and where the future itself (in the form of consequences) is known and therefore controlled and manipulated in advance. Theory is not belief because theory never sees itself restrained by its occasional status, it does not think its status occasional. With its global conception of itself, with its metaphysical confidence, theory has no need for self-revision. But if theory is in some sense like belief because it is also a form of practice, then the work of theory can only be the work of trying to convert (shape, force) experience into what theory wants to see in the world: an adequate object of its totalizing desire to rig the game of interpretation. Like belief, theory emerges from historical ground; unlike belief, theory cannot bear to live with history.

As Stanley Fish puts it in an essay whose "new pragmatist" conclusions I want eventually to challenge, theory would work as a general (rather than a "local") hermeneutics, an interpretive procedure which would always yield correct results if the proper steps were strictly followed. Fish argues convincingly that the model for "theory" (I'd say "traditional theory") is mathematics, a "rational activity" whose "constraints are not acquired through experience (education, historical conditioning, local habits) but are innate." The constraints of theory so conceived are necessarily abstract, general, and invariant. Fish's new-pragmatist definition of theory is pure William James. But his conclusion that theory cannot succeed because "it cannot help but borrow its terms and its content from that which it claims to transcend, the mutable world of practice, belief, assumptions, point of view," manages to be Jamesian while at the same time missing what I read as James's ironic political theme: that theory's very inability to be successful in its own terms has powerful historical consequences, that it is precisely its failure to leave history that ensures that theory is a practice and that theory always marks history with its imposing ambition.[4] The fully articulated pragmatism we find in James says not only that there is nothing but practice, but that practice carries with it the obligations of revision, that practice tends to force constant scrutiny of one's work in its context. This is so because the historical pressures at the site of practice produce a reflective (and dialectical) moment, let's call it ad hoc theory with a lowercase t, which is in turn tested by the practice to which it is necessarily returned.

So pragmatism teaches nothing if not responsiveness to contexts of work. When not so accompanied, our practice, including theoretical practice, becomes mindless work, and we become something like Charley Marlowe with his rivets in *Heart of Darkness*: which is to say that such work is not really mindless, but the hopeless effort of bad faith to escape from reflection on the situation of work and a form of intellectual cowardice. For Marlowe this means the hopeless desire to escape from reflection on the imperialist site of his activity and his responsibility at, and for, that site of work. The new-pragmatist demolition of theory is useful to a point: it shows us that theory, including its varieties after the new criticism, conceived and held in the traditional way, is not only defined by ahistorical hunger but doomed to perpetual inability to satisfy such hunger. But the new-pragmatist analysis, once it has uncovered that defining contradiction of theory (formalist desire, contingent setting of desire), concludes its own work too soon, not seeing that theory-desire's contingent setting in history is the ground of theory's real work, the ironic because unwanted object of its intention. The premature closure of new pragmatism's own analysis has this effect: it produces a style of dismissiveness which then comes around to haunt and seize antitheory, turning it into precisely the sort of theory that antitheory ought not to want to be—historically and politically blind praxis, theory (if you can imagine this) as a blithe-spirited Charley Marlowe.

Expressed most resonantly in key metaphoric moments, James's vision of pragmatism is irreducibly a vision of heterogeneity and contentiousness—a vision strong for criticism, self-scrutiny, and self-revision that never claims knowledge of a single human narrative because it refuses belief in a single human narrative and refuses the often repressive conduct resulting from such belief. James's fully committed pragmatism has no way of settling, once and for all, the question it constantly asks: Does the world rise or fall in value when any particular belief is let loose in the world?[5] When we act upon others or when others act upon us? By insisting that the question be posed that way, in nonacademic form (Does the *world*, not literature, not philosophy, rise or fall in value?), James is insisting that the consequences of belief reveal themselves most fully outside the immediate domain (in his case, the discipline of philosophy) of any particular belief's application. Like the father of pragmatism, C. S. Peirce, James is no philosophical ostrich with his head in the sand. He starts with the recognition that others believe differently and just as strongly.[6] James thereby puts us in a world of different and sometimes competing choices and conducts, and of different and sometimes competing stories, a world in which resolution could be achieved only in a final solution of criticism: by the forcible silencing of the competitor.

So the world according to James is a geography of practices adjacently placed: a heterogeneous space of dispersed histories, related perhaps by counterpoint, or perhaps utterly disrelated—a cacophony of stories—but in any case never related in medley. "The world we live in exists diffused and distributed, in the form of an infinitely numerous lot of eaches."[7] Overarching metanarratives, say Marxist or Christian, which would make all the "eaches" cohere—and so eliminate heterogeneous plurality—never tempt James. He is no utopian. (But neither is he a dystopian.) He believes that history conceived as teleological union is a late and nostalgic expression of classical aesthetics—the proleptic imaging forth, in the rigorous causal perfections of Aristotelian plot, of desired historical order, the harmony of time itself. Better, he believes, to think against Aristotle's preference for drama, better to prefer romance to drama, better to think that the "world is full of partial stories that run parallel to one another, beginning and ending at odd times. They mutually interlace and interfere at points, but we cannot unify them completely."[8] Together with his literary metaphor of narrative richness, James levels this backyard metaphor at the dogmas of monism: "It is easy to see the world's history pluralistically, as a rope of which each fiber tells a separate tale; but to conceive of each cross-section of the rope as an absolutely single fact, and to sum the whole longitudinal series into one being, living an individual life, is harder."[9] "It is easy," if you are James: James himself knew that the seeing of plurality, and the letting be of what you see, is not a matter of just opening your eyes to the facts and having a good attitude. His philosophical project is dedicated to the cause of getting others to see it his way while showing us, at the same time, the violent effects of seeing it otherwise, the bad attitude that necessarily accompanies seeing it otherwise.

History in James, as in his master, Emerson, is no monument that demands mimetic awe. Rationalism (a key word for "theory" in James) would force a mimetic role upon the text of the world: "On the rationalist side," James writes, "we have a universe in many editions, one real one, the infinite folio, or *edition de luxe*, eternally complete; and then the various finite editions, full of false readings, distorted and mutilated each in its own way." The effort of the rational textualist must be to make all finite editions somehow "correspond" to the *edition de luxe*. But the pragmatist gives us history in a complex metaphor both as text and as the liberation of textual work—a text, James writes, "in only one edition of the universe, unfinished, growing in all sorts of places, especially in places where thinking beings are at work."[10] For the pragmatic textualist, who is the bibliographer's version of the devil, there is only one text: the forever unfinished, decentralized text of history—forever supplemented, new chapters being written in all sorts of places by all sorts of people not especially in touch with one another. There is no work of "correspondence," only of "production." James's textual metaphor is an effort to speak against the political authority which masks itself in rationalist certitude and self-righteousness, which demands mimetic fealty, and which he specifically and frequently evokes after his involvement in the New England Anti-Imperialist League in royalist, militarist, aristocratic, and papal terms.[11] James's textual metaphor speaks *for* the liberation of the small, the regional, the locally embedded, the underdog: the voice that refuses the elocutionary lessons of cosmopolitan finishing schools. His unfinished (and unfinishable) text of history, authorized by no single author, is the text of American history as it ought to be—the multi-authored book of democracy in its ideal and antinomian form.

For James, then, there may be nothing more ugly than theoretical consciousness in the rational practices it authorizes. The lectures he delivered in late 1906 and early 1907 in Boston and New York, and then shortly after published as the book *Pragmatism*, bear the mark of a decisive moment in U.S. history: our first fully launched imperialist adventure, in the last years of the nineteenth century, in Cuba and the Philippines. Though pragmatism was inchoately present in his *Principles of Psychology*, he began to know his philosophy as pragmatism only after he found the political terminus of his thought in his anti-imperialist activism at the turn of the century. In the New England Anti-Imperialist League James experienced a direct and co-determinative connection between his philosophical principles and his political life. It was at that point, after his political turn—and not before, when it was abstractly possible for him to do so—that he began freely adapting from C. S. Peirce; it was at that point, and not before, that he began to understand empire as theory (as a kind of theoretical impulse), and theory or traditional philosophy as empire (as a kind of imperialist impulse). For James, the two impulses are measured and joined by the effects they produce in trying to cure the world of diversity.

James becomes the first in a hidden history of oddly connected American refusers of imperialism. The second was Wallace Stevens in "Anecdote of the Jar" of 1919, as read by a third, Michael Herr, in his book on Vietnam of 1970, *Dispatches*, in which the entire focus of American military power that was concentrated in the fortification at Khe Sanh was crystallized by Herr with Stevens' poem. Stevens, who found Dwight Eisenhower radical, is made by Herr to speak directly against the ideology of imposition and obliteration co-active in Vietnam with a strategy of defoliation. The textual expression of that strategy is the literal remapping of a country—"the military expediency," in Herr's ironic reflection on the sometimes mad and deadly relations of sign and referent, "to impose a new set of references over Vietnam's truer, older being, an imposition that began most simply with the division of one country into two and continued . . . with the further division of South Vietnam into four clearly defined tactical corps." Herr concludes by glossing Khe Sanh via the imaginative imperialism that was activated and subtly evaluated in "Anecdote of the Jar." "Once it was all locked in place, Khe Sanh became like the planted jar in Wallace Stevens' poem. It took dominion everywhere."[12]

James had written his own anecdote of the jar in the opening lecture of *Pragmatism*: "The world of concrete personal experiences to which the street belongs is multitudinous beyond imagination, tangled, muddy, painful and perplexed. The world to which your philosophy professor introduces you is simple, clean and noble. The contradictions of real life are absent from it. Its architecture is classic. Principles of reason trace its outlines, logical necessities cement its parts. Purity and dignity are what it most expresses. It is a kind of marble temple shining on a hill."[13] The marble temple shining on a hill is James's metaphor for traditional philosophy in its traditional project of representation: mind as correspondence, thought as reflection of real ontological structure, thought emptied of the messes of social time, thought historically uncontingent. But philosophy so conceived, James says, is not, despite its claim, an "account of this actual world." It is an "addition built upon it": a "sanctuary," a "refuge," a "substitute," a "way of escape," a "monument of artificiality"—"cloistral and spectral." All negative qualities, of course, and quite harmless, until we add one more characteristic which gives ominous point to all the others—James's shining marble temple of philosophy, like Stevens' jar of imagination, like Khe Sanh (like Bentham's Panopticon), is also a "remedy."[14] In this dismantling of the classic project of reason, what James wishes to show is that the product of rationalist method is not cool, contemplative representation—"theory" above the battle: it is *purity in action*. The shining marble temple is "round upon the ground" and it does not give "of bird or bush." Like the defoliating jar in Stevens' Tennessee, or the imposed references by which military need in Vietnam attempted to recreate the referent (we had to destroy that village in order to save it), theory classically conceived is the desire for a "refined object." And theory-desire, the desire for refinement, is a "powerful . . . appetite of the mind" which gets expressed as the *will to refine:* a chilling process when considered in the political contexts within which James writes.[15] In an eerie prolepsis of both Stevens' poem and Herr's reading of Khe Sanh as the "planted jar," James evoked his sense of the perversity of the American presence in the Philippines by describing it as an effort to "plant our order."[16]

I have to this point been emphasizing what I have called, a little misleadingly, James's political period, the late phase of his career when he could with some justice refer to himself as an anarchist. Actually this late phase represents a substantial change of heart which, if ignored, would obscure by suppressing not the nonpolitics but the more familiar American politics of his earlier career. Two historical points may be made, the first more or less factual, the second more or less speculative. In the late 1880s James responded to the protests of exploited labor in this country by telling his brother not to be "alarmed by the labor troubles here" (Henry was not "here"). Brother William went on to explain, in all seriousness, that the turmoil of strikes was "simply a healthy phase of evolution, a little costly, but normal, and sure to do lots of good to all hands in the end." If that response to the emergence of organized labor deserves to be characterized as academic in the worst possible sense of the word—how else to understand his application of Darwin?— then his remarks on the Haymarket Riot of May 1886 need another, less kind evaluation: in his response to that violent moment in our labor history James gave voice to American xenophobic paranoia. "I don't speak," he continues in the same letter to Henry, "of the senseless 'anarchist' riot in Chicago, which has nothing to do with 'Knights of Labor,' but is the work of a lot of pathological Germans and poles [sic]."[17]

The journey from "a lot of pathological Germans and poles," to James's critique of philosophy's shining marble temple on a hill, to Stevens' critique of the jar on a hill in Tennessee, to Herr's meditation on Vietnam, Khe Sanh upon a hill, perhaps began with John Winthrop's vision of the Puritan community as a "city upon a hill" and Winthrop's unwittingly ugly interpretation of that city when, years after he had coined the phrase, he banished Anne Hutchinson for antinomian heresy. Hutchinson: "I desire to know wherefore I am banished." Winthrop: "Say no more, the court knows wherefore and is satisfied."[18] The city upon a hill, a metaphor of community self-consciously visible and vulnerable, is revised in Winthrop's retort to Hutchinson into a metaphor of the imperial city rigorously and violently exclusionary—a structure of male authority, purity (Puritanism) in action, poised as a "remedy" against a radically individualist principle of resistance whose most famous American representative is female. Winthrop's revision, and its impersonal authoritarian devastation of insurrectionary female conscience, just may be (more on this later) the political unconscious of Jamesian pragmatism at its radical edge.

If Anne Hutchinson is the hidden moral and political mother figure behind James's pragmatism, then the not-so-hidden moral and political father figure behind his pragmatist celebration of sovereignty (personal and national) is Emerson—for intellectual and biographical reasons it could not have been anyone else— the Emerson who wrote that "whenever I find my dominion over myself not sufficient for me, and I undertake the direction of my neighbor also, I overstep the truth, and come into false relations with him. . . . This is the history of government—one man does something which is to bind another."[19] Emerson found the history of the word *politics* to be the history of a pejorative, coincidental with *cunning*; it meant the indenturing of others to the imperatives of power not their own, and (as Stevens would put it) the taking of dominion everywhere.[20] In his essay "History" (1841), Emerson argued by metaphorical sleight of hand that in the self's true (presumably American) domain there are no medieval relations of economic and political coercion, that the privileges of the spirit are radically open to all: "He that is at once admitted to the right of reason is made a freeman of the whole estate. What Plato has thought, he may think; what a saint has felt, he may feel; what at any time has befallen any man, he can understand; who hath access to this universal mind is a party to all that is or can be done, for this is the only and sovereign agent."[21] And with the agility of the socially critical punster, Emerson trained his wit in his famous "Nature" essay of 1836 on private property in the capitalist system, writing in a famous passage that though Messrs. Miller, Locke, and Manning may claim ownership of the physical property of their farms, the very best part of those farms their warranty deeds give them no title to: the "property" of vision is "owned" by the integrating eye of the visionary capitalist, the poet who alone can "possess," because he creates, the "landscape."[22]

The point of Emerson's compressed metaphoric recollections and attacks on feudal and capitalist modes of production is that the great human values are preserved only in the world of culture, because in that world the power that accrues from economic privilege—whether lordly or bourgeois—is presumably annulled, even though apparently culture can at no point annul the actual unfreedom and oppression that obtain in material society which, in Emerson's memorable phrasing, "everywhere is in conspiracy against the manhood of every one of its members."[23] "Society" for Emerson is synonymous with the surrender of "liberty and culture," with a process of coercion that sanctions the binding of many for the benefit of a few.[24] But culture is not a way of life intervening upon and shaping social, economic, and political relations: "culture" is rather an alternative to "society," wherein governments will continue to underwrite relations of domination. So culture for Emerson is simultaneously an idealist affirmation of freedom and truth in a democratic intellectual world of equal opportunity and an implicit denial that actual collective life can be the ground of those values. At its worst, and by virtue of what Herbert Marcuse would call its affirmative inward turn, Emersonian culture becomes an implicit validation (via benign neglect) of the real injustices rooted in real economic inequalities.[25]

What now appears most dated in Emerson's American repugnance for our European social origins, where the dream of America was hatched, was perhaps for his audience the most thrilling and the most duplicitous element in his writing. His clarion call for intellectual independence, sounded on numerous occasions—"We have listened too long to the courtly muses of Europe"—was intended to urge his fellow Americans on to the cultural end of the adventure, political independence presumably having already been secured.[26] But the overt message of "The American Scholar" and other essays which touch political themes directly is subverted time after time in Emerson's American revenge against the history of economic privilege. The American poet and the American scholar are the representative men who stand in for history's dispossessed and excluded in their desire to come into possession—for possession is power and power is freedom. In taking his revenge, the Emersonian poet asserts on behalf of all the mute and all the inglorious of all times solidarity in the transhistorical community of noble spirits and brilliant minds, for it is the Emersonian poet who underwrites the proverb of American proverbs that it is not where you come from that counts but who you are; it is he, the Emersonian poet, who celebrates the natural ground of privilege. But the retreat to the interior enacted by Emerson's various metaphors against ownership in both feudal and capitalist systems of production carries the unhappy message that cultural independence will not be the grace note of American history—in the citadel of subjectivity, where we contact the "sovereign agent," it will be the only independence we know.

In spite of Emerson's obvious delight in trumping the card of capitalism, neither the poet nor any other isolable individual finally owns anything, not even himself. The primary fact of Emerson's transcendental economy is not owning but belonging, not possessing but being possessed. That to which we belong ("the only and sovereign agent") and that by which we are possessed is no individual. What Emerson liked to call the "universal soul," or "Reason," or the "oversoul," he defined strategically, with a perfection of vagueness, as an "immensity not possessed and that cannot be possessed"—"we are its property." Whatever "it" is, whatever more specifically the word "immensity" signifies in Emerson's discourse, we can say that *it* is not quantifiable, that it cannot be economized as a "commodity." "It" is precisely that which cannot be made precise, specific, an object. It neither buys nor sells; it controls no labor power. It is instead a condition of release from possessive selfhood and the commodified consciousness of liberal political vision. "*It*"—this "immensity," a cliché in the rhetoric of the sublime—is revalued on American political ground as our possession by freedom, which Emerson (at his most hopeful) calls "the background of our being."[27]

In the crucial definition of personal consciousness that he offers in the first volume of *Principles of Psychology*, James chooses to ignore Emerson's rejection of all economic conceptions of selfhood. James finds (or thinks he finds) truly inalienable private property located at (and *as*) the core of selfhood. So the price of James's anti-imperialist vision of human heterogeneity may be the most radical of all possible alienation and disconnection, which he expresses as the first commandment of his capitalized psychology—thou shalt not steal individuality: "Each of these minds keeps its own thoughts to itself. There is no giving or bartering between them. . . . Absolute insulation, irreducible pluralism, is the law. It seems as if the elementary psychic fact were not *thought* or *this thought* or *that thought* but *my thought*, every thought being *owned*. Neither contemporaneity nor proximity in space, nor similarity of quality or content are able to fuse thoughts together which are sundered by this barrier of belonging to different minds. The breaches between such thoughts are the most absolute breaches in nature. . . . The worst a psychology can do is so to interpret the nature of these selves as to rob them of their worth."[28] Or, more emphatically still: "*In its widest possible sense . . . a man's self is the sum total of all that he can call his*, not only his body and his psychic powers, but his clothes, and his house, his wife and his children, his ancestors and friends, his reputation and works, his lands and horses, and yacht and bank-account."[29] But all of the things that we think we "own," James says, are "transient external possessions" with the sole exception of the "innermost center within the circle," that "sanctuary within the citadel," the "*self of all the other selves*," of which we can never be dispossessed: the "home," the "source," the "emanation" of "fiats of the will"—a feeling of an "original spontaneity," an active power within, without constraining ground, that becomes the ground of our personal freedom to say yes or no and a point of departure for James's anti-imperialist pluralism.[30] That feeling of original spontaneity is James's phenomenological postulate for the inviolability of self, or of a self that should be responded to as if it were and deserved to be inviolable.

What I think James knew is that his intellectual father's transcendentalist commitment to a community of justice and dignity beyond all those historical powers of oppression that Americans like to associate with the Old World could have no material site, not even here in the so-called New World. Emerson's "active soul," an ideal instrument, working directly, if at all, from mind to mind, never works in, on, or through the mediations of actual social arrangement. In the heat of James's anti-imperialist activity, Emersonian nonconformity was simply not enough—it lacked (my anachronism is the point) James's muscular pragmatism—for the disturbing implication of Emerson's divestiture of agency and sovereignty from the individual was political passivity, not political action. What James knew is that there can be no Emersonian practice. Any act of personal will over and above the organic act of transcendental selfhood is more than neither necessary nor appropriate; it is dangerous. Any act of would-be anti-imperialist will might become (ironically) a trace of the will of the imperialist that James and Emerson abhorred. But James's pragmatism is nothing if not a philosophy of will; of personal, not transcendental, agency; of personal, not transcendental, sovereignty that would and did risk (without guarantee of moral purity) frightening appropriation of its tenets. James took that risk because, unlike Emerson, he could not be satisfied with the interiorization of cultural power and the subjectification of freedom. James would make culture instrumentally powerful; he would make intellect politically decisive to the fate of society.

What ran deep in James and what beyond argument was altogether there in Emerson (let's call it the American instinct against the imperial social gesture), but which did not surface in James until late in his career, after he had been politicized, is a sense of American history and society as severely ruptured from its European origins and from European institutions synonymous with oppression: the Roman Catholic church, the army, the aristocracy, and the crown. James named these institutions as the true enemy of his philosophic method, which he sometimes late in his career associated with a Whitmanesque, unbuttoned, even anarchic notion of self-determination. Especially after 1900, James conceived of the role of the intellectual in specific American terms as one of guarding our freedom from those European institutionalizing impulses which might and *did* insidiously rebirth themselves here from the ("theoretical") "passion of mastery" and in the form of "national destiny," a slogan which speaks for efforts first to organize, on native ground, in a "big" and "great" manner (James hated those words) against the "molecular forces that work from individual to individual," then *over there* to bring light to the uncivilized: "national destiny" as the will to impose our sense of national story—plant our order—on foreign soil.[31] It was the American intellectual's duty, James wrote in numerous letters to the *Boston Transcript* in protest against our imperialist policies, to expose the empty but murderously effective abstractions of the party of Roosevelt (like our "responsibility" for the islands, like the "unfitness" of the Filipinos to govern themselves), and James was convinced that this could be done only if intellectuals in America developed class-consciousness as intellectuals: a class with presumably no reason to align itself materially with special interests because it stood, or should stand, for ideal interests only—by which he meant the preservation of radical individual freedom. Even in the United States this cannot but be characterized as an innocent view, but it is a view borne aloft in the morning freshness of the founding American myth—the democratic hope that with nothing resembling an aristocracy to encumber them, Americans in the new Eden had the right to think of the individual as truly prior to society. But at the same time James saw that in such presumably fluid social circumstances we could have no equivalent to a permanent presence (like an aristocratic class) responsible for overseeing the integrity of the social process as a whole. (Who, anyway, aside from Emerson, could oversee the integrity of antinomianism?) He nominated intellectuals for that role because he thought that in a society without those entrenched institutions within which European intellectuals found themselves, the American intellectual would wield "no corporate selfishness," and "no powers of corruption."[32] James underrated, though he did not ignore, the corruptive power of capital in fluid democratic contexts—he did not imagine that capital could bind intellectuals; he could not easily accept (though he witnessed) American intellectuals giving voice to the impulses of imperialism.

James *did* imagine the American intellectual as defender of a self that is, or should be, inaccessibly private property; a self that is, or should be, the motor principle of American anti-imperialism. Each of us, he writes in an essay called "On a Certain Blindness in Human Beings," is bound "to feel intensely the importance of his own duties and the significance of the situations that call these forth. But this feeling is in each of us a vital secret, for sympathy with which we vainly look to others. The others are too much absorbed in their own vital secrets to take an interest in ours. Hence the stupidity and injustice of our opinions, so far as they deal with the significance of alien lives."[33] The elaborate but symptomatic difficulty in making sense of James is coming to see that his overt commitment to the inalienable private property of selfhood, the original feeling of spontaneous action, the freedom felt within, is an inscription of a contradiction at the very heart of capitalism (and theorists of capital like Adam Smith) because property under capitalism can be property only if it *is* alienable—only if it can be bought, sold, stolen, and, when necessary, appropriated. James's political turn taught him that nothing was inalienable in the coercive world of imperialism, not even the secret self that we think we possess beyond alienation. He employs the language of private property in order to describe the spiritual nature of persons and in an effort to turn the discourse of private property against itself by making that discourse literal in just this one instance: so as to preserve a human space of freedom, however interiorized, from the vicissitudes and coercions of the marketplace.

James's anti-imperialism is American anti-imperialism; his philosophical term "pluralism" is an antithetical word signifying not so much what *is*, but rather resistance to the imperialist context of his work in the modernist moment. In other words, pluralism signifies what "is *not*" and what should be. His major effort is to combat the hegemonic discourse of a capitalism rooted in a democratic political context by appropriating the cornerstone economic principle of capitalism to the advantage of his counterdiscourse: a vision of human sanctity and difference central not only to his pragmatism but also to the originating myth of American political history. What James says in all but words is that if imperialism and capitalism on their own are capable of destroying the self, then in their unified American form they represent a global principle of structure, a world-historical menace of unparalleled proportions. In the name of pragmatism and the American dream, James wanted to turn America against the self-pollution of its foreign policy at the end of the nineteenth century; in such an act of self-criticism, he thought, we would subvert the economic and political postures which, by treating all human subjects as if they were objects, for all practical purposes convert us into objects who suffer degradations that nonhuman commodities cannot suffer. So James's quasi-Cartesian postulate of an interior spontaneity is not ontological but thoroughly instrumental. It is his great heuristic principle, the energy of his criticism, and the basis of his anti-imperialism.

After his political turn James could, in the same breath, speak against the rationalizations of theory and traditional philosophy as well as the theorizations of society, those political and economic arrangements of power that rob the self of itself by rationalizing the self in the name of capitalism and the commodification of human labor. Against the in-house economic imperialism which appropriated the self for capital in America, against his own earlier reaction to the Haymarket Riot, and against the international imperialism which denied self-determination to the Philippines and to Ireland, James brought his pragmatism as an emancipating critical force which would liberate the particular, the local, the secret self from intellectual, economic, and political structuralizations which would consume, control, deny all particularity, all locality, and all secret selfhood. James, to say it again, is no utopian: he has no vision of a future social arrangement that would ensure the safety of the self, no vision of the good collective. His pragmatism, Ariel-like, is emancipatory—it recognizes but does not capitulate to the suffocating and tyrannous world that Foucault described. It has nothing to say about where we should be, only about where we do not want to be.

James's Legacy—A New Pragmatism?

Does James's stance on the issue of traditional theory have any consequences of the sort that would bind intellectuals to the social contexts of their activity? Not an innocent question: my profession is theory-conscious, even theory-obsessed. Passion for and against theory seems unavoidable among those who come in contact with it: in the profession of literary studies as we know it, that means most of us. For since the late 1950s and the publication of Frye's *Anatomy of Criticism*, the American scene in literary criticism has been constituted by a controversy over the role of theory carried on with theological fervor by believers and scoffers alike. And since the summer 1982 issue of *Critical Inquiry* and the publishing of an article called "Against Theory," a new breed of scoffers, much to the delight of the old breed, has dominated the conversation. Unlike the old breed, however, this new breed comes cunningly armed with the intellectual skills associated with theorists in order to slay the dragon of theory and offer it up, lo! on the altar of the good old American philosophy, pragmatism itself. The movement in the United States drawing much attention now, even threatening to become fashionable, is the "against theory" movement; it is being associated everywhere with the names of Peirce, Dewey, and James; it is called the "new pragmatism."[34]

I think James would have found the "against theory" position beside the point (to put it gently) because he knew that there is no sense in being for or against what you cannot escape from. There is no escape from theory because, in James's characterization of rationalism, the theory of theories, theory is "an appetite of the mind"—part of the self.[35] We are all beset by the theoretical impulse, or theory-desire, as I have called it—by the need to make the place clean and well-ordered. In its simplest and yet most far-reaching implications, theory is the need to generalize, to overcome, to forget, and to obliterate differences: a description I'd offer as an equally fair characterization of concept formation (the obliteration of percepts) and of imperialism both as foreign policy and as a feature of the ordinary, casual imperialism of everyday life (the obliteration of persons). Since James's temperament is shaped by nominalist, empirical, and skeptical philosophical traditions, he believes that when theory-desire expresses itself by offering itself as an explanation of the concrete world, it must necessarily fail as theory, as explanation of the way things are at all times and in all places. The world just isn't the way theory says it is. So theory cannot have the consequences that it wishes. But it does have consequences because in an effort to make over into an image of its desire the heterogeneous world of history—the romance world of many stories that do not cohere—theory acts for worse upon the world.

The jaunty little dismissal of theory by the authors of the essay called "Against Theory" is irrelevant—but it is also something more: it is self-deluded. The enabling and self-trivializing assumption of "Against Theory" is announced in the essay's opening words: "By 'theory' we mean a special project in literary criticism." Knapp and Michaels say that "theory is not just another name for practice. It is the name for all the ways people have tried to stand outside in order to govern practice from without." They conclude that since no one can actually achieve that transcendental perch, no one should "try" to, and "therefore" the "theoretical enterprise" should come to an end.[36] That sort of conclusion, which seems so Jamesian, is not. What James says is that, though no one can actually get outside practice, the impulse to get outside is unavoidable because the practice of theory takes its point of departure not from a special venture of literary business, a "theoretical enterprise," as Knapp and Michaels suppose, but from the constitution of mind itself. One cannot "try" or "not try" to be a theorist. Theory is not simply a matter of intention or will or conscious agency. It is a matter of necessity; an impulse, an appetite. The effects of such unavoidable theoretical impulse can be the most heinous form of practice, with the most ugly sorts of political consequences. Theory—whether we call it structuralism or capitalism—is the desire which would be the "remedy" of difference. It cannot be dismissed. It can, however, be guarded against, and the method of vigilance is James's pragmatism, not "new pragmatism." Jamesian pragmatism is nothing less than the strategy for taking away rationalist theory's theoretical ambition, for encouraging us, in our impulses to theory, to recognize that we must live with differences, provisional utility, and the necessities of revision. Theory, so conceived by the old pragmatism, tentatively holding itself as *belief*, becomes a tool for getting our work done, for exploring the shifting situations we call history. But pragmatism (the vigilante within) is always on the verge of vanquishment, of giving belief over to theory (the totalitarian within).

In an effort to tame theory in the name of pragmatism, James seems to allow himself one theoretical moment, the sentimental essentialization of mind as Manichean battlefield—a struggle between traditional philosophy, or "theory," a male principle, and "pragmatism" (homage to Anne Hutchinson), which is a woman: the principle that "unstiffens" all theories and makes them useful, and a synonym for "himself" as woman in his untraditional philosophic activity. But James's essentialist portrait of mind as a conflicted androgynous unit is intended pragmatically, not theoretically, as a useful way to view, guard against, and maybe curb the aggressivity he found theoretical: aristocratic, churchly, European, and male, but not identical with the male gender. It is his way of encouraging self-critique, the braking of the ego; of saying that we have unshakable reason to worry; of encouraging the desire for the responsible life (the life that is responsive to its contexts) while specifying the content of responsibility with American liberal vision. James's figurative language tells us that pragmatism is a woman, but not identical with the female gender: pragmatism is democratic, pragmatism is Protestant, pragmatism is inseparable from the dream of America. Pragmatism is an epistemology for isolatos who experiment at the frontier, who work without the kingly privileges of tradition and the a priori, who in refusing the a priori of rationalism would also refuse all of the encrusted pre-capitalist social contexts that James associates with the history of philosophic rationalism. Theory, on the other hand, is a social elitist, theory is a masturbatory Old World gentleman who never gets his hands dirty, who cannot "unstiffen" himself. As the tool of tools, theory-erect would make unnecessary all other tools, all thinking, all revision, all worry because it is the machine for allegorizing and rationalizing and coercing all texts and all humans as instances of the same.[37]

The new pragmatists flounder on one of James's strongest insights—that theory cannot be identified with agency and the self-conscious individual, that theory is the sort of force that tends to control individuals by speaking through them. And so does James. What unifies and binds both ends of the pragmatist tradition is its political pivot, the ideology of liberalism. In the new pragmatism, the liberal commitment surfaces in the sentiment that theory can be dismissed, as if one could, as an autonomous individual, either will it away or will oneself into it. In James the liberal commitment surfaces in the belief that the central resistance to the hateful impositions of imperialism is generated autonomously in the molecular individual: molecular individualism is the great thing and it can be saved only by efforts of molecular will. The problem is that James treats epistemological and political rationalizations as if they were the same thing. The epistemological move to generalization may well be an "appetite of the mind," well-nigh unavoidable except in moments of radical Bergsonian cherishing of perceptual particularity. And the late James is very Bergsonian. But the economic and political move to generalize—the global generalization of labor known as capitalism—is not an unhistorical appetite; it is a locatable, historical phenomenon whose role tends to be blurred and repressed by James's liberal ideology of the autonomous self. The most powerful enemy of the self is not an irrepressible impulse but the economic imperative of capital rooted in and projected from collective interests. The category missing in new and old pragmatism is the category of class which tells us, among other things, that "individuals," including intellectuals, are also representations— vessels of power not originating in themselves and often directed against themselves.[38]

The typical liberal response to the destruction of selfhood that is synonymous with the commodification of labor at the economic level and the commodification of human relations in everyday life at all levels of human interaction is to ignore the historical action of capital in the American scene: the steamrolling of the individual in the name of individualism. The problem is collective, the antidote would seem to be collective, but it is precisely the decent collective that is unimaginable to the liberal mind, maybe because the underground of the liberal mind is really antinomian. When collectives are imagined by James, they tend to be represented as life-denying "system." James's celebration of individualism, whether in its modest liberal or its wild antinomian forms, must remain at the mercy of the systematic, capitalist appropriation of the individual. Since radical individualism in America can be seen, by definition, in no cooperative venture, it would appear that James needs to keep alive a threatening principle of generalization, always at the doorstep of individualism, in order that the radical individual may feel the isolated purity of its freedom. The idea of radical individualism in America derives much of its energy from the memory of our European origins—and capitalism, in James's America, is an ironic aid to that repressed memory of the ancien régime. If in one way James out-Marxes Marx, in another he un-Marxes him.

The really ironic thing about the recent "against theory" position, even in its latest and most clever formulation in an essay by Stanley Fish called "Consequences"—in which it is argued that neither theory nor belief can have "necessary" and therefore powerful consequences that we need to be responsive to and responsible for—is that its effort to bury theory has the consequence of reinstating theory-desire in its most naked form. The "against theory" position turns out to be the "for theory" position—a powerful expression of the very theory impulse that James so eloquently contextualized, but with none of James's feeling for its insidious and necessary impact on human behavior. The "against theory" phenomenon turns out to be a repetition, this time around in the name of *practice*, of the escape from history and political accountability so characteristic of the various formalisms that have dominated American critical thought since Frye. Whereas James counsels vigilance for the enemy within, the voices "against theory" counsel a dismissal of a nuisance from without, of recent academic origin, not realizing that they, too, like the rest of us, are the enemy, and in disturbing garb, especially when they write, as Fish now writes, without apparent awareness of the action that theory-desire takes upon their own discourse: as when Fish offers as an example of the irrelevance of theory "the case of two legislators who must vote on a fair-housing bill."

Fish offers this case hypothetically, as if such an example might conceivably have occurred to anybody—to, say, Locke or Hegel—or in any place, say in classical Athens or in feudal Europe. He argues that a legislator voting on behalf of equal access just might be a libertarian typically committed to individual freedom, that said libertarian might not side with the lobby which works for landlords and all others who like to rest their case on the rights of private property; while the utilitarian, who would ordinarily be committed to arguments on behalf of equal access, just might side with advocates of property rights as the only way to ensure in the long run the greatest good for the greatest number.[39] Fish's example is confusing because it is abstract; it never touches historical earth; it is an example offered in the analytical style of Anglo-American philosophy— a philosophical style which routinely rarefies "examples" like abortion, nuclear weapons, and capital punishment. Nowhere does Fish indicate awareness of what his language indicates against his intention—what his language speaks. At the level of his example's historical unconscious we find inscribed a discourse which must be made to say, against Fish's intention, that fair housing became an issue in the United States in the heat of the Civil Rights movement in the 1950s and 1960s. Within that historical locale, the position of the libertarian was almost always the position of the covert segregationist, the position that gave comfort, energy, and ideas to the racist who clothes his arguments with the rhetoric of property rights; while the utilitarian was almost always, within that historical locale, a proponent of social change who advocated fair housing as a way of making civil rights socially concrete for blacks, a position, in other words, that gave comfort, energy, and ideas to advocates of civil rights.

Fish's abstract antagonists on the issue of fair housing *might* conceivably, as he argues, have changed sides, *might* conceivably have taken each other's typical stance, thus demonstrating Fish's point—that it *might* not matter a damn what your position is, your practice *might* be otherwise. But in historical fact these antagonists almost never did change sides because their beliefs or theories or positions were politically and historically rooted, politically and historically determinate, in a moment which militated against such change, in a moment which extracted determinate consequences from the antagonists. Thus by reconceiving the problem of fair housing so as to eliminate its necessary relation to any concrete historical scene, Fish's discourse becomes theoretical—it would prove some general point about the impotence of self-conscious position taking, applicable for all times and all instances, and in so doing it would elide the differences in positions that produced the particular and potent forms of agony this country has experienced since the fifties and sixties. History exacts its revenge within Fish's discourse, and against his Anglo-American philosophical abstractness, and says not only that all ideas are rooted in specific social situations but that expressing ideas bears specific political consequences; Fish's discourse on consequences is a prime example, especially at the moment when it denies the consequential nature of having belief and theory.

What I am saying about Fish's most recent critical incarnation amounts to this: his treatment of the issue of fair housing is a betrayal of the strong historicism that he would elaborate, and it is a particularly destructive sort of betrayal which cancels out the only sort of political responsibility that a historicist can live with. Not the Kantian sort, which makes appeals to an ahistorical world of rights and moral imperatives; not the utopian sort, which appeals to a global community-to-be grounded in no particular time or locale. The political responsiveness that Fish betrays is to the very persons and historical community within which his nexus of terms—"fair housing," "utilitarianism," "libertarianism"—takes on determinate and powerful significance. Not just any historical community, but the very community within which Fish writes and within which his readers must receive him.

But the commanding question about the new pragmatism's consequences cannot really be pursued with justice at this moment. It is too new. I'll conclude, then, not with any statement about its consequences, which are not especially clear at this point, but with some remarks about its stance and its omissions. (1) However misled by the allurements of formalism, what was called theory in the United States in the sixties and seventies and in the early eighties has been the site in our profession of basic and often explosive questioning about the nature and role of literature. Marxism, deconstruction, feminism, psychoanalysis—these are the current terms of opposition to the status quo of the institution of literary study: these are terms of resistance that in various ways would take literature out of the vacuums of traditional humanism and traditional formalism and into the world of economics, power, gender, and class. The rhetoric of "against theory," therefore, at this juncture, cannot help but bring comfort, energy, and ideas to the enemies of change. The rhetoric of "against theory" is reactionary. (2) The "against theory" proponents are representative of a claustrophobic form of professionalism. They speak of "theory" as if it were the invention of literary critics and philosophers, a phenomenon of the academic institution merely. But the lesson of James is that theory is a phenomenon of everyday life in history and society, a phenomenon of all of society's institutions, and the name of a disposition whose consequences are revealed in oppression. The overly narrow, single (literary) institutional focus of the "against theory" professionals trivializes the social issues of theory, as James never did, and in the process trivializes the broader social role of literary study. In the name of practice, "against theory" gives us, once more, the ivory tower. (3) The constant accompaniment to James's criticism of theory and traditional philosophy is a commitment to anti-imperialism and an extended and troubled meditation on the fate of persons in a capitalist context. Fish's example of the two legislators and the question of fair housing looks like a splendid invitation, another social document calling for the intervention of historicized Jamesian conscience, but it is not. Despite the fact that his example has everything to do with the obsessive and intertwined themes of James's critique of theory—the sanctity of selves and the rights of property—Fish's point is that we can dance away, with impunity if we like, and keep on dancing away from the determinate responsibilities of belief that history thrusts upon us.

Since theory of the sort that James, Fish, and I are talking about works in the realm of probability, on culture and history, and not on nature, presumably the realm of rigorous causality and the classic object of scientific inquiry, it would follow that Fish's major point—that cultural theory has no "necessary" theoretical consequences—is logically correct. But his point is a trivial tautology unless pressed beyond its tautological truth that culture is not the realm of necessity. In other words, after all of contemporary theory's hermeneutical suspicions have been registered, after we have once again followed the lead of the early Roland Barthes who encourages us to break the conspiracy of silence by refusing to let culture be naturalized by the attitude of "it goes without saying," the question of probability remains. What might be the effect if a literary theorist got to that transcendental perch, got scientific? What has been the effect of imposing our will in Central America? Of making them hew, in James's terms, to our story? Or, in Fish's case, where the issue is also political, what might be the (probable) effect on his readers and students of his homogenization of the terms of struggle in the Civil Rights movement, especially in the context of the 1980s when so many of our students (with the aid of Reagan's Justice Department) seem convinced that racism in the United States was utterly routed everywhere by the late 1960s and that its last bastion is South Africa? The question about the literary theorist who would be scientific, the question about our political relation to the third world, and the question about Fish are not questions of the same order. But they all involve the effects of theorization: the costs of working to wipe out differences and otherness; the costs of trying to move over the realm of history, and command it from above. These costs are not the costs, or consequences, of theory as theory imagines itself and its effects; they are instead the costs, or consequences, organic to the effort of trying to succeed in the futile and inevitable adventure of theory. And they are real.

The new pragmatists maybe could learn a lesson from our godfather, Vito Corleone, who believed that one (preferably someone else) had to "answer" for one's actions. Don Corleone was a connoisseur of reason (as in "I will reason with him"; or as in "But no one can reason with him"). But the Don was no Kantian. Unlike the new pragmatists who assign self-consciousness no historical role, he knew that the sort of worry synonymous with self-reflection takes place in a context of other wills, not in some self-contained transcendental inner sphere, but in a context of situations that make vivid, sometimes vividly red, the consequences of taking "unreasonable" positions. Critical self-consciousness, in other words, is not a pointless activity of intellectuals too enamored of philosophical idealism, but a necessity for getting on with others in the world—a necessity even for intellectuals.

If the political unconscious of the new pragmatism is liberal (in its wild phase, antinomian), its explicit political content runs all to indifference and the professionalism that would make itself a world apart. James, an integrated intellectual, a professional with an organic sense of the relation between philosophy and all other institutions, who called himself a me-liorist because he thought his world needed changing and could be changed for the better, would find in the new pragmatism the thoroughgoing satisfaction that he had excoriated in Josiah Royce: the confidence that this is the best of all possible worlds. James not only thought otherwise, but thought that the process of change must be initiated close to home, in self-worrying critique. The new pragmatism, on the other hand, would stand one of the most ancient of Western maxims on its head. It says in all but words: "The unexamined life is the only life worth living." Here at last, moving with the tides of the times, is the basis for a literary criticism of the eighties.

CHAPTER 3

Writing after Hours

Money is a kind of poetry.

WALLACE STEVENS

The centuries have a way of being male.

WALLACE STEVENS

Junk is the ideal product. . . . The junk merchant does not sell his product to the consumer, he sells the consumer to his product.

WILLIAM S. BURROUGHS, *Naked Lunch*

Part One: Patriarchy against Itself—
The Young Manhood of Wallace Stevens

> Get money. That way you can concentrate on your work and
> not have to worry about earning a living while you're
> creating.
>
> HAROLD ROBBINS

> Masculinity imagines itself poorly, or imagines itself, at
> most, only by feminizing itself.
>
> PHILLIPPE LACOUE-LABARTHE

*I*n what is advertised as a "controversial coast to coast best-
seller," most men who were asked, "How would you feel if
something about you were described as feminine or womanly?"
said (surprise) they'd be angry. Consider these voices from *The
Hite Report on Male Sexuality*:

> Enraged. Insulted. Never mind what women are really like—I know
> what he's saying: he's saying I should be submissive to him.

> To be called "like a woman" by another man is to be humiliated
> by him, because most men consider women to be weak, and a man
> doesn't want to be considered weak.

> Chagrined. I may appear soft, but I carry a big stick. So watch out.

> If I was described as having something "like a woman's," I would
> be outraged. I would defend my masculinity almost automatically. I
> wouldn't like being compared to a woman's *anything*. [1]

About two seconds of reflection should be enough to convince
most of us that what is offered in *The Hite Report on Male Sexuality* as the representative testimony of contemporary American men is, in fact, representative: our relations with women
are problematic, those with ourselves something worse. What
Shere Hite does not call attention to is an intriguing recurrence
in many of the responses: the question is heard as a charge, and
it is imagined to be coming from another male. The basic point

now seems to me inescapable, though to say "inescapable" is in no way to say that the history of literary theory and criticism has found it so (or that I have always found it so). One way of understanding that history is to read it as a series of ingenious escapes from the basic point which is economic and sexual (in that order, the order of repression) and which goes something like this: What we know as "femininity" is internally linked to what we know as "masculinity" because both designations are highly motivated cultural constructions of biological difference that do powerful social work at the moment when they are lived, when they constitute the barely conscious and barely reflected upon substance of belief. The political synonym for "belief" is "ideology" in the particular sense of a constructed thing which nevertheless feels natural and is never (or is only rarely) experienced as a thing bearing interested human intention. The basic ideological point has to do with social engenderment, and it means, among other things, that if you're male you must police yourself for traces of femininity. If you're male it means, among other things, that the great dread is not so much that another man might call you feminine or womanly (in our culture, a pretty dreadful prospect) but that you might have to call yourself feminine or womanly. The political issue of gender has recently been the special concern of feminist criticism, and eventually, after a long look at Wallace Stevens, I'll address feminism directly, in what may be its institutionally most potent form.

I

In 1914, after a hiatus of some fifteen years, a period of poetic self-silencing in the pursuit of economic success, Wallace Stevens went public again with his poetry. In between his years at Harvard (1897–1900), when he published frequently in undergraduate magazines, and his move to Hartford, Connecticut, in 1916, when he made his initial appearances in the newly emerging little magazines of literary modernism, Stevens led a double life in New York City. The lion's share of his waking hours was spent trying (and mainly failing) to earn a good wage—and by "good wage" I mean a wage that would enable him to resume the comfortable upper-middle-class style he was accustomed to living in Reading, Pennsylvania, where he grew up, and in Cambridge, Massachusetts, where he was supported by his father's faithful checks. In the late hours of evening during his New York years he read and occasionally wrote verses; on weekends he took marathon walks in the country of twenty to thirty miles. In this period between Harvard and his appearances in the little magazines fell his courtship of Elsie Moll. It went on for about five years, not because she held him off (the opposite appears to have been the case), but because he was not about to be married until he felt himself economically secure as his father had defined economic security for him. Part of his courting of Elsie involved sharing with her what he called his "secret" passion for poetry. In a letter written to her about a year and a half before the appearance of "Sunday Morning," and with deceptively light tone, Stevens touched what should have been a central issue of *The Hite Report on Male Sexuality*. In effect, he called himself feminine or womanly:

> I sit at home o' nights. But I read very little. I have, in fact, been trying to get together a little collection of verses again; and although they are simple to read, when they're done, it's a deuce of a job (for me) to do them. Keep all this a great secret. There is something absurd about all this writing of verses; but the truth is, it elates and satisfies me to do it. It is an all-round exercise quite superior to ordinary reading. So that, you see, my habits are positively lady-like.[2]

Stevens' designation of verse writing as "positively lady-like" (and I note that the term "lady-like" feminizes in the direction of the leisured class: he is not talking about working women) on the face of it makes no sense to readers like ourselves whose feel for poetic history tends to be limited to the canonical powers. For not only the great figures but almost all the figures of English and American poetry that we know and he knew or might have known (he knew most) were male. The most powerful poetic presences of his young manhood were Keats and Tennyson on the English side and the Fireside poets on ours. Moreover, when Stevens wrote to Elsie of his ladylike activity, Whitman had at last won acceptance. The curious thing about Stevens' letter is that without even a gesture of argument the heavy fact of male literary authority is simply set aside. The facts do not count in my case, he is implying, and by so implying in effect he asks us to set aside the mainstream argument of American literary feminism in *The Madwoman in the Attic*—that poetry is the most privileged of male literary territories—because something other than the leisured male privilege of English literary history is at work in Stevens' life. Verse writing is for me, Stevens suggests, a thing for ladies. It is absurd that *I* do it. I am an American male. I have to be practical.

But there were other poetic forces in Stevens' young manhood, and their gender complicates his male literary inheritance and begins to make sense of the sexual and literary self-deprecation that he voiced to Elsie. Those poets who have not survived in the canon of American poetry—those ever-mournful, ever-self-renouncing, and, in the culture of Stevens, ever-present women (especially present in newspapers)—define the poetic female as a special kind of American womanly cultural agency, maybe even the agency of culture itself. So disseminated was this figure of the woman poet that Mark Twain could count on his readers to recognize her in his collective send-up in the Emmeline Grangerford episode of *Huckleberry Finn*. ("She warn't particular, she could write about anything you choose to give her to write about, just so it was sadful. Every time a man died, or a woman died, or a child died, she would be on hand with her 'tribute' before he was cold. She called them tributes. The neighbors said it was the doctor first, then Emmeline, then the undertaker.") Emmeline Grangerford was a type of the poet that Stevens could not admire and yet could not help (at some level) but assume as a figure of himself, so pervasive was her cultural presence when he was beginning to think of a life as a poet.[3]

In spite of the effort, then, which marks most of his letters to Elsie, to master issues of gender, vocation, and money with flippancy of tone, Stevens registers and unmasks, against his desire, what proved to be the unmasterable situation that he'd prefer to submerge in "the gaiety of language," to use his phrase, which is supposed to, but can't, redeem his social *malheur*. His "absurd" habit of verse writing embodies this unavoidable structural contradiction in bourgeois culture: as it brings forth feelings of pleasure ("it elates and satisfies me to do it") while engaging him in the sort of exertion synonymous with work ("a deuce of a job"), it triggers at the very moment of pleasure the negative judgment of his macho superego because this job can bring no economic support, cannot earn the characterization "work"—hence is really no job at all. His "absurd" habit of verse writing necessarily forces upon him a feeling at odds with his maleness—the feeling of the sexual other within, in the mask of poetic culture: the lady poet. So when we ask, just who is this "me" made happy by verse writing? the embedded cultural logic of his letter to Elsie makes us answer that Stevens' "me" is in some fundamental sense a ladylike, economically unproductive "she." Elsie could be entrusted with the secret. Elsie would understand.

Fifteen years earlier Garrett Stevens, successful lawyer, small businessman, and a poet himself (the first Wallace Stevens, as it were), had sent his son, then at Harvard, this letter. It would haunt his son's young manhood:

> Our young folk would of course prefer to be born like English noblemen with Entailed estates, income guaranteed and in choosing a profession they would simply say—"How shall I amuse myself"— but young America understands that the question is—"*Starting with nothing, how shall I sustain myself and perhaps a wife and family— and send my boys to College and live* comfortably in my old age." Young fellows must all come to that question, for unless they inherit money, marry money, find money, steal money or somebody presents it to them, they must *earn it* and earning it save it up for the time of need. How best can he earn a sufficiency! What talent does he possess which carefully nurtured will produce something which

people want and therefore will pay for. This is the whole problem! and to Know Thyself![4]

A few years after he received this letter, while toiling unhappily in the competitive world of New York journalism, Stevens in fact requested guaranteed income from his father so that he might pursue another kind of career in writing, one that could not be economically productive: one which could not sustain himself, much less a wife, family, a college education for his sons, and a comfortable old age. His father refused his request.[5] The son of Garrett Stevens had begun to understand, but apparently had not yet learned to live with, the primary lesson in American history that was to be his burden as it was the burden of most of young America's males. His father was passing on the middle-class wisdom of Poor Richard and Horatio Alger that to be born an American is typically to be born without a sustaining economic past: to start with nothing, even if your father (like Garrett Stevens) has sustained himself, a wife, and has sent his boys (not his daughters) to college, because such a father in achieving such accomplishments was likely to have exhausted most of what he had earned. What little he might pass on would never be enough for his son to sustain himself, his wife, etc. The aristocratic model of English poetic history which motivates the argument of *The Madwoman in the Attic* does not pertain in the United States because to be born an American is to be born into a context where literary patronage virtually does not exist and where your padre cannot be your good padrone. I have done it, Garrett Stevens was saying to his son, now prove your manhood by imitating me to the letter.

As a high school senior, and showing considerable promise of being his father's son, Stevens took first place in a speech contest by celebrating, in a rising patriotic rhetoric, the self-made man—the "one grand result of Democracy, which feudalism, which caste, and which monarchy can never know." "We cannot help but admire the man," he continued, "who with indomitable and irrepressible energy, breasting the wave of conditions, grows to become the concentration of power and worth."[6] Of course when he gave voice to this founding American ideology and ever-recurrent immigrant's dream of America—what could it mean to be an American and not dream this dream?— Stevens himself was no self-made man who had breasted the wave of conditions: he was in fact on his way to Harvard, he had experienced the pleasures of summer camp, good books, excellent food, and a mother who did not have to spend eight to ten hours a day, five or six days a week, in a factory, and who mothered him and his siblings dearly. At least until he was forced to move into the world on his own, he would have no experience of the economic terrors of self-making and would likely have trouble even imagining the consequences should his energy for economic self-making prove to be anything less than indomitable and irrepressible. Garrett Stevens' upper-middle-class daughters might have to face economic terror, too, if, say, they failed to marry someone like their daddy—or if, say, refusing the gender typecasting of their society, they struck out on their own, in efforts to become self-made women.

Stevens' move to New York in 1900 forced him to bear witness to the thinness of his middle-class insulation. Shortly after getting there he entered into his journal a reflection on a Harvard graduate he had never met but of whom he had heard much, one Philip Henry Savage. This journal entry echoes his prizewinning high school speech, it echoes the Poor Richard letter his father sent to him at Harvard, and it touches a new theme. This would-be ruggedly independent new American man would somehow, if he could, join his aesthetic sense, already heavily cultivated as a teenager and at Harvard, to what he was beginning to see as the unavoidable economic plot of his existence:

> Savage was an admirable fellow. Mason calls his attempt at self-support "praiseworthy though quixotic!" This is absurd. Savage was like every other able-bodied man—he wanted to stand alone. Self-dependence is the greatest thing in the world for a young man & Savage knew it. I cannot talk about the subject, however, because I

know too little about it. But for one thing, Savage went into the shoe business & still kept an eye on sunsets and red-winged blackbirds—the summum bonum.[7]

Very soon Stevens would know much more about the subject. His New York years (1900–1916) quickly became an effort to achieve Savage's sort of balance of necessity and pleasure, business and play, act and perception, not because Stevens was reading Kantian aesthetics, but because that sort of schizoid balance ("the summum bonum") was the very thing that his socialization as the son of Garrett Stevens taught him to desire. The story of his New York years was mainly a story of his failure to achieve the summum bonum, or of his success if weekend Emersonianism must suffice. The means of self-dependence pursued Monday through Friday; things not for themselves alone but for his self, pursued and savored on Saturdays and Sundays:

> The roads are strewn with purple oak leaves, brown chestnut leaves, and the golden and scarlet leaves of maple. I doubt if there is any keener delight in the world than, after being penned up for a week, to get into the woods on such a day—every pound of flesh vibrates with new strength, every nerve seems to be drinking at some refreshing spring. After one has got home, how delicious to slip into an easy chair & to feel the blood actually leaping into one's pulses, a wild fire, so to speak, burning in one's cheeks.[8]

One way of mitigating this solution of the "weekend"—a therapeutic as well as a temporal concept in bourgeois life—and of joining his vocation with his avocation, or so it seemed to Stevens, lay in his first choice of career in journalism, a field which he tried, with the assistance of his Harvard teacher Barrett Wendell, as soon as he got to New York. The guiding principle behind his choice seems to have been this: Write all the time, write sometimes because you want to, and write when you must, for a living, but write. He quickly learned, however, that the monetary rewards of journalism were erratic, the writing assignments mainly a grind, and his future as a journalist just too chancy. All of which was brought sharply into focus for him in the depressing spectacle of a funeral of a fellow journalist who also wrote fiction that he respected. Stevens found the affair "wretched, rag, tag, and bobtail"; hardly anyone went to the church. Those in attendance were obviously lower class. A few literary types showed up, but in appearance it was impossible to distinguish them from the nonliterary and merely poor. Stephen Crane deserved better: "As the hearse rattled up the street over the cobbles, in the stifling heat of the sun, with not a single person paying the least attention to it and with only four or five carriages behind it at a distance I realized much that I had doubtingly suspected before—There are few hero worshippers. Therefore, few heroes."[9] Crane's funeral gave Stevens a glimpse of a possible writerly future. Stevens entered law school.

Three years later, in August of 1904, and about a month after being admitted to the New York bar, he wrote a retrospective meditation in his journal on the perilous comforts of middle-class life as he had known it. Theodore Dreiser couldn't have done it better. This journal passage marks the birth of Wallace Stevens as class-conscious and self-conscious economic man for whom the American dream is no longer an abstraction; Wallace Stevens—real-life brother of some of the most compelling figures in modern American fiction: Carrie Meeber and G. W. Hurstwood in *Sister Carrie*, Thomas Sutpen in *Absalom, Absalom!*, Jay Gatsby. What makes Stevens different and maybe more typical—neither Dreiser nor Faulkner nor Fitzgerald would tell his story—is his sense that he has been expelled from Eden, that his particular form of the American dream involves the recapturing of a lost social and economic status that he had never earned but which he had nevertheless enjoyed, the resumption of a life that had fashioned the mode of his desire and had given him a taste of the good life. Suddenly he felt a shocking solidarity with the poor who had hitherto only repulsed him in their filth and poverty (the sight of Italian immigrants had once made it impossible for him to finish a snack of clams on the half shell); he was coming to know a new sort of closeness with those who had hitherto made him feel faintly disgusted when they sat too near him on commuter trains. At the age of twenty-five Stevens came to know economic difference and the peculiar privilege of middle-class life in America. The Italian immigrants he saw in Greenwich Village, like the bums in the Bowery he observed on his walks in the city, might dream the dream of upward mobility—they could sink no lower economically. The fabulously wealthy of his time, legends even then—like the Carnegies, the Mellons, the Rockefellers, the class Fitzgerald called, simply, "the very rich"—could pass out dimes in the streets if they liked (and they did). *Their* children, whatever spiritual descents they might experience, could look with impunity upon the poor: they would never be one of them. But Stevens, and those like him, knew better than to dream the dream of upward mobility. Passage into the realm of the Rockefellers was not realistic; a repetition of one's father's economic status was more likely and it was clearly desirable over the other possibility which is the special privilege of the middle class: the possibility of economic descent. The dream of the middle class in America is the nightmare of downward mobility: Stevens' version of the nightmare concludes with an effort to resist it, with what in his writing is an almost never expressed impulse, the utopian urge toward classless society.

The mere prospect of having to support myself on a very slender purse has brought before my mind rather vivid views of the actual facts of existence in the world. There are astonishingly few people who live in anything like comfort; and there are thousands who live on the verge of starvation. The old Biblical injunctions to make the earth fertile and to earn one's bread in the sweat of one's brow are one's first instructions. True, it [is] not necessary to start from the soil; but starting with nothing whatever—to make a fortune— is not wholly inspiring after a fellow has spent more or less time lolling about. It is decidedly wrong to start *there* with one's tastes fully developed & to have to forego all satisfaction of them for a vague number of years. This is quite different from beginning as other men do. It is more like being up already & working down to a certain point. Another phase of the thing is that when one has lived for twenty-five years with every reasonable wish granted & among the highest associations—starting at the bottom suddenly reveals millions of fellow men struggling at the same point, of whom one previously had only an extremely vague conception. There was a time when I walked downtown in the morning almost oblivious of the thousands and thousands of people I passed; now I look at them with extraordinary interest as companions in the same fight that I am about to join.[10]

So for this middle-class professional, endowed with capitalist values through his father, in part against his literary desires, the inescapable question pressed upon him first by family and then by his New York experience is this: How can I turn some part of myself (my "talent") into a commodity that people will want and "therefore pay for"? The choice of profession need not "amuse," it need not give pleasure (much later in his poetic career he would insist that the supreme fiction must give pleasure), but (as Father said) it must pay. To "Know Thyself," according to Garrett Stevens, is to know yourself as economic man, fit for the hurly-burly of the marketplace where the big boys slug it out. To "Know Thyself" for Garrett Stevens' son meant that in finding his productive talent he would prove his masculinity in general and prove it in particular as equal to his father's. But knowing himself also meant knowing that he was given pleasure by his verse-writing talent—and to know himself that way as a young man meant to feel himself as the potential subverter of his official role as a young American male. Only leisured women and leisured men (like men and women in the great tradition of English letters, or fortunate ladies and gentlemen in the American tradition), could do what he wanted to do. Modernist poetics in the United States, especially Stevens' version of it, is sexually and economically framed (in both senses) from the beginning. Modernist poetics in the United States begins with the great problem of the comfortable bourgeois world: the antagonism of duty and happiness. Modernist poetics in Stevens is a feminization of the literary life motivated by capitalist values, and, at the same time, a struggle to overcome this feminization which (in our culture) is more or less equivalent to the trivialization of literature and the literary impulse.

Garrett Stevens was by most standards an unsuccessful poet, and in the end his failure in business was so disastrous—he went bankrupt—that his son had no choice but to "stand on his own two feet." His son's life and career were therefore at once imitation and stunning transcendence of the father. A brilliant success in two areas, Stevens' bifurcated career perfectly realized the hegemonic aims of his capitalist socialization. Assiduously "masculine" in his pursuit of economic fulfillment—Stevens worked well beyond retirement age because he had no intention of ever retiring—in his aesthetic life he cultivated the self-abnegating virtues that his society relegated to the "feminine" sphere: in other words, he cultivated "culture" itself in the sense that capitalism shaped for that term. So the genteel virtues of culture that Stevens was heir to (feeling, sensibility, self-renunciation) functioned as a critique of capitalist willfulness and greed, but critique at a safe distance; critique that could not function as intervention and trigger of social change. The realm of ("affirmative") culture, so well contained outside the realm of economic action, becomes a rationalization of the order of things. The life of Stevens was an expression at once of the ease with which that contradiction could be sustained and of the inescapable discontent of an existence in which schizophrenia is normalized as the structure of everyday life.

2

> Complacencies of the peignoir,
> And late coffee and oranges in a sunny chair
> And the green freedom of a cockatoo
> Upon a rug. . . .

Those who read Wallace Stevens know that the woman evoked in these opening lines of "Sunday Morning" and then debated with so strenuously and unfairly is not to be taken as the representation of a real woman. We have been taught that she represents the traditional religious impulse—the need, as Stevens phrased it in the poem, "for some imperishable bliss"; a conservative figure who sums up all at once the resistance to Darwin, the resistance to the aesthetes, and the resistance to the higher criticism: a traditional muse, maybe, but one who must be symbolically put in her place, because she stands against the very literary and intellectual styles that a young modernist in the early twentieth century is supposed to be comfortable with. But she may also be Stevens' muse, the first appearance of his interior paramour, part of Stevens himself—a suggestion made in passing by Harold Bloom.[11] And much of what Stevens' critics up to and including Bloom have said about her is persuasive. The preponderance of scholarship is ample testimony that "Sunday Morning," in its atmospherics and in its ideas, is a conventional poem, very much of its intellectual period: a late-nineteenth-century set piece on behalf of the religion of art that happened to be written in New York City in 1914 and published in 1915 in Harriet Monroe's *Poetry*.

Before I make her a figure of something else, however, like a figure of the muse or of religion or of a deep-seated (if repressed) impulse in the poet, I prefer to dwell on the obvious unspoken of Stevens criticism. The "she" of the opening lines of "Sunday Morning" is a comfortable woman of class, whose expensive and leisured femaleness Stevens insists upon. By their peignoirs ye shall know them, as well as by their associated commodities, the good things that money can buy. Her cockatoo, her rug, her coffee, her oranges: these, to put a wicked twist on some later lines of the poem, these are the measures of her soul. The coffee, the oranges, the cockatoo—these are not, appearances to the contrary notwithstanding, natural things in themselves, those pure "comforts of the sun," self-sufficient sensuous indulgences that Stevens urges her to partake of as substitute for religious impulse. For the coffee, the oranges, and the cockatoo are bought things filtered through the economic process: nature mediated by human labor—in the specific instances of Stevens' opening lines, by laborers who do not, but only because they cannot, sit about on Sunday morning in their smoking jackets and peignoirs, sipping coffee and nibbling on a dietetic breakfast. These sorts of laborers don't tend to go on diets, nor would they be taking late breakfasts. They'd be where the lady thinks she ought to be—at church. The coffee, the oranges, and the cockatoo are things like rugs—all metonyms for value in its commodity form—because they are all things for sale.

"All New York, as I have seen it, is for sale—and I think the parts I have seen are the parts that make New York what it is."[12] Stevens wrote that in a depressed mood shortly after moving from Cambridge. Everyday life in New York dramatized for him consumer capitalism as a frustrating spectacle of surreal narcissism: "Everybody is looking at everybody else—a foolish crowd walking on mirrors."[13] In this social setting, desire assumes mimetic form, and all commodities—privileged lives are a form thereof—become the mirrors of romance, promises of fulfillment quite beyond the explicit use of commodities: entries into an existence definitively more pleasurable than one's own, and available for a price. The world of New York, a "field of tireless and antagonistic interests," is the ultimate marketplace: Stevens called it "fascinating but horribly unreal"—he meant "unfortunately real," I think, because so destructively tempting.[14] Only nature is exempted by him from his mimetic economy of desire, but only because (he notes this sardonically) winds and clouds are not "generated in Yorkville" or "manufactured in Harlem."[15] "Sunday Morning's" site of production is New York, and the poem comes, in fact, at the end of almost fourteen years of mostly unhappy New York life. We cannot really locate the elegant interior and the woman of "Sunday Morning" there, but we can place Stevens in New York, in shabby elegance, within a room of his own. The interior decoration in Stevens' little apartment bore pictures of desire of what he thought "most real" and (in the heart of the city) most not there.

> The carpet on the floor of my room is grey set off with pink roses. In the bathroom is a rug with the figure of a peacock woven into it— blue and scarlet, and black, and green, and gold. And on the paper on my wall are designs of fleur-de-lis and forget-me-not. Flowers and

birds enough of rags and paper—but no more. In this Eden, made spicy with the smoke of my pipe which hangs heavy in the ceiling, in this Paradise ringing with the bells of streetcars and the bustle of fellow boarders heard through the thin partitions, in this Elysium of Elysiums I now shall lay me down.[16]

The verbal control and lightness of touch on display in this as in so many of his journal entries and letters prefigure the relaxed authority of his poems. Leisurely ease and satisfaction, witty power over circumstances and self-control (*happiness* is probably the word I want), these are things he needed most to feel and sought to create for himself in everyday life. The writing of Wallace Stevens, in journals, letters, essays, and poems, enacts that quest for happiness with a verbal prowess so striking that the existential absence of happiness—the thing that most moves the writing—tends to get hidden. The contentment he communicates to us in the journal entry about his protected little apartment is a veiling of the feelings of being out of place in a world wholly involved with getting and spending and which he can't help but encounter daily on the streets of New York. The young Stevens smoking his pipe in his room meditates on what is presumably *not* "generated in Yorkville" through the mediation of rugs and wallpaper, what *might be* generated in Yorkville. The world of aesthetic enjoyment, though often identified in his journals with experiences of art exhibits and of nature—not nature in a vacuum but nature as a motivated negation of New York: what he walked away from on weekends—this aesthetic world of the weekend is not enough in itself to alleviate the dissatisfaction Stevens felt through the workweek. His radical desire was for the aesthetic Monday through Friday, and he got it (in bourgeois fashion) at night in his apartment, an interiorized, private place, in the middle of New York, where decor and furnishings delusively appear to be freed from the "field of tireless and antagonistic interests" and are not therefore meditated with Marxist X-ray vision as products of economic leverage and exploited labor, but rather felt as things in themselves. Commodities so cherished are not heaven but the image of heaven—Stevens calls it Eden—where the delights of commodities are even more keenly felt (like stolen kisses) thanks to the thinness of partitions that do not block out New York. It is worth emphasizing what ought to be clear: Stevens' room is not explicable in Leo Marx's terms as a garden whose satisfactions are stoked by the invasion of the machine. It is a place whose objects of pleasure are machine-made. The phrase for all of this, "commodity fetishism," belongs to Karl Marx, but some of its subtlest implications belong to modern American writers. Commodity fetishism—the hedonism of bourgeois man bought at the psychic expense of a repression of the economic process which gives rise to commodities—is the point of departure for Stevens for an experience that would not be commodity-bound, the basis of an experience that would be radically liberated not only from commodities but also (in his room in the city) from natural objects as well (Stevens' walks in the country were sometimes spoiled by evidence of human presence) and, finally, that would be liberated even from the determinacies of gender, class, and human agency.

For Stevens the road to transcendence was often paved with commodities—by his habit in later life of collecting objets d'art from abroad and bringing the most satisfactory of them into his private bedroom. It was a road paved by the consciousness that felt its freedom in owning and in so owning could withdraw the thing owned, hide it away from the economic field of interests where things were often lost. The successful insurance executive who bought fine things for his room from Ceylon, in the 1930s and 1940s, makes his first extant appearance in his Harvard journal when he writes, "it is a great pleasure to seize an impression and lock it up in words: you feel as if you had it safe forever."[17] He made another appearance a few years later in this letter to Elsie when he told her: "You know that I do with you as I like in my thoughts: I no sooner wish for your hand than I have it—no sooner wish for anything to be said or done than it *is* said or done; and none of the denials you make me are made there. You are *my* Elsie there."[18] Buy it, with your money or your mind, but buy it and make it safe. Ezra Pound's modernist shibboleth "Make it new" becomes in Wallace Stevens, "Make it private."

Stevens' early letters and journals take us into the social kitchen of his poetics. They show us the process, not quite perfectly submerged by the poems, within which and from which he wrested—almost literally pulled free—his moments of aesthesis as interiorized moments of impression isolated from social time and severed from all human contacts, and preserved as images, autonomous thinglike perceptions driven by a will to purity. The aesthetic for Stevens is a lyric process of making interior, from the real space of the streets of New York to the private space of his room and then into the psychic space of consciousness (perilously sealed now to the outside) where pastoral experience can be made safe. In his room, literal and psychic, the pastoral can be had any time, any place. Aesthesis as the formation of impression is the repression of New York—a process of levitation which first transforms the bums in Washington Square into "crows in rainy weather" before taking the final subjective leap into the atmosphere (I mean the "air") of an impressionist painting and the experience of color abstracted from all objects:

> The other morning as I came home I walked up to Washington Square to take a look at the trees. The birds were just beginning to cheep & there was a little warm wind stirring among the leaves. I was surprised to find the large number of people who were sleeping on the grass and on the benches. One or two of them with collars turned up & hands in their pockets shuffled off through the sulphurus air like crows in rainy weather. The rest lay about in various states of collapse. There must have been a good many aching bones when the sun rose. The light was thin and bluishly misty; by the time I was in my room it had become more intense & was like a veil of thin gold.[19]

In light of the vocational anxieties he expressed in New York, the passage on the rug with the peacock woven into it from Stevens' journals and the opening lines of "Sunday Morning" (a poem written in New York) when placed side by side unveil a decisive scene for modern American poetry: the author as economic as well as sexual transvestite. It is a densely entangled scene because it compresses and fairly smothers in sensuous detail issues of gender, the commodity, and religion: the lady in her peignoir, the cockatoo upon her rug, and the dream of Palestine, site of Christian catastrophe. One of the traditional questions of scholarship on the poem—is the cockatoo real or is it a pattern in the rug?—becomes irrelevant when the poem's and the poet's social mise-en-scène is taken into account. Traditional Stevens criticism raises the question because it wants to know how to take "green freedom." Is Stevens being ironic about nature, or literal? Is nature really his realm of freedom? But real or imagined—cockatoo "upon," not "in," a rug suggests a real cockatoo—the phrase "green freedom" embodies an ironic intention directed not toward the bird as representation of nature but toward the woman's relationship to the bird, a relation that point for point repeats Stevens' relation to his peacock in a rug and his forget-me-nots in wallpaper. A pet cockatoo (whether female or male, the sound of freedom is phallic, cocky: it will become transformed, later in the poem, into the sound of men chanting naked in a ring), a pet cockatoo upon a rug is a bought bird in captivity. Not so much an ironic bird as a pathetic one. The pet cockatoo, like those roses in the rug, is a sign of a relation to nature that expresses androgynous desire (peignoired and pipe-smoking Wallace Stevens) for the green freedom of an impossible natural autonomy. In Stevens' middle-class settings of freedom, "green freedom" represents maximum desire. It is that setting of freedom as pathos-for-freedom that points to "Sunday Morning's" logic of displacement which moves the lady (and the poem) from the "complacent" limits of hedonic pleasures (commodity-bound) to the Christian extinguishment of all things and all pleasures in a procession of the dead that ends the first section of the poem—the ascetic renunciation of the worldly, the final freedom promised in silent Palestine: "Dominion of the blood and sepulcher."

Renunciation of the worldly is the feminine way in Stevens'

culture, and it is also the way of the poet who (like himself) defines his writing against the economic: romantic anticapitalism in the high-modernist moment is difficult to distinguish from feminine anticapitalism. So Christian fulfillment in "imperishable bliss" is the coded and displaced form of one kind of poetic impulse—for Stevens, a ladylike feminization of writing that must renounce not only the commodity but ultimately also the world of the senses because his sensory experience is fatally mediated by commodities. Feminine renunciation is a radical impulse that he feels (the impulse, as he wrote in his journal, to be "all dream") but that his male obligations tell him he cannot choose.[20] His images for his relation to poetry and to the woman of his life (lock up the impression, lock up Elsie) tell us that at some level he wishes to choose not the way of renunciation but the way of power, not the ascetic extinguishment of the worldly in Christian glory but the feeling of power over the worldly: lock up and make safe everything you value—your impression, your woman, and the fine things you import from Ceylon. The only image of himself as woman that he can tolerate, therefore, is an image of female power. He can be like a woman and bear it if he can be like the presiding woman evoked in "The Idea of Order at Key West," the single artificer of the world in which she walked, the god of modernist desire as autonomous God the Mother. The issue is power, and the freedom that power purchases for Stevens, in all senses of the word "purchase."

In "Esthétique du Mal," a poem published almost thirty years after "Sunday Morning," Stevens wrote that "The greatest poverty is not to live / In a physical world." Through the lens of that thesis Stevens in his room and the lady of "Sunday Morning" in hers slide together into a single image. They live "inside," surrounded by things that have been refined, picked, caught, shipped, fashioned: representations of nature drained of their naturalness. In "Sunday Morning" Stevens imagines two forms of liberation from that kind of production, both forms perfectly suited to the needs of a secular middle-class poet. His first imagination of liberty is offered in the second section of the poem under a definition of "divinity"; the second is offered in the seventh section as a vision of community. The first form of liberation is offered as resolution for the peignoired woman; the second is offered presumably as resolution for the peignoired woman's desire for paradise, but the community imagined is homogeneously male and in some sense homosexual. Both forms of liberation are utopian: they are offered as the possible, in future tense. Both imagine perfection in sensuous, erotic, and natural settings. Both imagine a return to the physical world from an impoverished, oddly unreal, and sometimes neurasthenic Prufrockian middle-class existence. Stevens' nature walks on weekends brought him back to physical life—vibrating flesh, refreshed nerves, pulsating blood that made his cheeks burn with color. In sections 2 and 7 of "Sunday Morning" Stevens imagines the transcendence of the social and sexual differences that troubled and defined his young manhood.

The first of the passages is the more radical of the two. Not only gender difference, but agency itself, the apparently autonomous subject, as both site of gender and the perception of gender, is obliterated:

> Divinity must live within herself.
> Passions of rain, or moods in falling snow;
> Grievings in loneliness, or unsubdued
> Elations when the forest blooms; gusty
> Emotions on wet roads on autumn nights;
> All pleasures and all pains, remembering
> The bough of summer and the winter branch.
> These are the measures destined for her soul.

These lines owe something in particular to the coordinated naturalism and anti-institutionalism of Emerson's address to the Harvard Divinity School, and much in general to Emerson's other paeans to self-reliance. Just as in Emerson it is not the self conceived of as autonomous agency or individuality that is the god, not at all that sort of self that is being relied upon, so in "Sunday Morning" "herself" is not identified with divinity. We cannot lose our way if we stick by the quiet precisions of Stevens' language: divinity lives "within" herself, it is housed there, as it may be in any agent, female or male, as Emerson argued. Divinity is affective consciousness but not consciousness coincidental with "subjects" or individuals who feel and remember that they feel. No grammatical sloppiness but a philosophical sharpness shapes the lines "All pleasures and all pains, remembering / The bough of summer and the winter branch." The dangling modification (who is remembering?) is a deliberate suppression of the actor who remembers, because it is not an actor who is the true subject of remembering, grieving, elation, pleasure, or pain. Divinity is the subject of the lines, but divinity is not *a* subject. Divinity is "selfhood" that cannot be translated into gender or, by the ideology of liberalism, into autonomous agency. Stevens' language is erotically provocative (a gusty, wet, blooming passion), but neither genital differentiation nor any other sort of differentiation is anywhere, in this passage, indicated by his language.

If no subject, divinity may be something like an intransitive verb because it takes no object. The passions, grievings, and moods have no intention: they are directed to nothing in particular. Divinity so redefined by the very structure of Stevens' syntax is a transcendental in opposition to the transcendence of Christian tradition (the dead in heaven). This is a divinity whose heaven is the earth, where feeling is the expression of natural process, where nature is the motor principle of expression: not passions for or about rain, but "Passions *of* rain." If no actor, then no subject; if no worker, then no product; if no gender difference, then no male or female roles; if no labor, then no economy: this is the condition which Stevens envisions as "her" destiny. The image of destiny that Stevens delivers is critical; it is a judgment upon the social site of "Sunday Morning's" production: the antagonistic world of men and women where everything is for sale. Syntactically and existentially the mood of these lines is imperative: "Divinity must live within herself."

This vision sounds final because it imagines an end to the oppression and divisiveness of gender within capitalist economics. In so imagining that end it promises a destiny which one has trouble taking seriously, perhaps because the one who must take it seriously is one like ourselves—one for whom the oppression and divisiveness to which "Sunday Morning" is in part addressed remain firmly in place. This vision of the promised end feels like the end of the poem, but it is not the end. Perhaps it seemed even to Stevens that as utopian visions go this one's referent was too subjective, its sexuality too disembodied, too idealistic even for this strong son of Emerson. Stevens' utopian vision in the second section of "Sunday Morning" does not address a new world of labor and human relations, sexual and otherwise, where, as he put it in the third section, "The sky will be much friendlier . . . / A part of labor and a part of pain."

In his second apocalypse, in the seventh section, Stevens returns us to the world of labor, gender, and genital sexuality— now phallically renewed:

> Supple and turbulent, a ring of men
> Shall chant in orgy on a summer morn
> Their boisterous devotion to the sun,
> Not as a god, but as a god might be,
> Naked among them, like a savage source.

As a vision of the future this passage is so astounding, or so absurd, and for so many (like me), so seductive, that it has stunned into silence some seventy years of commentary on Stevens. I mean silence on the plain sense of the passage and on the enhancement of that plain sense by the social and sexual context of Stevens' young manhood. But Stevens' absurdity is important absurdity because it is not personal and because it joins mainline American literary visions of male utopias: certain raft passages in *Huckleberry Finn*, the "Squeeze of the Hand" chapter in *Moby-Dick*, Rip Van Winkle's fantasy in the Catskills of men at play, many, many things in Whitman and, more recently, the Brooks Range conclusion of Norman Mailer's *Why Are We in Vietnam?* What Stevens imagines for the social future is a place without women; men who work, but whose work cannot be distinguished from the homoerotic pleasure of sexual indulgence (Stevens, a keen etymologist, would have known the kinship of "orgy" with an ancient Greek word related to "work"); men who work nakedly—and in their nakedness bear no signs, as the peignoired woman bears signs, of social difference. Their nakedness and their arrangement in a ring speak the language of fraternity (brothers, but no sisters) and equality. And they chant: in community they create a fundamental poetry—a devotion to a "lordly" nature that is spun out in the sentimentality of choiring angels, a metaphor taken away from traditional Christianity and transvalued with outrageous deliberation into the music of pagan naturalism. The contradictions of Stevens' early life and poetry—work, poetry, and nature itself, the conventional realm of female authority—all are reclaimed for a masculine totality, fused in an image of masculine power: Father Nature.

3

The embeddedness of "Sunday Morning" in the political and economic materiality of Stevens' America, through the specific historical circumstances of his biography, has long been obscured by the literary history of the poem: the embeddedness of "Sunday Morning" through its network of allusions in a sort of literary materiality. The presence in the poem of Shakespeare, Milton, Keats, and Tennyson ("The Palace of Art"), among other worthies, has been explored with useful results, but the activity of so historicizing Stevens within English and American poetry has been carried off in the quasi-theological abstract atmosphere of idealism, high humanism, formalism, and (more recently) the new idealism of the intertextual method (both Derridean and Bloomian) of anxiety-ridden historicisms: as if literary history were an autonomous process; as if poets engaged their dead poetic ancestors, and only their dead *canonical* ancestors, in direct dialogue; as if what Harold Bloom calls "the poet" in a human being could be usefully segregated because the poet within is somehow free from the economic and sexual being who might marry, have children, and need to earn a living; as if the historical company of poets were actually disencumbered from the entanglements of their nonpoetic histories; as if the sophomore survey of English literature were an adequate representation of the process of literary history. Stevens' most distinguished critics, Harold Bloom and Helen Vendler, have led the way by proceeding as if they had never read the poet's letters and journals, or as if, having read them, they had come to the conclusion that the worldly life they found portrayed therein pertained to somebody else. And the theory and practice of the best known and most influential of American literary feminists (Gilbert and Gubar, Elaine Showalter) give us no respite.

"Sunday Morning" is not only encumbered from the "outside," as it were. Its very language does battle with various discourses of idealization from late-nineteenth-century American gentility to the critical culture of Bloom and Vendler. Stevens mounts a counterrhetoric against the words of idealism (holy, divinity, lord, seraphin, Jesus, freedom, soul) by bringing those words into the poem and bringing them to earth: freedom is green, soul is passion, the lord is the sun, angels are well-built men. Stevens' struggle with religious ideality, given voice by his leisured lady's need for Christian fulfillment, is simultaneously a struggle against what for us must be a mostly buried literary ideality—the meaning of Keats as Keats had been reconstructed by the powerful literary tastemakers of Stevens' youth. Renunciation, as the need for fulfillment beyond society, economics, and nature, is "Christian," it is "poetic," it is "feminine," and the name of renunciation (especially in Stevens' early poetry) is "Keats." The allusive representation of Keats in "Sunday Morning" is the literary site of convergence of Stevens' economic and sexual anxiety, his ladylike poetic self-consciousness, and his desire to make himself a poet of broad cultural relevance against the authoritative voices of his literary scene. The literary historicity of "Sunday Morning" is no autonomous alternative to its economic materiality; rather it turns out to be both its intensive clarification and its critique.

R. H. Stoddard, Richard Watson Gilder, E. C. Stedman, Henry Van Dyke, G. E. Woodberry, and their friends—no longer the names of American literary powers—dominated our poetry and criticism from the death of Whitman and the passing of the Fireside group to the emergence of the little magazines of modernism and the early poems of Frost, Stevens, Eliot, and Pound. The "genteel" circle, as they would later be caustically dubbed, were antididactic literary theorists who preferred Poe among nineteenth-century American poets and championed him against the public-minded eloquence and rhetoric of Longfellow and Bryant; they were anticapitalist social critics who stood against industrialism, utilitarian ethics, bourgeois man, the entrepreneurial spirit, and their representation in journalism and in realist fiction, that dark duo of the literary spirit for which their genteel scorn was unsurpassed except by their opposite numbers in England: Yeats, Ernest Dowson, and Lionel Johnson.[21] And as editors of powerful magazines like the *Atlantic* and the *Century*, as anthologists, critics, literary historians, poets, and translators, they enforced their taste. To their strong American echo of English aestheticism, the genteel group added a native dose of renunciation which purified their aestheticist inclination of any Paterian sensuousness for its own sake or any sake. In the atmosphere of late-nineteenth-century Anglo-American Hegelianism, these Americans were ascetic aesthetes who cultivated a search for the ideal that entailed a rejection, Manichean in force, of the world and the body in the world. Poetry for them was the name of a literary purity that, unlike the prose of fiction or of the essay, would neither minister to the new self-made man nor bring remuneration from the world of capital. The poet who best represented this purity and at the same time its potential subversion by the temptations of capital and the flesh was Keats. So the rhetorical target of Stevens' modernism is not some presumably old-fashioned sense of the poetic, as in Yeats's exemplary modernist formula in which imagination always opposes rhetoric and action, but the effete modernity of his genteel contemporaries who pre-echoed most of the canonical modernist literary and social biases.

"Sunday Morning" in its literary historicity bears little if any anxiety over the power of a predecessor lyricist. It is instead full of contempt (not too strong a word) for his culture's representation of Keats as a poetic ideal that would divide Stevens against himself. Stevens' fight is to win poetic space from contemporary poets and critics. If "Keats" was a word signifying freedom from bourgeois economic contamination, then, at the same time, and by the force of a deadly cultural logic, "Keats" was also a word signifying sexual otherness to the econo-machismo of Stevens' culture—not freedom to be masculine in some other, perhaps healthier form, but the loss altogether of a culturally readable and culturally acceptable masculinity. This "Keats"—not the poet Stevens read and admired, but the poet recreated by genteel attitudes—would deny Stevens his writerly masculinity in a representation of the poetic vocation that in making it autonomous within capitalist society thereby makes it at best feminine and at worst desexualized. In his Harvard journal Stevens makes the point with this incisive remark whose immediate target might appear to be popular women poets like Frances Osgood and Lydia Sigourney, but whose true object is Stedman and his friends, the male vehicles of both literary feminization and literary asexuality. "Poetry and Manhood: those who say poetry is now the peculiar province of women say so because ideas about poetry are effeminate. Homer, Dante, Shakespeare, Milton, Keats, Browning, much of Tennyson—they are your man-poets. Silly verse is always the work of silly men."[22] The power of those silly men to affect the cultural unconscious of their time might be measured precisely there, with Stevens saying, in so many words, that he knew better, and yet while knowing better nevertheless played out his literary youth as if he feared that he just might be one of those silly men who would be denied poetic manhood.

Not one of your man poets, genteel "Keats" was often crystallized in images of flight. If T. E. Hulme's later attack on the romantics is overstated (he said they were always flying up into the circumambient gas), it is right on target for the romanticism of Stedman and company who turned Keats into a "superb blue moth" and the great odes into the music of "ethereal passion."[23] In fact, the idealization of passion is something like a key to understanding the genteel ethos, and Woodberry's title for a volume of poems, *Ideal Passions*, can stand as the secret subtitle of all their works. Not surprisingly, the publication of the Fanny Brawne letters made passion, apparently not of the ethereal sort, the riveting issue of genteel commentary (public and private) on Keats. Keats's sexual innocence had to be protected at all cost—it was the symbolic mark of what poetry had to be: the safe haven of ideality in a world that the genteel cultural critics found epitomized by the marketplace. Gilder, alone in his room reading the Fanny Brawne correspondence, tells us that he smashed the volume to the floor and cried;[24] Stedman, in an exemplary essay, concocted (*pour l'occasion*) formalist theory in order to save Keats the poet from Keats the man (shades of Harold Bloom): the man might have been passion's slave, Stedman had to admit it, but "If you would know an artist's true self you must discover it through his art."[25] In another essay, which suppresses its author's anxieties not at all, Van Dyke—sounding a little like Stevens, in masculine discomfort—first exempts Keats from the world of the stock exchange, then defends him against the suspicion that he was a "feminine poet" ("the quality of extreme sensitiveness to outward beauty is not an exclusive mark of femininity"), but then must admit that Keats was "not a virile poet, like Dante or Shakespeare or Milton," and may never have become one. On the other hand, Van Dyke is eager to point out (as we watch him sift through the sexual options) that Keats was no senile poet who celebrates "the impotent and morbid passions of decay"—his goddess is no "decrepit Venus sinking into the gutter." Van Dyke's solution to the question of Keats's sexuality is ingenious: Keats is a "juvenile poet," a writer of "springtime." With no sense of what a bawdy reader might do with his remarks, Van Dyke declares the poetry of Keats "small in bulk and slight in body." Van Dyke's Keats died a sexually suspended twelve-year-old, "sensuous in every line, yet free from the slightest taint of sensuality."[26]

Like the father of the poet, Stedman was an early version of Wallace Stevens: he wrote treatises on poetic angelism while working as a Wall Street broker. Stedman, author of *The Nature and Elements of Poetry*, and editor of a history of the New York Stock Exchange, is the forgotten predecessor of the poet who wrote *The Necessary Angel* while drawing a vice-president's salary at the Hartford Accident and Indemnity Company. Stevens' career from its beginning is a troubled expression of an effort to overcome the trivializations that were thrust upon bourgeois writers like himself who could not help but define themselves in self-trivializing terms. But Stevens did not go gently into the good night of modernism, and in "Sunday Morning" his protest is lodged most powerfully in his effort to recover poetic self-respect, whose name was necessarily phallic, from poetic self-trivialization whose various names were "Keats," "femininity," "Christianity," and "ideality."

The Keats who appears allusively in "Sunday Morning" is at once mythic weapon to be deployed against Stevens' contemporaries and the representation of what Stevens most feared he'd be forced to become—the genteel poet of a debilitating modernism which reserves literature for the weekend when productive males presumably might have time to consume it and even produce it ("arts and leisure"). "Keats" is present to "Sunday Morning" in sections 4, 5, 6, and 8, where he is evoked for "visionary south" ("Ode to a Nightingale"), for Porphyro's heavy breathing and heavily fruited offering to Madeline ("The Eve of

St. Agnes"), for the timelessness of arrested natural processes and acts ("Ode on a Grecian Urn"), and for the somber twilight fluttering of swallows that closes the moody meditation of "To Autumn." In each except the last instance, the unmanned Keats of Stevens' culture is made to speak through the unhappy consciousness of Stevens' dreaded alter ego with whose desires Keats is allusively identified—the yearning lady whose need for the imperishable is projected in the whining tones of genteel idealism. Stevens' comebacks to Keatsian yearning are delivered in a debunking, even hectoring voice, no less cruel because only implied: It makes you sad that "men sit and hear each other groan"? You say that "palsy shakes a few, sad, last grey hairs"? You're telling me, my good woman, that "youth grows pale and specter thin and dies"? That "Beauty cannot keep her lustrous eyes / Or new Love pine at them beyond tomorrow"? Face it: love (this in reductive delight) whispers only "a little out of tenderness." But the hammer blow, twice dealt, comes in the form of an existential proverb: a proverbial alternative and rewriting of the most famous of Keatsian adages, "Beauty is truth, truth beauty." Stevens says: "Death is the mother of beauty, hence from her, / Alone, shall come fulfillment to our dreams / And our desires." From such mockery Stevens moves in section 6 to his reading of the urn poem as a desperate exercise in sublimation. To replay Keats's lines in more sexually suggestive language, as Stevens does, is to establish the distinction between himself and his genteel readers of Keats as the liberating distinction between maturity and adolescence.

> Does ripe fruit never fall? Or do the boughs
> Hang always heavy in that perfect sky,
> Unchanging, yet so like our perishing earth,
> With rivers like our own that seek for seas
> They never find, the same receding shores
> That never touch with inarticulate pang?

Those suspiciously anthropomorphic rivers flow toward the sea, but they never get to pour their waters in because the ever-receptive shores ever recede, ever back away from all penetration. The voice of sexual culmination will never utter the pleasure of its "inarticulate pang," because it will be forever poised at pleasure's very brink. This is "happy happy love"?

Stevens' fullest response to genteel Keats comes in the seventh section, in the vision of supple and turbulent men who chant in orgy. The transitions between sections of "Sunday Morning" are abrupt at best, not narrative or logical. In the blank space between sections 6 and 7 Stevens seems to say to the lady of Keatsian yearning (and with maximum intention to shock her): Now consider this as a vision of paradise. In its literary context, this seventh section begs to be read as an effort to drown the skinny boy soprano of genteel Keats with the generous Italianate amplitudes of Walt Whitman, whose sexual frankness kept him at the margins of genteel culture. The Whitman who is being recalled is the poet of "Song of Myself," section 11. Stevens' complacent woman from section 1 of "Sunday Morning," the sign of Christian desire emerging first as a response to a leisured context of consumption, then modulated into the sign of a de-eroticized Keats, is now (in the blank space between sections 6 and 7) transformed into the poem's presiding point of view, the consciousness of Stevens himself in the mask of Whitman's wealthy, lonely, voyeuristic lady who imagines her/himself in the classic male position ("they do not ask who seizes fast to them, / They do not know who declines with pendant and bending arch"); who both dreams on the friendly twenty-eight young men bathing by the shore and "sees" the supple and turbulent men of "Sunday Morning" chant in orgy: "She owns the fine house by the rise of the bank, / She hides handsome and richly drest aft the blinds of the window." Coming as it does on the heels of the Grecian-urn-dominated sixth section of "Sunday Morning," and its maliciously painful picture of religious paradise as unculminated Keatsian foreplay, the effect of "Sunday Morning" 7 is to say to the "silly men" of Stevens' positively ladylike culture that poetry is Whitman, not Keats—masculine, not feminine, not asexual. The poetic is nature reclaimed not as the great Mother creator but as the

Father phallic progenitor—section 7 says this with no poise of phallic confidence but out of desire for phallic confidence: desire not for the domestic and the commodity-dominated but for the communal, the heavenly as phallic song—for the music of nature as the sound of a phallic freedom that replaces the silence of disembodying Palestine. Not richly dressed, but naked:

> And in their chant shall enter, voice by voice
> The windy lake wherein their lord delights,
> The trees, like seraphin, and echoing hills
> That choir among themselves long afterward.

In the final, eighth section of "Sunday Morning," as the prophetic voice proclaims the death of God, Stevens takes on Keats directly, creating his distance not by mocking what Keats has been made to stand for but by crossing the breathless naturalism of Keats's closing lines in "To Autumn" with analogical music: the hard-earned particularities of Keats, so resistant to paraphrase, become in Stevens' response the eminently paraphrasable deer, quail, and sweet berries which ripen in the wilderness—all, as Helen Vendler laments, "allegorical instances" of Nietzschean messages of finitude, freedom, and isolation.[27] Stevens' "casual flocks of pigeons" figure anxiety not for English nightingales but for American waterfowl: the closing lines of "Sunday Morning" are a rewriting of the clear and hopeful teleological text of William Cullen Bryant's famous poem which Matthew Arnold, who understood the cultural power of literature when he saw it, called the finest lyric of the nineteenth century. As Stevens' pigeons descend into darkness they form a sign which, however ambiguous, calls for translation just as Bryant's waterfowl does and as Keats's swallows, gnats, and robins do not. Stevens' deployment of natural phenomena, in other words, is an instance of his rhetorical intentions, his "disguised pronunciamento," as he put it in "The Comedian as the Letter C." As a student at Harvard, he learned to distrust (in a thickening fin-de-siècle atmosphere) overtly moralizing art—exposed pronunciamento, as it were. He recoiled from Bryant and the Fireside group because, as he put it, the "New England school of poets were too hard thinkers. For them there was no pathos in the rose except as it went to point a moral or adorn a tale. I like my philosophy smothered in beauty and not the opposite."[28] But we have to say back to Stevens that disguised pronunciamento is still pronunciamento, and philosophy smothered in beauty is still philosophy, not the opposite of philosophy. And he knew it. Aestheticist theory—"the sensuous for the sake of sensuousness," perception for the sake of perception—Stevens found to be "the most arrant as it is the most inexcusable rubbish." "Art," he argued, "must fit with other things; it must be part of the system of the world. And if it finds a place in that system it will likewise find a ministry and relations that are its proper adjuncts."[29] Vendler finds a desecrated (because covertly didactic) Keatsian voice at the end of "Sunday Morning," not a voice that merely purrs in sensuous revelry as Keats had in the autumn poem which Stevens evokes, but a voice that actually speaks to someone, is not merely "over-heard," and in so speaking conveys *thought* (formalist abomination) about the role of artistic sensuousness in a world in which young intellectuals of Stevens' time conceived of Jesus as a man who died, and of his grave as no entrance, no "porch," but the end of the line. Stevens' modernism is not hostile to canonical modernism's twin bête noir: rhetoric and the will. He is not failing to become the Keats who has been idolized by anti-intellectual Keatsophantic formalists from E. C. Stedman to Cleanth Brooks to Helen Vendler; even though his American predecessor Fireside poets would have recoiled from his exotic lushness, he is trying to be a poet who would nevertheless succeed in assuming their mantle of cultural ministry—the cultural power that the Fireside poets had assumed for themselves and wielded throughout the American nineteenth century. It was the mantle of cultural authority, honor, and centrality that neither the economic nor the aesthetic culture of Stevens' young manhood—neither his father nor Stedman—could have recognized.

4

The issue of Stevens' sexual identity as a writer—his effort to phallicize poetic discourse—is not just related to but just *is* the canonical modernist issue of poetic authority: the cultural power—or, increasingly, for the poetic modernist—the cultural powerlessness of poetry in a society that masculinized the economic while feminizing the literary. In the context of Stevens' America the nonutilitarian emphasis of aesthetics and literary theory since Kant and the early romantics—initially a badge of honor, a political protest, as Raymond Williams has shown,[30] a critique of capitalist values on behalf of a higher usefulness in the healing of self-alienated bourgeois man (in Coleridge's definition of imagination's function: the unification of the whole soul of man)—increasingly this nonutilitarian emphasis in the modern idea of literature becomes, by the testimony of the modern poets themselves, the mark of poetry's social irrelevance. At the turn of the century in the United States and under the guidance of Stedman's genteel theories, feminization, social inutility, and poetic autonomy are just so many equatable ideas marking the marginalization of poetry in the name of the very modernism whose cultural ambition would be so very great, a modernism which would find, in Stevens' words, a "ministry" in the world. "Poetic autonomy": not some sealed alcove but at once the sign of alienation felt by writers from Keats to Stedman *and* the sign of a critical desire to engage and shape society while being beholden to none of the institutions which degrade work and all human relations, especially those between men and women. The cultural discourse that Stevens was heir to encouraged him to fantasize the potential social authority of the literary as phallic authority and to desire that the poetic should be endowed with social power within a social formation that cannot itself permit such endowment. In the literary culture that Stevens would create, the "phallic" would have been not the curse word of some recent feminist criticism but the name of a limited, because male, respect for literature.

The Harvard journal entry of 1899 which declares confidence in the eternal manliness of real poetry and the letter to Elsie Moll of 1914 which muses on the absurdity of his verse-writing habits, so ladylike, enclose two other letters to his wife-to-be, one of July 1908 in which manhood as an artist is seen as coincidental with major, canonical status, and another one of August 1911, in which he imaginatively sees himself cut down artistically and sexually, by Gainsborough, for being a painter of fans.

> We gabbled about Michael Angelo—he, for—I against. And don't you agree with me that if we could get the Michael Angeloes out of our heads—Shakespeare, Titian, Goethe—all the phenomenal men, we should find a multitude of lesser things (lesser but a *multitude*) to occupy us? It would be like withdrawing the sun and bringing out innumerable stars. I do not mean that the Michael Angeloes are not what they are—but I like Dr. Campion, I like Verlaine—water-colors, *little* statues, small thoughts. Let us leave the great things to the professors—substitute for majestic organs, sylvan reeds—such as shepherds played on under cottage windows. . . . A fancy, at least. I need not agree with it tomorrow, if I do not care to.—But there are many fancies. They do not last. Tonight, after dinner, for example, I thought I should like to play my guitar, so I dug it up from the bottom of my wardrobe, dusted it, strummed a half-dozen chords, and then felt bored by it. I have played those half-dozen chords so often. I wish I were gifted enough to learn a new half-dozen.— Some day I may be like one of the old ladies with whom I lived in Cambridge, who played a hymn on *her* guitar. The hymn had thousands of verses, all alike. She played about two hundred every night—until the house-dog whined for mercy and liberty.[31]

> . . . my trifling poesies are like the trifling designs one sees on fans. I was much shocked, accordingly, to read of a remark made by Gainsborough, the great painter of portraits and landscapes. He said scornfully of some one, "Why, the man is a painter of fans!"—Well, to be sure, a painter of fans is a very unimportant person by the side of the Gainsboroughs.[32]

To get Michelangelo and Shakespeare and all "phenomenal men" out of your head means self-consciously choosing minority (lesser things, little statues, small thoughts) in full awareness, with your eyes on what constitutes majority: on precisely what you fear you do not have—the majestic organ of a phenomenal man. And Stevens' confident wit can neither cover up nor take the place of his imagined lack of vocal size because wit of his kind has historically been the sort of low virtue that poets substitute when, for whatever reasons, the high serious subject is just not available. The poetics of minority in Stevens is inaugurated with the imagination of insufficiency. To get Michelangelo and Shakespeare out of your head means banishing the sun for the stars, it means choosing the pastoral—not culture and the city, the traditional province of the long poem and the poet of epic ambition. It means becoming like one of those old ladies he lived with in Cambridge who played thousands of verses on her guitar but with the added gift for innumerable variations so that the house-dog would not whine for mercy and liberty: small but multitudinous pleasures. The withdrawn sun returns in "Sunday Morning" along with some phenomenal men in pastoral context; the guitar and the poetry of theme and endless variations will return in the first of many efforts in Stevens' later manner to write the long poem, a major poetry, "The Man with the Blue Guitar." But to become minor and to like it is never to title a poem "Notes toward a Supreme Fiction" and in so doing tell all that you feel small, but can imagine a big thing. To become minor and to like it is never to have to call your poems "poesies," or to characterize them as "trifling," or to think of what one does—what makes one what one is—as similar to an expendable item of luxury that ends up, like a fan, in the hands of leisured ladies. Or worse yet: not even a fan but a decoration on a fan. It is never to put your manhood into jeopardy by letting yourself be the wimp who was put down by Gainsborough. To think well of yourself as a minor light is never, with all editorial time virtually run out, to write in panic to your publisher, Alfred Knopf, and tell him to change the title of your first volume to *The Grand Poem: Preliminary Minutiae.*[33]

If it is possible to condense the anxieties of a career into one line it would be this one from "Sunday Morning"—"She makes the willow shiver in the sun." That may be the central line of the poem because it speaks of a desire to make a delicate and subtle moment of perception and perceptual pleasure into a grand and urgent thing: the redemption of our lonely finitude. The line projects *an* image while celebrating, implicitly, and at the same time, the possibilities and values of *the* image as medium of perceptual acuteness; it urges the necessity of perceptual acuteness because it is the antithetical major clause which completes a long series of piled up subordinate phrases of depressing implication; death is the enabler of the percept, and the percept in natural context, borne and preserved by the image, makes it all bearable:

> Although she strews the leaves
> Of sure obliteration on our paths,
> The path sick sorrow took, the many paths
> Where triumph rang its brassy phrase, or love
> Whispered a little out of tenderness,
> She makes the willow shiver in the sun.

That last line blends the urge of aesthetic minority, a poetics of small pastoral impressions, with the commanding rhetorical tone of the cultural medicine man who has been entrusted with a culture's well-being—as if the fate of society depended upon what Stevens later would call the "yes" that is uttered after "the final no," a little thing, "No greater than a cricket's horn" or a "petty phrase."[34] With Pound and Eliot, no other modern American poet believed that what his society thought so "little" of (as in "belittle") might mean so much.

There is evidence to suggest that what pushed the marriage of Elsie Moll and Wallace Stevens in the wrong direction, at least from her point of view, was his decision to publish the "secrets" of his poetic character that he had once entrusted her with: those little handmade volumes of verses, written as special gifts of courtship. The poems were their bond. The poems—the act of writing them and the act of giving them to a womanly audience of one—brought Stevens and Elsie together by giving life to what his father and the culture his father mediated for him would have called the "woman" within Elsie's suitor. In the private place where Stevens felt that he could be himself, the poems were an expression both of domestic tranquillity and of his feeling of himself, as individual, that he could not separate from the domestic site of that feeling: "I certainly do not exist," he wrote to her before they were married, "from nine to six, when I am at the office. There is no everyday Wallace, apart from the one at work—and that one is tedious.—At night I strut my individual state once more."[35] Until he went public with his poetry Stevens had not violated the sentimental norms of cultural femininity, but had accepted them in perhaps a more radical fashion than even America's sentimental novelists had accepted them. They published; they sold in big numbers; the "damned mob of scribbling women" made money, as Hawthorne wrote with some envy. In effect, Stevens told his wife-to-be, I am complete when the values of hearth, home, and poetry are united at the site of our living together. This is one way to read his correspondence with Elsie Moll, the woman he addressed in his letters as his "country girl," his "little girl," his "lady," his "Queen," his "Princess," his "second self," his "Muse," and his "Bo-peep," which he sometimes conflated with "Pete," his nickname in college— "Bo-pete."[36]

Stevens knew himself well enough to describe the act of writing to Elsie as an act of "self-communion."[37] So to go public with his poetry (from her point of view) was to breach the alliance of poetry, home, love, and marriage, and to dishonor the bond, to betray her and himself, the two that should be one, and therefore to betray the marriage itself by exposing little Bo-peep—exposing Elsie, his "Muse," the poetic-as-pastoral-as-feminine—to the world of men and power, and in such betrayal (now his point of view) convert the poetic into the pastoral as masculine: the major, the canonical, ministry in the world. As lover and husband, as economic man and aesthetic man, Stevens occupied the contradictions of his culture. There is an emancipatory implication in his unhappiness as a young man,

and the story of his early life and career sometimes tells a tale
of radical social discontent.

5

Even in the economic and sexual terms through which I have
tried to give some coherence to Stevens' story, I find coherence, in the end, elusive. But maybe that kind of effort to make
sense of "Sunday Morning" and Stevens' young manhood makes
its strongest historical and political statement right there: the
points where interpretive coherence fails turn out to be, at least
for this reader, the very points where, as Stevens begins to lose
command of his rhetoric and argument, his poem takes an unexpected turn. For example, Stevens naturalizes the commodity
without seeming to be aware that he is doing so—converting
the lady's oranges and cockatoo into "comforts of the sun"
("pungent fruit and bright green wings"). And that sort of forgetting of the labor process that produced her comforts is surely
socially representative forgetting, especially on Sundays when
Christians give thanks, but generally not to their fellow human
beings. It is rather the next conversion—from commodity to
so-called comforts of the sun and then to the "Things to be
cherished like the thought of heaven"—that most intrigues me
because it is the beginning of the undoing of the poem's overt
rhetoric.

In the traditional reading of "Sunday Morning" which pits
poet against yearning woman, macho existentialist against repressed feminine religiosity, the specific "Things to be cherished like the thought of heaven" are "things" of an earthly
paradise that is supposed to be an alternative to old-fashioned
heaven: "things," in this poem's insistently debunking materialist rhetoric, are supposed to take the place of "thought"
of an immaterial place, even of the immaterial place itself.
But neither earthly "things" nor the possibility of naturalized
subjectivity, however lushly evoked as "Passions of rain," can
grant sufficient solace for the lady. She wants "imperishable

bliss." To continue a little longer with this fiction that the poem is a dialogue between a male and a female voice, she seems to know that "things" *like* the thought of heaven are only "like"—substitutive satisfactions (in Freud's phrase), and so never wholly satisfactory. She continues to yearn and "her" yearning in two crucial places becomes "his." In those two moments the fiction of antithetical male and female dialogue is exploded. The poet becomes "lady-like," his rhetoric loses its naturalistic ground and begins to levitate toward what it most wishes to debunk.

The first spot of rhetorical unsettlement occurs in the foggy allegory of section 3. Jove, poor Jove, didn't have a mother to suckle him. Another god, whose name also begins with a *J*, did: his death mustn't, however, become a reason to mourn his absence (he never was). It should rather be the celebrating occasion of our creative presence (we made him). When we realize that, then the sky, a "between" place, which some say divides us from heaven, becomes part of our place, the one and only place—"A part of labor and a part of pain . . . Not this dividing and indifferent blue." In the poem's overt philosophical intention, the two lines I have just quoted make perfect, summarizing sense. But there is a line between those two that I've deliberately omitted and that makes sense neither in my little allegory of the history of the gods nor in the poem's general orientation. The line reads: "And next in glory to enduring love." Endurances (with the special exception of endurances of seasonal change) are what this poem is against. Stevens sets them in the context of feminine desire in order to denigrate them. Yet this line asserts the glory of one particular, imagined endurance and says that enduring love would bring ultimate fulfillment. And more: the line not only asserts the ultimate value of enduring love but compares enduring love to what is not strictly comparable with it—glorious earthly paradises of change. "Enduring love" is not just more glorious than that—it is the earth's negation, the very thing that he would choose if such love were a matter of choice, and a metonymic stand-in for all negations (like traditional religion) that would replace earth with heaven. In an essential way, the poem becomes confusing, and this confusion can be focused in the comparative "next in glory," which posits a continuity of natural and ideal values, and implies the happy proposition that all choices are in some sense good choices, when in fact Stevens is arguing the opposite: for discontinuity of natural and ideal realms and the unhappy proposition that only one choice is a good one. The irony of the comparative is that it puts the values of the lady in the mouth of her rhetorical antagonist at the moment when he is trying to sustain his contrary discourse.

The initial occurrence of "Death is the mother of beauty" (in section 5) appears to swing the poem back on track by negating the great feminine negation ("enduring love"), but the second elaborated occurrence of this aphorism at the end of section 6 reinstates the so-called female desire for enduring love in the figure of the mother (Stevens' mother died three years before the publication of "Sunday Morning"):

> Death is the mother of beauty, mystical,
> Within whose burning bosom we devise
> Our earthly mothers waiting, sleeplessly.

Stevens' biography here erupts into the poem, making him speak against his poem's male/female contest of voices, making him conceive of his readers as radically like him—an audience composed wholly of bereft children, specifically of bereft males, sons who have all lost their mothers and who are all projecting their mothers on the other side of death waiting for them in transcendental space, worrying, refusing to sleep until they (we) come safely home. I read the aphorism "Death is the mother of beauty" in its second appearance this way: My mother's death is the mother of beauty, my mother's death is itself a mother—a substitute mother that shocks me, as all death must, into cherishing the earth. My mother's death is therefore the birth of my imagination, the necessary angel of earth, yes, but I have only one mother and this substitute does not suffice.

I need to see her again, my real mother, whose death enabled the birth of my poems, knowing that I cannot. So I will invent her there, "devise" her waiting for me—in heaven, site of all enduring love. The full-throated phallic song of earth (section 7) follows, now all the more powerfully when we see what it is that Stevens is trying to forget.

He knew that you can't get your mother back, even if she's not dead, and he also knew that you can, if you're male, find a pretty good substitutive satisfaction for her:

> This has been a busy & therefore a profitable week. Tonight I received no assignment & so I am in my room. I almost said at home—God forbid! The proverbial apron-strings have a devil of a firm hold on me & as a result I am unhappy at such a distance from the apron. I wish a thousand times a day that I had a wife—which I never shall have, and more's the pity for I am certainly a domestic creature par excellence. It is brutal to myself to live alone. . . . I don't know—sometime I may marry after all. Of course I am too young now etc. as people go—but I begin to feel the vacuum that wives fill. This will probably make poor reading to a future bachelor. Wife's an old word—which does not express what I mean—rather a delightful companion who would make a fuss over me.[38]

The story of Stevens' early life and career sometimes tells a tale that it doesn't appear to know it is telling, of discontent radical not in the usual senses of left politics but in the etymological sense, "radical" because such discontent is alleviated only by a return to the origin, by a son's desire for his mother's breast that would, if granted, simply set aside all of his male obligations in the world of capital.

Reflections on Essentialist Feminism

I began with a distinction between biological and social engenderment that has nearly become the de rigueur departure for feminist cultural analyses. "Femininity" and "masculinity," to say it again, are internally linked social constructions of basic biological difference. The purpose of this act of construction, if I can speak of a social process as having intention, is the conversion of biological difference into hierarchical opposition. Social constructions of gender (or of anything else) are freighted with ideological content which varies historically, geographically, and culturally, even though the positional relation of one gender to the other (the relation of domination) appears to remain constant. History, in other words, as repetitious sexist drama: the authors of *The Madwoman in the Attic* are not unconvincing when they claim a radical coherence of all writings by women. But in a spirited, sympathetic, and (to me, at least) mostly persuasive deflation of a number of major American and French feminist literary reputations, Toril Moi, a Marxist feminist, makes in her book *Sexual/Textual Politics* just the sort of point that Sandra Gilbert and Susan Gubar will occasionally make in theory but cannot live by:

> It has long been an established practice among most feminists to use "feminine" (and "masculine") to represent *social constructs* (patterns of sexuality and behavior imposed by cultural and social norms), and to reserve "female" and "male" for the purely biological aspects of sexual difference. "Femininity" is a cultural construct: one isn't born a woman, one becomes one, as Simone de Beauvoir puts it. Seen in this perspective, patriarchal oppression consists of imposing certain social standards of femininity on all biological women, in order precisely to make us believe that the chosen standards for "femininity" are *natural*. Thus a woman who refuses to conform can be labelled both *unfeminine* and *unnatural*. It is in the patriarchal interest that the two terms (femininity and femaleness) stay thoroughly confused. Feminists, on the contrary, have to disentangle this confusion.[39]

Moi's statement seems right on target but a very small part of it may conceal a disabling contradiction in the writings of the most well known American literary feminists and their followers, and in the work of a younger wave of feminists who are at the verge of open revolt against their mothers. I notice that Moi relegates "masculinity" to a parenthesis and then proceeds to elaborate her theory with respect only to the cultural genealogy of femininity, with respect to what was and is being done to women. Parenthetical masculinity in Moi's discourse signifies a certain equality with femininity, both being social creations and not conditions of nature. But the parenthetical can function as an expendable afterthought, and in too much feminist criticism that is exactly the fate of the "masculine," however rhetorically understandable that may be, given the history of sexism, which is hard, of course, to distinguish from history. The impression that Moi and many of her sisters leave (though Moi knows better) is that women are history's privileged victims: as if the female is subjected to social construction by a maleness that operates out of a socially uncontaminated free space; as if male authority to oppress is a one-way street; as if male power stands outside the arena of oppression as its originating god-the-father-of-patriarchy: serene, monolithic, omnipotent, natural, coolly paring its mandarin fingernails.

The logic of Moi's statement demands that I say that I wasn't born a man, I became one. Seen in this perspective, patriarchal oppression also consists of imposing certain social standards of masculinity on all biological men, in order precisely to make us believe that the chosen standards for masculinity are *natural*. A man who refuses to conform can be labeled both unmasculine and unnatural (or ladylike, as Stevens labeled himself). It is in the patriarchal interest that the two terms (masculinity and male) stay thoroughly confused. Cultural critics of both sexes interested in the issue of liberation need to disentangle *this* confusion as well.

You probably can't help but notice that in my replay of Moi's statement I am trying for a pithy summary of the theoretical point, and its implied polemic, submerged in my reading of the early career of Wallace Stevens. And you can't help but notice a certain absurdity in what I've said in my revision of Moi— an absurdity embedded in patriarchy itself, which I'll try to disentangle this way: the ancient social process called "patriarchy" consists also in the oppression of patriarchs; the "interest" of patriarchy lies also in the confusion of men, in teaching men who will not conform how to alienate and despise themselves, and even men who do conform. A little deconstruction goes a long way. Patriarchy against itself dismantles itself from within, its intention overridden, captured, and wounded by the very structure of sexual relations it would set in place and manipulate. Patriarchy does not and cannot understand the self-subverting consequences of what it conceives of (to use Moi's word) as its "interest." If we can speak of a social process as having intention, then we have to follow through and say that it also has an unconscious.

If history, as Gilbert and Gubar argue, is a repetitious sexist drama (not easy to argue otherwise) with men in the plot-controlling role of the oppressor, and women in the role of selfless victim, then history may be in danger of being translated by some of our most influential feminists into Manichean allegory, and the very category that Moi and others invoke in order to explain the transformation of biology into history—she calls it, interchangeably, the "social" or the "cultural"—this category will be banished almost as quickly as it is invoked. With the social banished behind the scenes, history begins to look very much again like biology, biology like metaphysics, and the writing of feminist literary criticism like a ritual of scapegoating propelled by paranoia. At some destructive level history does look like Manichean sexual allegory because the biological difference does make a difference. It is in the interests of patriarchy (not feminism) to convince us that *that* difference is the only difference that can make a difference; the critical method proper to patriarchy (not feminism) is naturalistic, ahistorical: a formalism of gender.

In *The Madwoman in the Attic* (1979) Sandra Gilbert and Susan Gubar produce (in this order) a feminist poetics, a reading of literature by English women through the nineteenth century, with special emphasis on novelists, and, in a substantial closing section, a reading of nineteenth-century poetry by women, with special emphasis on Emily Dickinson: all of this—seven hundred pages' worth—as prelude to a study of literature by women in the twentieth century, in the context of modernism, a book they call, with no hint of dystopian depression, *No Man's*

Land, the absurd negative of Stevens' absurd no woman's land. In addition, Gilbert and Gubar have recently published what is being talked about (not without heated debate) as a definitive anthology of women's literature (but not quite: "the tradition in English," as they call it), under the imprimatur of Norton—in matters anthological, the hegemonic house of college collections of literature. Since the publication of *The Madwoman in the Attic*, Gilbert has taken off from her pages on Dickinson and nineteenth-century poetry by women and has begun to write on the course of American poetry, with her point of departure a comparative treatment of Whitman and Dickinson and her object a theory about the sexual shape of modernist poetry in America. Stevens is one of her favorite modernist examples.

Beginning with an often compelling but I think fatally flawed account of patriarchal power and its metaphors of authority, ownership, and the pen as penis—patriarchy's celebration of male autonomy, akin to God the Father Almighty—Gilbert and Gubar end with a visionary assertion of matriarchal power and its metaphors of authority, ownership, and (ultimate mixed metaphor) the pen as vagina: a celebration of female autonomy, God the Mother Almighty. Gilbert and Gubar use the terms female and feminine interchangeably, with a preference for "female," as Moi notes with exasperation, thereby tipping us off to their central assumption which Gilbert calls "bracingly ontological."[40] Here and there in *The Madwoman in the Attic* there is some drift from the happy metaphysics of feel-good ontology, toward the social ground of sexual role construction, but in the main they stick to the traditional philosophical meaning of ontology. For Gilbert and Gubar the male and the female constitute two autonomous, really separate realms of being. The self-coherent identity that patriarchy presumably enjoys, in their imagination of patriarchy, haunts the image of woman that they fashion. Their understanding of patriarchy emerges most clearly not when they treat it directly but as they construct their envious counterideal, the flip side of the patriarchal coin in liberal society—the self-coherent and self-creating woman writer, hiding behind the self-renunciatory posture that patriarchy forces her to take: woman as she should be, after the "renew[al of] our lives" which literary study in Gilbert's feminist mode is supposed to make happen.[41]

There is, or will be (Gilbert and Gubar slide around on this point), not *a*, not *many*, but "the female imagination," a favorite phrase of theirs, which is the source for the single archetypal tale that woman tells because she must tell it, her gender so dictates, and that Charlotte Perkins Gilman has already told in paradigmatic form in a short story called "The Yellow Wallpaper."[42] "The female imagination" authorizes woman's literary autonomy. But what exactly *is* the female imagination and the supposed literary autonomy of woman that it authorizes? Like patriarchal theorists before them, Gilbert and Gubar gloss female imagination and female literary autonomy with sexual autonomy. Biology is the ground of unique psychic difference. In their discourse "sexual autonomy" is translated variously and repeatedly with a series of metonyms like "interiority" and "subjectivity":

> "her own autonomy, her own interiority"
> "her stubborn autonomy and unknowable subjectivity"
> "her subjectivity, her autonomy, her creativity"
> "her own sense of self"
> "her own vocabulary, her own timbre, . . . her own viewpoint."[43]

So "she" is not comfortably "autonomous," but stubbornly so, insisting on autonomy against male authority and male autonomy. But stubborn autonomy (and now the Bloomian chickens come home to roost) is anxious autonomy, not sure of itself: no autonomy at all, as Bloom knows. "Her" subjectivity (or autonomy or interiority or creativity: they are the same) is knowable only to herself and to other women like Gilbert and Gubar who are its privileged interpreters. It is by definition unknowable to men who are closed out by the terms of Gilbert and Gubar's Manichean sexual ontology. So my first general point about *The Madwoman in the Attic* is that, though patriarchy and matriarchy differ in spelling only by a single letter, in the visionary discourse of Gilbert and Gubar they often differ not at all. For it is not just rhetorical emphasis but real commitment to the presiding metaphor of patriarchy that comes through the leitmotif *her own, her own, her own.* Females own themselves in the interior (their private property), which no patriarchal male (a redundancy), no matter how much real estate he owns, can ever take away. Cunning patriarchs, of course, are pleased to permit the sisters to own their interiors. To insist on autonomy and ownership, as Gilbert and Gubar do, is bluntly to insist on the values of the phallus that patriarchy invents.

My second point about *The Madwoman in the Attic* is that its unintended identification of matriarchy and patriarchy is identity with a familiar difference. The claim that Gilbert and Gubar make on behalf of the female writer rests on their inability to keep from assenting to what they do not want to assent to, a keystone premise of patriarchal thought that grants the male the natural authority of reason and the female the natural debilitation of reason known as emotion, which the male (woman-born) is afflicted with but can transcend through the discipline of dialectical exercise: in the classical world it was called philosophy. I am rehearsing the old Platonic foundation of Western thought and its distinguishing and generative opposition between male and female which produces other oppositions, like that between philosophy and the mimetic arts of poetry; objectivity and subjectivity; and, in the political realm, the opposition significantly enhanced and reconstituted in the bourgeois era of sexism between a public sphere of action (civil involvement, economic pursuits, government) and a private sphere of domesticity where women, when they are not engaged in nurturing activities that prepare the male for his public life of "significant action," can indulge "contemplative purity" in the pursuit of poetry, religion, and other opiates of the lady's world.[44]

On numerous occasions Gilbert and Gubar express their repugnance for this last variant of patriarchal thinking, but at a deep theoretical level they accept it with gusto. In a crucial passage, in an effort to deflect an inescapable critique of their method—a method which says that there are themes in women's writing not to be found in men's—they disarmingly grant the critique, allow that men, too, have dramatized such themes, like feelings of imprisonment and escape. But then, almost in the same breath, they attempt to recoup their notion of a unique female thematics with the stunning assertion that men like Donne, Coleridge, Wordsworth, Byron, Keats, Poe, Dickens, and Tennyson can deal with the theme "more consciously and objectively than the female writer can." When *they* write about imprisonment and escape, men are really writing about impersonal matters of theology, epistemology, the nature of the psyche—they might be making, as Byron does in "The Prisoner of Chillon," "a political point about the tyranny of the state." Moreover, "though male metaphors of imprisonment have obvious implications in common . . . such metaphors may have very different aesthetic functions and philosophical messages in different male literary works." Women writers, Gilbert and Gubar believe, have trouble being objective and unemotional, really write about themselves, about the personal as the private, about what has actually gone on in their lives. Since all women have essentially lived one life, all women writers have the same "unconscious or conscious purpose"—the telling over and over again of the same tale of "their own distinctively female experience" (a literature of their *own*).[45]

It requires only modest critical generosity to envision the transformation of Gilbert and Gubar's sexist ontology of despair into historical categories that offer a little hope for change. Their examples of male privilege can often be coaxed to speak for another conclusion. Thus: it is historical rather than biological privilege and dominance that grant men the socially produced "freedom" of an "objective" stance in the world, while historical oppression has forced women into obsessive and repetitive inwardness, an apparent archetypal unity of experience (the "same conscious and unconscious purpose"), the option of the public sphere and its liberating variousness having been historically inaccessible to them. Male "health" and female "madness" are products of this social arrangement. Traditional male writers can take epistemology, theology, and politics as subjects because traditionally males have had the option, mainly denied women, to enter the public domain, as theologians, clergy, politicians, and philosophers. In other words, if the problem is primarily political then there is a reason for feminism, and the political actors who would alleviate the problem should call themselves feminists, rather than, say, genderists, because feminism better names and has historically so named the problem. On the other hand, to go with Gilbert and Gubar's ontological construction of the issue is to say that there is no political solution to biological warfare. To write the sentences I've just written with even modest self-consciousness is to realize how dated they are. They are dated because feminism in the twentieth century, in its official and implicit forms—practiced without notice by fellow travelers—has been doing its work.

Even the most schematic account of the changing faces of patriarchy, with attention to its aesthetic dimension, will tell us something about the socially specific but unexamined underpinnings of *The Madwoman in the Attic*. Let's try this schema: with his argument on behalf of the contemplative attitude that he thought poetry encouraged, Aristotle in the *Poetics* wished to demonstrate that poetry was like unto reason, the very reason aspired to by ruling-class men but endangered according to Aristotle's predecessor by mimetic poetry, a womanish sort of thing which watered and fed the passions. Aristotle argued that the distance of tragic drama from its existential and biographical sources—its imposition, in the form of plot, of causal order upon those sources—underwrites its ability to expel emotion. Mimetic poetry could, after all, play a role in the education of (male) leaders—Aristotle, a man of his times, thought women defective in the soul, so unfit to lead. Mimetic poetry need not be censored in the city-state, after all, because its function was to assist the birth of reason and the production of rational knowledge: precisely Plato's theory about the function of non-mimetic poetry. Numerous of Aristotle's Renaissance heirs in Italy and England (Mazzoni and Sidney are exemplary instances) did not miss the point that Gramsci and other Marxists would make centuries later: they would affirm in ingenious detail that the poetic genres played a necessary political role in the sustaining of hierarchical social order—the training of ruling-class leaders, the consoling of the underclasses. The genres could help to make the state safe for the status quo.

If the typical position of Renaissance Aristotelianism is that poetry sustains dominant political power by playing the conservative role of cultural enforcer, then somewhere in the late seventeenth and early eighteenth centuries (there are many theories about this), and with a vengeance in the nineteenth century whose literary terrain preoccupies Gilbert and Gubar, the aesthetic is theorized as an adversarial cultural agency, a potential voice of revolution directed not (of course) against the classical city-state or feudal society but (the evidence is too ample to need citing) against the social world invented by capitalism and against everything, including patriarchy, which sustains and forwards its purposes by a life of "significant action." Contemplation, the imagination, and renunciation are poised against action, the will, and ownership, by mostly male poets and theorists from Shelley to Yeats, not for the better education of the new patriarchal authorities of capitalism, but for the subversion of capitalist powers and values altogether. The beauty and goodness of selflessness, which Gilbert and Gubar read as a patriarchal plot to imprison women, was a favorite idea of male romantics who would have been stunned to learn that their talk about selflessness and negative capability proved that they were really repressed women, or secret feminists made so by capitalist pressures. They thought they were putting poetry on the side of the human (both sexes) as weapon against the dehumanization wrought by the new capitalist order. The hegemonic strength of capitalism was quickly proven, however, in the patriarchal appropriation, virtually simultaneous with the growth of romantic alienation, of romantic rejectionist aesthetic. The aesthetic of contemplation, imagination, interiority, subjectivity, and renunciation was soon encircled, then converted into bourgeois value. So this is the fate of Kantian disinterest: the essentials of romantic aesthetic were like unto a passive and presumably nonproductive woman. In Tennyson's "The Palace of Art," a major Victorian expression of (and lament for) the feminization of culture, a poem clearly behind the writing of "Sunday Morning," alluded to many times by Gilbert and Gubar as metaphor for patriarchal economic and aesthetic power (they conceive of it as an overwhelmingly male palace of art), the palace is the place of a stagnant, inactive female soul. But Tennyson's private female soul, synecdoche for all leisured females, is also a metonym for all male artists—that was the cultural lesson of capitalism most deeply embedded in his poem.[46]

Tennyson's guilt is of his class—he should have been doing his duty in the foreign service, or some such ruling-class career. His guilt is also the sign of capitalism's victory over the aristocracy: it had captured the aesthetic and turned it into the shame of those (male and female both) who traditionally practiced the poetic arts. Against Tennyson's ruling-class shame we might set the working-class anger of Whitman, who thought Keats betrayed his humble origins by trying to sound like some privileged college gentleman who lived in libraries, fed off his father's inheritance, and constantly dropped the names of the gods and goddesses of twenty-five hundred years ago. Whitman, who thought Tennyson an asexual wimp, revolted against the feminization of poetry not with a life of significant economic action—the wisdom of *his* class—but in the name of poetry and the class (his own, the masses) for whom the male poets (who hung out at Cambridge) or the lady poets (Twain's cloistered attendants on the deathbed) never spoke and who were providing the arms and legs of industrial capitalism. Thus, my third general point about the authors of *The Madwoman in the Attic* is that their failure to specify the social and economic ground of the feminization of literary activity leads them to posit a hostility of so-called male and female literary traditions that runs contrary to the unified relegation of male and female poets to the junkheap of uselessness, or to the uses of leisure-time (weekend) entertainment in the culture of capitalism in the nineteenth century and in our day. The "feminization" of the literary that occurred under the social conditions of capitalism in the nineteenth century bears heavily on men, especially in the United States on middle-class men of literary bent. The reason for this is not that capitalist ruling-class conspirators met behind closed doors in order to instruct their cultural agents to feminize the literary; the reason is that middle-class males of "culture" are virtually by definition, in a capitalist environment, the chief architects and agents of cultural feminization; architects, therefore, of their own schizophrenia, and the career of Wallace Stevens—which falls socially between the embarrassment of Tennyson and the resentment of Whitman—is an American paradigm.

My fourth general point about *The Madwoman in the Attic* is that its authors naturalize the mainly comfortable and mostly privileged economic situations of their favorite nineteenth-century women writers. In so doing they sometimes forget or repress and at other times appear deliberately to want to trivialize the different and not-so-comfortable economic situations of other writers, male and female. Their preoccupation with biology as the supposed ground of psychic difference of "woman" with a capital letter leads them to elide the social origins of sexual role differences. They like to start with a psychosexual proposition and then without mediation leap to the literary, which is supposedly both mirror and epiphenomenon of the psychosexual. In their preface, Gilbert and Gubar say this: "For not only did a nineteenth-century woman writer have to inhabit ancestral mansions (or cottages) owned and built by men, she was also constituted and restricted by the Palaces of Art and Houses of Fiction male writers authored."[47] For the nineteenth-century women writers they treat, that goes almost without saying (especially the part about having to inhabit those mansions). But what of the men and women writers—and nonwriters—who did and do live in cities, not in pastoral splendor, in dwellings owned neither by their fathers nor by their husbands or lovers or uncles or aunts? Gilbert and Gubar write movingly of the psychic suffering of privileged women, but they have so little grasp of the cultural advantages that such women (or men) have who happen to be fortunate enough to live in mansions or cottages owned and built by men—to whom they are related by blood or marriage—that they are led to the surprising generalization that upper-class women have been, in their words, "Denied the economic, social, and psychological status ordinarily essential to creativity," and "Denied the right, skill, and education to tell their own stories with confidence."[48] They are right: it is a fact that women of all classes in the nineteenth century did not enjoy the social and political status that men enjoyed, but it seems unnecessarily insensitive to women *and* men from unprivileged backgrounds to say that women of the upper classes were denied the economic and social state essential to creativity just because upper-class men had advantages they didn't have. What is beneath this view of the plight of upper-class women is the great animating myth of essentialist feminism: that a poor man always has it better than a rich woman. Women's psychological status, in the light of Gilbert and Gubar's theory of a totalitarian patriarchy, *is* less than conducive to creativity—though the brute fact of what Hawthorne called the "damned mob of scribbling women" implies a less efficient patriarchy than Gilbert and Gubar would allow, or, to give the point a Foucauldian twist, a patriarchy that wanted to produce in the nineteenth century a hegemonic sentimentalist discourse, not silence. Their point that women can't tell their stories with confidence is probably true. On the other hand, we have learned from Bloom that lack of confidence is the hallmark of the so-called male tradition. Bloom or no Bloom, the writer who tells his or her story (or *anything*) with ease is a rarity: probably more a rarity among women writers, though I would be surprised if Alice Walker and Jane Austen are equal sisters in insecurity.

The canonical women writers Gilbert and Gubar treat were without exception not denied the social and economic status that marks the English literary tradition, nor were they denied the skill and education to write the novel of manners, or poems (like Emily Dickinson's) that knowingly draw on the Bible, the English metaphysicals, and Emerson, among other difficult and highly literate sources. Austen and Dickinson have nothing in common with working-class and middle-class women and men who were and are on the margins of literacy, who had to put out in sweatshops and came home too exhausted to do much of anything, much less write novels with titles like *Mansfield Park* or *The Portrait of a Lady*. Gilbert and Gubar's notion of underprivileged women, "the less gifted sisters" as they phrase it (and let us note the naturalizing metaphor of "gift"), consists of those whose pressing needs forced them "to go out into the world as governesses." That women who are denied a classical education at Oxford or Cambridge may have been handicapped in the contest for the lyric laurels, may have felt forced to write prose fiction because it did not demand a classical education (so they argue), these facts, much insisted upon by Gilbert and Gubar, cannot deny the overriding fact that Austen, the Brontës, and George Eliot were educated sufficiently to write what have become classics of English fiction, while others of the brothers and sisters were not. Dickinson, they finally admit, was not *forced* to lock herself up in her room. Exactly: most women and men don't have the privilege of being crazy in that way. Gilbert and Gubar allow that any "moderately intelligent young woman" in New England "seeking independence" could have become the equivalent of an English governess (an American "schoolmarm"), there were other careers besides writing, but "moderate intelligence" is only one of the conditions of that option, and being a school teacher in nineteenth-century America was rarely an option for the underprivileged.[49]

The aristocratic social model simply saturates the analyses

found in *The Madwoman in the Attic* and blinds its authors to any other sort of social experience and any sort of literature not rooted in the English country house. Gilbert's visions are literally visions of "lords" and their "beautiful stately ladies" whose obligation is to "silence." Here is Gilbert describing her awakening to a gathering of English department chairmen: "The treasures of Western Culture, it began to seem, were the patrimony of male writers, or to put it another way, Western Culture itself was a grand ancestral property that educated men had inherited from their intellectual forefathers, while their female relations, like characters in a Jane Austen novel, were relegated to modest dower houses on the edge of the estate." The point, I guess, is to get to the center of the estate, to get into the mansion—own it yourself. Wherever the writers of the stories of shopgirls were situated—those stories were to be the future of fiction, Virginia Woolf argued, because the middle class was the future of society—those writers were not situated *there*, at the edge of the estate: especially if we can imagine the tellers of those tales of unprivileged life as themselves coming from the unprivileged classes.[50]

All of which brings us at last to Gilbert's theory of American poetry—"classless" in a way Marx never dreamed. Whitman and Dickinson are her originating giants, the father and mother of male modernist and female modernist American poets. And they are originals in at least two senses. They are first of all Americans who are original as America itself is original—historically belated in relation to English and continental societies. They are also would-be original *poets* who find themselves not only belated vis-à-vis European poetic traditions but also alienated from the Anglophiles within, the American poets of Fireside fame (Bryant, Longfellow, etc.). Whitman and Dickinson were so alienated from the poetic norms of the day, Gilbert argues, that they both wrote what their contemporaries and Gilbert call "not poetry." Whitman and Dickinson are the first expression in poetry, then, of Emerson's call for an American literature not tuned into the courtly muses of

Europe. But they are different, too: Whitman came out of a problematic working-class family, while Dickinson was born into a genteel and financially solid situation, just the sort of "cultivated New England family which fostered the careers of men like Bryant, Lowell, and Emerson": she was from "the 'right' class," Gilbert admits, "a privileged daughter, a sort of Yankee princess." But these differences of social, economic, and cultural origin are quickly done away with. Ontologically bracing psychosexual theories have no use for the sociological perspective that Gilbert occasionally lets herself indulge. Whitman's feelings of marginality might be traced to social sources, but then so could Dickinson's. Genteel daughters could be well-read, but they were taught ladylike reticence in matters of publication. (Maybe they were supposed to keep quiet, but our literary history in the nineteenth century shows that many overcame literary repression with a vengeance and loosed a tidal wave of language.) Gilbert concludes that Dickinson must have found herself in a position of "privileged marginality not unlike Whitman's." So what seems like an important social difference is really a social sameness: Whitman and Dickinson were both marginalized by their social experiences, however different those experiences were, and we can safely ignore their social origins altogether because they were led by different routes to what Gilbert thinks were the same feelings of alienation. Would the sexual difference of gender that distinguishes Whitman and Dickinson itself have had different consequences had their family contexts been reversed? Would a working-class Emily Dickinson have written at all? These are questions that cannot be pursued within Gilbert's framework of assumptions. The critical method of patriarchy, the formalism of gender, ahistorical, naturalistic, is the critical method of Gilbert's history of American poetry.[51]

Since the sexual difference is the only difference that makes a difference for Gilbert, she can move directly to the literary level, to Whitman and Dickinson as writers, sans all mediation. There she finds that genre directly expresses one of the genders and directly suppresses the other. Whitman, for all his originality, had to "fortify" his threatened masculinity through covert allusions to the major (essentially male) genres of English poetry; Dickinson, because she is a woman, cannot do that. Hence it is she who is authentically alienated, she the authentic American original, the true fulfillment of the Emersonian dream of a radically American literature, the mother of all authentically original American poetry in the twentieth century. Since her "not poetry" constitutes a rejection of all poetic forms hitherto known to men, it is her poetry, not his, that is truly innovative (Whitman seems more original than he is) because her verse moves toward what Gilbert calls the "undifferentiation of prose" which is "implicitly maternal," literary feminism's version of Freud's oceanic feeling and the female alternative to the clean, tidy, uptight and well-controlled world of male poetic genres. The point is deliciously confirmed for Gilbert when Whitman, in apparent reversal of an earlier position in which he defines the male genitals as the authentic poems ("This poem drooping shy and unseen that I always carry, and all men carry"), late in his career says that the true poem is a vagina: "Unfolded out of the folds of the woman man comes unfolded. . . . Unfolded only out of the inimitable poems of women can come the poems of men"—"Unfolded" and *duly obedient* (this last phrase of Whitman's Gilbert italicizes without a trace of humor). No male poet, including Whitman, can live with the truth, Gilbert believes, the priority and authority of the female. Male modernist poets following in the footsteps of Walt Whitman quickly repress the thought; female poets, following Dickinson, reject all poetic tradition, therefore all male authority: they are the real avant-garde of modernism. And Stevens is no exception to the rule: his poems are not formally innovative—they are rather spineless reshufflings of traditional poetic genres which are intended to "fortify" his imperiled work. By everywhere reversing the usual macho clichés, Gilbert's rhetoric invents the new clichés of macha. It is Dickinson who can face the music and dance—she requires none of the varnishing illusions supplied by genre. Dickinson, therefore, not Whitman or Stevens, has real balls.[52]

In the end Gilbert's economic metaphors of culture are forced into a seriousness which her kind of feminism (a new name for essentialist humanism) seems never to have intended for them; these metaphors are haunted by their own countereffects which undo her argument by revealing its inability to successfully suppress history, real economic determinants, and the fully socialized sexual identity. She writes that the "treasures" of Western culture are the "patrimony of male writers," a "grand ancestral property that educated men had inherited from their intellectual forefathers," and that the literary female relatives of those men were necessarily relegated to "modest dower houses on the edge of the estate." And let us note again that Gilbert's sexual-economic allegory of culture is confined by another metaphor—that of the aristocratic family: this sexual struggle for power is all in the wealthy family. If that is so, however, then how can it be the case that the distinction between male and female writers (as she insists in the next sentence) is one between "male patrimony" and "female penury"? A dower house of English literature, after all, or even an actual dower house hardly amounts to penuriousness by any standard, especially not within the English aristocratic model that shapes her argument. What Gilbert's argument must ignore are those experiences of English writers (male and female) who never even get close to dower houses, in real or literary estate, and whose literary and other property was never ancestral because they inherited nothing. But Gilbert must do more than ignore those experiences: she must appropriate real economic penuriousness as metaphor for the spiritual sort that characterizes the situation of the aristocratic lady of literary aspiration in the nineteenth century (penuriousness of the leisured class). This argument becomes bizarrely inappropriate when it is imposed on American literature, and she so imposes it when she turns her attention to Wallace Stevens whose "A Postcard from the Volcano" she finds attractive because it employs what looks like the same metaphor of the ancestral mansion. Stevens' poem would appear to clinch her argument in its modernist American extension. Gilbert describes the tone of this poem as "wistful"; it is, but she has no persuasive account of a context for that tone. For her it is just there as a kind of oddly sad note in the generally confident and free-floating phallic music of literary patriarchy.[53]

Stevens is meditating on not having heirs, or on not having heirs who can acknowledge him as the patriarch, or on not being able to pass on his patrimony and in the same act transmit his authority and create himself as the patriarch; all of the above. Strange new patriarch, who bequeaths not an anxiety of influence to his children (who he imagines will not recognize him as their father) but an anxiety of not influencing to himself, as he imagines his nonsurvival as a writer, imagines his inability to become canonical, part of the tradition; imagines his failure to become one of "your man-poets." What shall we say of *this* male's relation to his patrimony? What is patrimony, anyway, that cannot be bequeathed to one's children as it was bequeathed to oneself? Probably patrimony that never was bequeathed, patrimony, then, that never was patrimony. Gilbert's feminist categories break down, at this point, because they cannot attend to the American circumstances of this poem's production: the early 1930s when Stevens bought his first home, gracious in space, but no mansion; a middle-class life in which he inherited no real estate from his father; a life, in other words, whose only mansions were metaphorical. And even those were radically in doubt: in the early thirties Stevens, then past fifty years of age, could look back at his first and only volume of poems, published in 1923, at age forty-four, and contemplate the almost nothing written or published in between. And he could look forward and imagine himself childless: not "my children" but

> Children picking up our bones
> Will never know that these were once
> As quick as foxes on the hill.

He could look forward and imagine himself unacknowledged by a generation of writers who feel no burden of history; his golden style repeated in blithe ignorance and ease:

> Children,
> Still weaving budded aureoles,
> Will speak our speech and never know. . . .

Patriarchy? Patrimony? Grand ancestral property? Dower houses? It would be hard to think of terms less appropriate to the description of Stevens or any number of other modern writers in the United States. Gilbert and Gubar's theorization of gender is in fact compromised by the conditions of canonical literary production in nineteenth-century England; these conditions are now, in Gilbert's recent work, being projected as the conditions of American writing.

"A Postcard from the Volcano," published in 1936, is produced by a double career, driven by a double desire for literary and economic substance and staying power—that, I believe, is where its wistfulness comes from. This doubleness of desire is generally the circumstance of Stevens' writing, but circumstance only; not explanation. "A Postcard from the Volcano" is a modern American male instance, not harsher, or bleaker, than the instances of Emily Dickinson, but different.

Part Two: Penelope's Poetry—
The Later Wallace Stevens

I

Even in 1938, when he had behind him *Ideas of Order, The Man with the Blue Guitar*, and the difficult period following the publication of *Harmonium*, when it seemed he might be finished, when he was writing almost nothing; even in 1938, when he was beginning to experience a personal literary renaissance and an onset of personal affluence dramatically highlighted by the collective disaster of the Great Depression (he was making better than $25,000 a year), at fifty-nine years old, Wallace Stevens continued to speak, as he would speak to the end of his life, in the contradictions and with the denigrating self-consciousness that shaped his early sense of himself as a writer who had also to be responsible to his role as married, middle-class male citizen—his father's son:

> The few things that I have already done have merely been preliminary. I cannot believe that I have done anything of real importance. The truth is, of course, that I never may, because there are so many things that take up my time and to which I am bound to give my best. Thinking about poetry is, with me, an affair of weekends and holidays, a matter of walking to and from the office. This makes it difficult to progress rapidly and certainly. Besides, I very much like the idea of something ahead; I don't care to make exhaustive effort to reach it, to see what it is. It is like the long time that I am going to live somewhere where I don't live now.[54]

The new note in this rehearsal of his old and definitive conflict comes in toward the end and it brings uneasy resolution. Not desire for anything particular, but desire without an object exterior to itself, the sheer feeling of desire as the ground of his pleasure. But not quite: for he needs to posit an object of hope beyond longing that will bring longing to an end, but he doesn't care to make an "exhaustive effort to reach it" because he doesn't really care "to see what it is." The object that he won't go all out to reach is ostensibly the poetry that he might write, those poems that will not be preliminary, that will not be an affair of weekends, holidays, and those few hours just before and after work, walking to and from the office. One way of phrasing the odd theme of Stevens' later career, the odd and necessary game that he plays with himself, is to say that it is constituted by a double desire—to *want* to write poems of real significance and, at the same time, not to want to *write* them.

My sense of the tonality of this entire passage from a letter written in 1938 is shaped by its last sentence: "It is like the long time that I am going to live somewhere where I don't live now." The pain in that remark I want to call structural because the "It" that is like "living somewhere else," the writing he would do had he sufficient world and time, would be embedded in a social context that would be "its" enabling, "its" nourishing ground. *Would:* the entire passage is marked by an implicit subjunctive mood and is itself an example of the kind of writing that it tries to characterize—writing that is preliminary to the realization it imagines but does not quite want: preliminariness being the condition that Stevens wants to transcend and yet the condition that it is necessary to sustain if fulfillment, the problematic object of his hope, is to be deferred.

What, more specifically, can be said about the imagined social context of an imagined writing that would bring utter fulfillment? It is a place ("where I don't live now") that wouldn't subject him to demands that now rob him of time and force him to give his best (make him feel "bound") to others. But if the imagined context is a place to live without constraints, it is also and most quintessentially *time* itself in the sense of a delicious process of living his life in such a way that fulfillment will be "long." Not the ecstatic arrest of desire's movement when it gets what it wants—culmination and then what nobody wants, the aftermath of anticlimax—but ongoing ecstasy ("the long time that I am going to live somewhere where I don't live now"). The wistful pathos communicated in the passage derives from Stevens' desire not to be resigned and his implicit admission that he must be resigned to a life of quiet despair because his life and writing feel contained and dominated. The title of one of James T. Farrell's novels (via A. E. Housman) is almost perfect here: *A World I Never Made.*

Not that Stevens wouldn't have wanted to unmake and then remake his world. But no one, I trust, will accuse him of being a revolutionary writer—even to say the words *Wallace Stevens* and *revolution* in the same breath seems ridiculous, extremely so, yet what shall we call the urge that is being expressed in that key sentence ("It is like the long time that I am going to live somewhere where I don't live now") and specifically in the analogy that says in so many words that writing the way you really want to write is like living in the way you really want to live and you are not doing either, nor will you ever do either as long as the course of your everyday life continues to run as it always has. Underneath the analogy is the proposition that writing is the expression of a material ground at once personal and social. The particular mix of feeling in this passage, desire and fatality, might have been a kind of subjective political nitroglycerin. But it never went off. Stevens was never able to believe that the social ground of his life and writing was itself unstable, never able to believe that the personal subjects it contained and restrained (like himself) might in their discontent make it unstable, explode its structure by refusing the very thing that keeps in place social structures that produce unhappiness: by refusing acceptance of social structure as unalterable fact, like a thing of nature; by refusing, therefore, resignation to the structure.

Stevens' writing tends to wander unhappily between criticism and utopia. If his desire is without clear utopian object, then so is his dissatisfaction, so is his frustration without sharply viewed critical object. Resignation to unhappiness is a massive repression in Stevens, from his young manhood to his last years, of the personal choice that affirmed commitment to the system of his unhappiness. "Repression," an easy word to use in literary circles, does no justice to the devious rhetoric of repression, that social production of a system which "teaches" (manipulates) its subjects by giving them a discourse for saying "happy" when they mean unhappy:

> If Beethoven could look back on what he accomplished and say that it was a collection of crumbs compared to what he had hoped to accomplish, where should I ever find a figure of speech adequate to size up the little that I have done compared to that which I had once hoped to do. Of course, I have had a happy and well-kept life. But I have not even begun to touch the spheres within spheres that might have been possible if, instead of devoting the principal amount of my time to making a living, I had devoted it to thought and poetry. Certainly it is as true as it ever was that whatever means most to one should receive all of one's time and that has not been true in my case. But, then, if I had been more determined about it, I might now be looking back not with a mere sense of regret but at some actual devastation. To be cheerful about it, I am now in the happy position of being able to say that I don't know what would have happened if I had more time. This is very much better than to have had all the time in the world and have found oneself inadequate.[55]

If "repression" better than "resignation" captures the psychic quality of this letter of 1950, then "rhetoric of repression" is better than either, because "rhetoric" suggests that Stevens is caught up in a situation in which he is both the target and the speaking subject of a systemic intention, its very medium, the self-subverting speaker of a kind of newspeak in which regret over not doing what you most want to do—and what, really, is "mere" regret?—and willed superficiality (choosing not to go to your depths, your "spheres within spheres") all somehow add up to a "happy and well-kept life." But we have to say that neither "repression," nor "resignation," nor even "rhetoric of repression" can do justice to the lucid and self-stinging consciousness that says "well-kept" and "To be cheerful about it," to the man who is not cheerful, knows he's not, and knows precisely the costs of his life and can somehow bear those costs because he believes ("of course") he has chosen them. And maybe that is the supremest of all of Stevens' fictions: the sustaining feeling that the life he so often felt he suffered, he chose; that social necessity, in fact, is freedom.

When Stevens said in the letter of 1938 that he would like to do something of "real importance," he was at once alluding to his negative feelings about *Harmonium* (a book mainly of little things) and the desire that he felt, in the months when he was preparing *Harmonium* for press, to write the long poem, a desire no doubt in great part propelled by his assessment of his early work. The long poem would be the benchmark of a culturally significant poetry, a poetic proof of manhood because a proof of social power. The course of Stevens' intention as a poet can be traced in two letters written forty-two years apart; the change is from self-deprecating lyricist, and a poetry of decorative frivolity, to philosophical consciousness of his age, and a poetry of necessary knowledge; the change can be charted in the occurrence of a single word. Consider this line from a letter that I quoted above, in which Stevens compared himself with Gainsborough: "my trifling poesies are like the trifling designs one sees on fans."[56] Compare that with this response to Renato Poggioli, who needed some clarification about certain stanzas of *The Man with the Blue Guitar*, a poem Poggioli was translating beautifully for an Italian edition: "I desire my poem to mean as much, as deeply, as a missal. While I am writing what appear to be trifles, I intend these trifles to be a missal for brooding-sight: for an understanding of the world."[57] This comment is to serve Poggioli as a sort of explication of *Blue Guitar*, stanza 24, which reads:

> A poem like a missal found
> In the mud, a missal for that young man
>
> That scholar hungriest for that book,
> The very book, or, less, a page
>
> Or, at the least, a phrase, that phrase,
> A hawk of life, that latined phrase:
>
> To know; a missal for brooding sight.
> To meet that hawk's eye and to flinch

Not at the eye but at the joy of it.
I play. But this is what I think.

The change in the career of a "trifle" appears radical: from effeminate "trifling poesies" to missal, from a trivial thing in the hand of a comfortable lady to the book of books in the hand of a fevered young man, from decorative nonsense to world-penetrating knowledge: the original trifle somehow become sacred text. How more dramatically could Stevens have elevated his conception of poetic function—yet note that he insists on, really, the continuity of trifling things ("I intend these trifles," these poems, these playful stanzas of *Blue Guitar*, "to be a missal"), as if the aborted purposes of his "horrid cocoons" (his metaphor for his earlier poems) might somehow still be redeemed, the miscarried insects reimplanted in the nourishing environment of a longer meditative form, so that their potential might finally emerge, be realized. The passage that I allude to from *Blue Guitar* catches Stevens in his later manner: it enacts not the sensuous immediacies of perception ("the spruces rough in the distant glitter of the January sun"), nor erotic linguistic festivity ("concupiscent curds" whipped in "kitchen cups"), but the immediacy of a kind of thought indistinguishable from desire; pleasure reimagined now as something almost final, almost ultimately good, the fruit of fulfillment yet to be gripped; the pleasurable object of desire semiobscure, barely but forever out of reach. The effect of later Stevens, especially in the long poems, is of someone discoursing on some tremendous urgency, the thing most needed—poetry, the poem, the supreme fiction: but not a person—without ever being able to make it clear what the thing is, though getting close, without ever experiencing the fulfillment that the thing might bring, though getting tantalizingly close. If poetry is the object of Stevens' desire ("I desire my poem to mean as much . . . I intend these trifles to be . . ."), then the central fact about Stevens in his later manner is that he was not writing "poems," according to the implicit definition of the poem we find in *Harmonium*, a book in which he delivered and didn't just hope for poetic payload. What he is writing is a kind of pre-poetry, a tentative approach to the poem, an enactment of desire not as a state of mind, with all the inert implications of the phrase "state of mind," but as movement, and not movement in a straight line, as if he could see the end of the journey, but a meandering sort of motion: desire as improvisational action which gives us a sense of starting, stopping, changing direction, revising the phrase, refining the language, drafting the poem and keeping the process of drafting all *there* as the final thing because the finished thing can't be had ("The very book, or, less, a page / Or, at the least, a phrase, that phrase, / . . . that latined phrase"). Bad later Stevens sounds like a lot of boring talk from a long-winded lecturer who never gets to the point. Wonderful later Stevens draws his reader into the improvisational song of desire, a writing about itself in the sense that the "itself" is longing as language eking itself out, each phrase a kind of blind adventure going nowhere, an infinite and exquisite foreplay. So what is before foreplay? His version of the bourgeois quotidian, "the effect of order and regularity, the effect of moving in a groove . . . railroading to an office and then railroading back." Above all the police, who "are as thick as trees and as reasonable. But you must obey them.—Now, Ariel, rescue me from police and all that kind of thing": as if the police were not only who they are but also a *kind* of thing, a metaphor of the social world for which only "books make up. They shatter the groove."[58] But only in books. And what is after foreplay, anyway? Necessarily the end of desire, the police and all that sort of thing: reasonableness, the groove, no play.

In *Blue Guitar* 24 Stevens shapes at once a double and a doubled image: at the base, the figure of the young man under maximum agony of desire—ecstatic need matched by ecstatic book. The figure of the young man, the scholar finding the book, discarded like detritus in the mud, not writing the book; this figure is at all points repeated by the figure of the poet writing of the young scholar, the poet leaning in late with mounting anticipation, looking for the poem, not writing it in the sense of planning it out, or intending to write it by realizing a pregiven structure ("perish all sonnets"),[59] but having it come upon him, out of nowhere—a surprise like the poem that Stevens wanted to fly in through the window.[60] This second image of Stevens himself brooding over the scholar of brooding sight rhythmically replays the scholar's hungriest hunger (his wanting to know) in a lurching rhetoric not only improvisational but repetitively so (that book, the very book; a phrase, that phrase, that latined phrase), a rhetoric verging on stutter—and on excitement that would extinguish all language—then crystallized without warning into the metaphor of the hawk of life—improvisation resolved into major chord—an eye keenest for life's smaller pulses. That hugest banality of literary modernism—that poetry is a substitute for religion—is openly affirmed only to be radically reduced, shaved almost to nothing (from book to page to phrase): a missal, yes, but for the purpose of brooding upon the mouse in the grass. At that very point of minimalist pathos, an abrupt shift to maximalist grandeur (who could have predicted this escape from the literary police of continuity?)—a shift embodied in the infinitive form of the verb which, in Stevens, is the linguistic shape of desire in itself, a mode of transcendence, the sacred text of longing without end, amen. A hawk of life, that latined phrase. Colon. To Know. Semi-colon. To know without a subject of knowing: to know without an object of knowing, purely to know. "To know" and "To meet"—not conjugated, not in time.

Then to turn from the "joy" of such keenness of sight, to turn away from the hawklike eye, pure in its brooding over living detail, to turn away in a kind of instinctive reflex—you "flinch" not at the eye, the vehicle of aesthesis, but at the joy of aesthesis, because what you think you most want, and do want, you really don't want when you get it because having it means the end of improvisation. To have joy is not to have the joy of anticipation. I play. But this is what I think. Those flat declaratives of the last line, made even flatter by the heavy caesura which separates them, speak joylessly with a sort of staged yawn of the poet's withdrawal from joy and of his imagination of joy that he fears will go stale because all joy eventually must.

So where does this poetry of the desire for poetry finally go? Nowhere at all, as it mustn't. To write a long poem out of such intention, without plot or historical subject or philosophical system, is to write the epic of bourgeois interiority, wherein the life of the spirit is hard to distinguish from the special sort of desire stimulated in the time and place of first-world consumer capitalism: when the life of the spirit is subjected to endless need for the new which alone can break us out of the grooves of boredom. What we want is to be thrilled: "What I want more than anything else in music, painting, and poetry, in life and in belief is the thrill that I experienced once in all the things that no longer thrill me at all. I am like a man in a grocery store that is sick and tired of raisins and oyster crackers and who nevertheless is overwhelmed by appetite."[61] Stevens gourmandized with epicurean delight—he frequented gourmet grocery stores in search of the most expensive, the most exotic, the most sumptuous; he saw, he bought, he ate. His later poetry is a form of gourmandizing, but deliberately teased out and emptied of satisfaction, a sustaining of overwhelming appetite: the thrill sought is the promise of thrill, not the thrill bought. At the poetic, if not at the economic, level of his existence, he found a way to supply the spirit by resisting consumption: a life of indulgence, a poetics of asceticism tempted.

The passage from his correspondence that I've just quoted on the grocery store has been centrally quoted by Helen Vendler, Queen of Formalism, as evidence for her humanist perspective: "It is not possible," she says, "for us to be without desire; we cannot help but engage in that process that Freudians call idealization. . . . All human beings engage in poesis in constituting an imagined world to live in; and the engagement in poesis is coterminous with life. To be alive is to desire." Stevens on the grocery store, therefore, is Stevens expressing desire in old age—that's what it feels like to be old and still to desire.[62] What is wrong with Vendler's thesis is what is right about it: it is so true, so reasonable, so abstract, no one would disagree with it. But it can't pinpoint the literalness, the specificity of Stevens' discourse. Grocery stores of the sort that Stevens frequented are not timeless objects of experience: "To enjoy the fine things of life you have to go to 438 ½ East 78th St., two floors up in the rear, not three floors, and pay $6.00 a pound for Viennese chocolates. One of the men in the office here got talking to me about tea the other day. I asked him what kind of tea he used. Oh, he said, anything that the A&P happens to have."[63] What he felt about supermarkets he also felt about department stores, labor unions, classes, apartment houses, and any and all forms of life and literary expression that partook in the slightest of generic regularity ("perish all sonnets").[64] Genres, schools of writing and music ("There is no music because the only music tolerated is modern music. There is no painting because the only painting permitted is painting derived from Picasso or Matisse"), mimesis, literary modes, standardized and disciplined production of all kinds—in a word, the generalization of everyday life and the generalization of literary life for Stevens all added up to one thing: the potential destruction of an original life of one's own and of an original literature of one's own, the twin goals he announced in a letter long before he wrote his meditation on old age and desire.[65] The new, the original, the spontaneous—that was the source of a vital and pleasurable life: those were the values most denied him in advanced capitalist society. For Stevens to imagine himself satiated on raisins and oyster crackers, in a grocery store where only raisins and oyster crackers are available, is for Stevens to imagine himself without thrills, to be sure, in the ennui of old age, to be sure, but old and without thrills in a specific way, in a gourmet consumer's version of hell: not just anyplace, but here, and now, for a man who thought that buying a pair of pajamas at Brooks Brothers was a partaking of the "bread of life" "better than any soufflé."[66] His late poetry of deferred desire is not the escape from gourmandizing, it is its perfection. Writing after hours is the spiritual pause that refreshes but does not alter the life of getting and spending.

To write the long poem, then, is by definition to string together a collocation of moments and to create a book of moments which hangs together by the force of desire for moments, the moving into the moment, the moving out. Such a long poem, so-called, is only delusively different in scope from his earlier things. Stevens did not advance in scope, ambition, or high seriousness. Of course, like his critics, who take their cue from him, he liked to think he had. (He wanted to call his collected poems "The Whole of Harmonium"—a wonderfully resolved, teleological construction of the life of a writer who had once toyed with calling *Harmonium* "The Grand Poem: Preliminary Minutiae.")[67] He even considered, in his later years, the possibility that his sort of poetry could be theorized, become an object for study; he spoke with friends of the possibility of an endowed chair at Princeton in the theory of poetry.[68] But he knew that the one thing you can't do with surprises that fly in through the window is to theorize them. He knew that improvisation formalized is something else.

2

The standard generalization about Wallace Stevens' poetic development is that as he grew older he put on the vocal weight which enabled him to transcend the mere aesthetic perfections of his earlier poems—so sensuously full, so exquisitely achieved, so intellectually empty. Aside from Yvor Winters and his few (and ever fewer) devotees it is hard to find serious readers of Stevens who don't believe that he actually grew up as he grew older and that the proof of his maturity lies in his later long poems where (so it goes) he at last achieved the requisite (churchly) tone of high seriousness and important human reference. That old contention of Stevens' critics is strongly echoed in a wider cultural dimension in the self-reflexive song of canonical modernism, in the full terror that modernists feel for their own social relevance. Beginning with aestheticist principles, modernists ask, with an art that presumably turns its back on the world, refuses representation, turns inward to sensation and impression, as Pater urged, how can we put art back in—give it connection, power, or, in Stevens' words, "a ministry in the world"? Whether they write poems, narratives of character, or narratives of ideas called critical theory, that's long been a panicky question of literary modernism. And the story I am telling about Stevens and his culture is maybe the most vivid example that I can give of an anxiety framed by this classic contradiction of the middle-class world: on the one hand, our retreat to the interior, whether of our homes, our families, or our writing—wherein we indulge the sentiment that our private life is our authentic life—and our concurrent disavowal of all possibility for happiness in the public sphere, or in relationships not sanctioned by the public sphere; a retreat, a disavowal, on the other hand, incessantly accompanied by an incipiently explosive dissatisfaction with all private (and aestheticizing) solutions to pains whose sources are not personal and which require keen attention to history's plots. Georg Lukács's excoriation of the subjective and plotless qualities of high-modernist literature is perfectly just as far as it goes. But what it leaves out is one of the most interesting things about high modernists— their pre-Lukácian discomfort with what they suspect as their own self-trivializing ahistoricism.

Reviewers of Stevens' first volume said over and again, in so many words, that he was a precious little aesthete—that he had nothing to say and, even worse, that his poems were on principle mindless: maybe gemlike, but also without point. These negative assessments bothered Stevens but not for the usual egoistic reasons. The fact is that he had heard it all before. His reviewers had only uttered publicly what he was telling his friends in letters in the months when he was deciding on the contents of *Harmonium*, reading over all he had written in the previous decade, thinking about what to keep in and what to keep out. He was saying in those painfully self-conscious days that his poems were "horrid cocoons from which later abortive insects had sprung"; they were "witherlings"; "debilitated." At best, "preliminary minutiae"; at worst, "garbage" from which no "crisp salad" could be picked.[69] Stevens, at forty-four, would not be one of those writers who could by reading his old things over gather sustenance. He was one of those modernists who suffered from a severe originality neurosis whose sources were equally literary and economic, whose obsessive force was determined by equally decisive experiences of the literary avant-garde and the decadent edge of consumer capitalism. As his master category of value, originality simply makes nonsense of the conventional modernist opposition of aesthetics and economics because it not only prized the new as the different, the rare, and the strange, but could and did find triggering releases of pleasure equally in original poems and in exotic fruits bought at a specialty market for gourmet shoppers. He was one of those writers who find their old things just old—and psychically unprofitable to reencounter. And given the significant social role he had imagined and would imagine for poetry from his Harvard years on to the end of his life, his judgment upon what he had actually managed to produce from his late twenties through his early forties must have felt bitterly ironic. Yet, I think, not really despairing. For even as he condemned himself in self-disgust, he was allowing himself the hopeful fiction of organic growth. He might be looking at abortions but he could imagine and believe in the possibility of full-term birth and teleological perfection both for himself and for his poetic project—a distinction which became harder and harder to make as he absorbed the full failure of his marriage to Elsie Moll.

His project was not wrong from the start. The origin was in fact good. His beginning as an aesthete, if only a beginning, in the delights of pure perception and linguistic riot, was yet the right sort of beginning. For him the aesthetic was an isolated moment, withdrawn from the social mess and forever free from didactic and political translation. As he grew older and more critical of the canonical modernism he partly endorsed, he began to believe that if the autonomous aesthetic moment was to become the urgent and compelling moment he always felt it inherently to be, then it would somehow have to carry its purity beyond itself, back into the social mess, to his rhetorical target: the culturally and economically privileged readers who, like himself, needed to transform the basic joyless conditions of their existence. "It Must Give Pleasure" is the title of the final section of *Notes toward a Supreme Fiction*. *It* must give pleasure because little else does. He declared in a characteristic moment in the essays he wrote in the later years of his career that poetry helps us to live our lives, and lucky for us that it does—we get so little help from anyplace else. He once told his wife that the nine-to-five working-day Wallace was nothing—the sources of his authentic selfhood were at home, quite literally: the site of his marriage and (for this aesthetic burgher) the site of poetic activity. But when love and marriage parted, making his marriage an empty form, his writing became the final source of selfhood: his last resort. The fate of his poetic project turned out to be indistinguishable from the fate of pleasure. The most poignant and definitive image I've ever seen drawn of what Stevens became as a man, after his marriage collapsed, was drawn by Stevens himself in a letter written in his seventieth year: "We have a very good time here. We go upstairs at night long before dark. Nothing could be more exciting than to sit in the quiet of one's room watching the fireflies."[70] The "we" referred to, Elsie and himself, is a "we" long limited to pronominal designation. In fact, "we" are not having a good time. As "we" fades to the impersonal "one," Stevens is relieved of the embarrassment of openly saying to his correspondent "my room." They go upstairs long before dark to separate bedrooms they'd chosen many years before—Elsie to do God knows what, he never tells us, he to watch the flashing of fireflies in their mating game,[71] to feel excitement that he can't share except with his interior lover, his own creative impulse, whose power to bring him "vivid transparence" he defines as the power of peace itself: poetry, Stevens' ultimate mating game, a game best played with only one player in the game, a last resort but also a best resort because in this game reliance on another is not a possibility.

The idea of the long poem became attractive to Stevens in the prepublication period of *Harmonium* because it promised to resolve the painful and difficult-to-disentangle questions of his literary stature and his marriage (hard to call it his love life), neither of which he could separate from his economic role as a male, from the social disease that I have called econo-machismo. The long poem, not the small pleasures of minority—those little things he had praised of Dr. Campion and Verlaine—could be the signature at once of his maleness and of his cultural relevance, a figure of his emerging social prowess at a time when he began to have doubts about his sexual prowess.

"Witherlings," that coinage for his early poems was just right: a live thing too soon dead, dried up because unnourished by what it most needed but could not from itself generate— a sustaining environment of thought. "Witherlings": literary modernism's great ideal, autonomous life, as aborted life. And "witherlings" in another sense, a thing withered in the human sense of the metaphor: the thing in question, now, not a tender shoot of plant life but an intention to speak and to act—*the aesthete as minister*—stunned into silence and paralysis (as in: he was withered by her scorching tone). The long poem, which would speak discursively as well as be, could never be figured by a decoration on a trivial thing (like a fan) in the hand of a leisured woman—the decoration, like useless autonomous art, a signifier of leisured life; the fan, an indulgent necessity (like autonomous art) for those unused to and unwilling to sweat and whose cultural advantages (like the experience of autonomous art) presuppose economic advantages. Real men, like Gainsborough, paint landscapes and portraits, not decorations on fans; real men, if they write poetry, go for the long poem of public (epic) import, not the small lyric of bourgeois delight. The poet who in his thirties felt himself marginalized by his social context as a ladylike dabbler in after-hours verse writing would become in his imaginative life at least (or is it at most?) a Latin lover courting what has to seem for the male modernist a forbidden woman, the epic muse who not only inspired but also had been possessed by a special sort of man, the sort embodied by Homer, Virgil, Dante, Milton. With those types she was obviously well bedded; could she be persuaded to try somebody new and so apparently ill-endowed for the task of epic loving? Could ladylike Stevens become one of those he had once called "your man-poets"? He wasn't sure and he marked his doubts with a humor which is always the sign (if we can trust Robert Frost's surmise about this) of virtually unbearable and unshareable inner seriousness: "I find this prolonged attention to a single subject has the same result that prolonged attention to a senora has according to the authorities. All manner of favors drop from it. Only it requires a skill in the varying of the serenade that occasionally makes one feel like a Guatemalan when one particularly wants to feel like an Italian."[72]

In the time between the publication of *Harmonium* (1923) and his second volume, *Ideas of Order* (1935), specifically in the period between 1923 and 1930 or so, or for about seven years, Stevens wrote hardly anything. His literary sterility in those years can't be explained by the largely indifferent and hostile reception of *Harmonium*; bad reviews didn't silence him because he was their virtual author. In "The Comedian as the Letter C," his first attempt at a long poem, Stevens was a previewer of *Harmonium*'s reception, more harsh than any of his actual reviewers. The "Comedian" is a severe and hilarious reflection on a poet, like himself, who seemed to him to deserve the deflating mockery of epithets like "lutanist of fleas" and "Socrates of snails," as well as sexually caustic allegorization as a skinny sailor trying to conduct the sublimely frightening music of a sea storm with a pathetically inadequate little baton: as if poetic and sexual inadequacy were somehow each other's proper sign.

Self-disappointment and the need to think through self-revision are better but not sufficient explanations of his literary silence: if he was experimenting with new longer forms and new ambition, he was doing it in his head, or in drafts which no one will ever see. He certainly wasn't trying out his new self in the little magazine scene whose editors constantly requested his work and likely would have published pretty much anything he might have given them. By 1923 he was a respected avant-garde writer whose attractiveness was enhanced by his privacy and mysteriousness. He turned down many requests for poems; he had nothing to give. And while he was imagining but doing very little about earning his poetic manhood he was living out and doing a great deal about earning the sort of manhood that his American middle-class superego taught him to desire or pay the price in guilt.

From 1924 to 1932 he lived in a noisy two-family house, on a busy street in Hartford. In 1932, having saved up enough, he bought his first and only house (for $20,000, in cash). In this period he became a father who did what typical working fathers do—exercise their fatherhood after supper and on weekends, or precisely during those times when this father, unlike most working fathers, wanted to but couldn't do the reading and writing which were the basis for his other career. One of the few poetic exhibits we have from this period is an occasional verse, done for Valentine's Day 1925. It is an offhanded, sweet little thing, as its genre demanded, but nevertheless an elegy for his recent poetic death dipped in bitters, in which he tries to rationalize his quotidian obligations as a new kind of poetry, expressed in doggerel, the perfect representation of the well-grooved routine his everyday life had become. Not the poetry of everyday life, but everyday life as poetry:

> Though Valentine brings love
> And Spring brings beauty
> They do not make me rise
> To my poetic duty
> But Elsie and Holly do

And do it daily—
Much more than Valentine or Spring
And very much more gaily.[73]

In this post-*Harmonium* period he seems to have made his greatest effort—in which he succeeded—to rise to the corporate top of his business world: the right sort of thing to do for a man with family responsibilities, who was sole source of the family's income, who wanted his own home, and who liked really nice things, like oriental rugs. But poetry was power and freedom over circumstances—Stevens, like most writers since the late eighteenth century, needed to believe that—and the more financially unstable the writer, the more he believes that proposition of aesthetic idealism, the promise that there will be refuge even in the filthy prison house of capitalism. Stevens undefensively knew and admitted and even celebrated another, more commonly held proposition: that money was power and freedom, too. Cultural capital, money of the mind, is good, even if it is the opium of the intellectuals: it is a *kind* of money. But money itself, ah! money itself, whatever it is, it certainly is not a *kind* of money. The logic, which Stevens never resisted, is that money is a kind of poetry. In 1935, the middle of the Depression, when he was earning $25,000 a year (roughly the equivalent of $200,000 a year in our terms), when, in other words, he'd made it financially—after 1935 his poetic production simply mushroomed—he wrote this to a business associate:

> Our house has been a great delight to us, but it is still quite incomplete inside. . . . It has cost a great deal of money to get it where it is and, while it is pleasant to buy all these things, and no one likes to do it more than I do, still it is equally pleasant to feel that you are not the creature of circumstances, but are (at least to a certain degree) the master of the situation, which can only be if you have the savings banks sagging with your money and the presidents of the insurance companies stopping their cars to ask the privilege of taking you to the office. For my part, I never really lived until I had a home, say, with a package of books from Paris or London.[74]

Unlike most writers in his romantic tradition he knew that feelings of power and freedom in imagination were precisely the sorts of effects produced by a capitalist economic context in those (writers and intellectuals) who hate capitalist economic contexts; he seemed to know that aesthetic purity was economically encased; that imaginative power was good, to be sure, but that economic power was a more basic good because it enables (as it makes us desire) both the aesthetic good and the aesthetic goods (books from Paris and London) that he required. Can cultural power, however acquired and whatever its origin, turn on its economic base, become a liberating and constructive force in its own right? Believing in that proposition is not the opium of intellectuals, it's our LSD. Yet it may not be completely naive to think that art and intellect are forces of social change. Marxists, of course, think so; on the other hand, the textbook critics on the Christian New Right, who practice a different sort of hermeneutics of suspicion, also think so; even T. S. Eliot thought so. It is possible that the addiction I allude to is a necessary addiction, a need of literary types to "turn on" politically because all the while we fear our political irrelevance. Stevens himself constantly chewed over the idea, and though he tended to reject the notion that literary force is also political force—the artist has no social role, he said more than once in his letters of the thirties and in his essays—it may be that the deep intellectual unity of his later career was produced by his encounter with radical thought in the thirties. Stevens emerged from that encounter thinking that Stanley Burnshaw's Marxist critique of his work was intelligent and probing—a fact contemptuously buried by Bloom and Riddel, among other champions of the poet; he emerged believing in the social responsibility of his poetry, everything he says to the contrary notwithstanding. How more responsible (and guilty) can you get than, on the one hand, to write the rarefied lyric that Stevens writes, and, on the other, to assert that poets help people to live their lives?

What Burnshaw's critique of *Ideas of Order* did was to crystallize for Stevens his own class position and at the same time that of his ideal and (as it would seem to him) inevitable audience.[75] Stevens found Burnshaw's review "most interesting" because it "placed" him in a "new setting." That new setting, the "middle ground" of the middle class, is the socio-economic space of those who are both potential allies and potential enemies of class struggle. Burnshaw's insight into this "contradiction," as he called it, of the middle class—into, really, the undemarcated and therefore (at best) confused quality of class struggle in the United States—is matched and one-upped by Stevens in a letter written shortly after he read Burnshaw in *The New Masses*:

> I hope I am headed left, but there are lefts and lefts, and certainly I am not headed for the ghastly left of *Masses*. The rich man and the comfortable man of imagination are not nearly so rich nor nearly so comfortable as he believes them to be. And, what is more, his poor men are not nearly so poor.[76]

In the United States, the middle ground is vaster than Burnshaw thinks and the high and low grounds are narrower and not as melodramatically in opposition as the Manichean metaphors of Communist party rhetoric would make them out to be. As the poet of the middle ground, of those not subject to revolutionary hunger (we need the pun), whose basic sustenance was more or less assured (the "more or less" assuring also a conservative anxiety, a willingness to rock the boat ever so gently), it was Stevens' "role to help people"—people: the middle class is easily universalized in American discourse—"to help people live their lives. [The poet] has had immensely to do with giving life whatever savor it possesses."[77] To supply savor is to supply aesthetic, not biological, necessity: to supply what Marx in *The German Ideology* called the "new needs" (or felt lacks) of women and men after their life-sustaining necessities have been met and they begin to produce not only their sustenance but also the means of reproducing their sustenance.[78] At the point at which leisure becomes real and, in the same moment, really problematic, "we" need a civilized poet. Stevens believed it to be a need of cultural life and death whose satisfaction would determine our "happiness," or lack thereof, outside and irrespective of our political state (which for the middle class rhymes with fate).

It was also in this period of his economic growth and literary self-critique that one of the crueler jokes of literary history that I know was played out. Stevens, a major figure in the insurance business, according to those who know, the best in the field of surety bonds in the country, developed a serious case of rising-executive sickness: high blood pressure bad enough that he was advised not only to lose a great deal of weight but also to get to bed as early as possible on the faultless medical theory that a sleeping man's pressure can't help but be good. Stevens assented to the advice: so after supper there was the noise of a two-family house (the landlord had young children), there was the new baby, there were the domestic chores he regularly pitched in on, then lights out at nine. The joke is that the blood pressure problem was so serious that this well-connected insurance executive could not buy life insurance, not then, not ever—and the "then" I refer to was 1929, 1930, 1931, etc. One reason he worked well past retirement age, practically to the day he died, is that he liked his work (there can be no question about this). Another reason was that he had to because there was one part of his material context—the physiological part—over which he could not become master. Add to that his unquestioned and perhaps unquestionable feeling, which was something like an unavoidable affective accompaniment of his patriarchal formation, that it was his duty to take care of Elsie and Holly. And given the situation of those three, it could not have been otherwise. At these levels his brute material situation was not subject to his personal manipulation: his literary power could not touch it.[79]

3

I have alluded more than once to two of Stevens' poems written for his interior lover—one of them, "Final Soliloquy of the

Interior Paramour," much better known than the other thanks to the unequivocal commitment to the subject of imagination which its title announces. Stevens' readers have liked nothing better than to bypass the personal and material levels of his writing, and in this late metapoetical reflection we appear to be given license by the poet himself who seems to tell us that his real subject (poetry itself) is and has been all along unencumbered. "Interiority" appears to mean in "Final Soliloquy" and in his discourse at large what it has tended to mean in the history of philosophy since about Descartes—that ideal realm of the spirit where the new bourgeois man feels historically untouchable, his freedom guaranteed now by its last best defender, the aesthetic itself, in the moment that Foucault, with the able assistance of Orwell, has defined as the moment of the disciplined society. The message that Stevens' critics read in his work is that high-formalist literature is the ground of human freedom which, though threatened and drained by everyday life in the world that capital makes, can be nourished and protected by literary experience, and literary experience alone, and especially experience of a writer like Stevens who is exemplary because he provides us, at once, both the theory and the practice of a redemptive imagination. The fundamental hope in Stevens is political—though neither Stevens nor his critics are comfortable with that word: it is conspicuously absent from their discourse—and he is politically hopeful, moreover, in the idealist tradition running from Schiller to Marcuse in which the aesthetic is the antithesis to the totalitarian story Foucault narrates in *Discipline and Punish*, but an antithesis that may well be one of the subtlest effects of an incipient totalitarianism and its culture.

But it is the other poem that I allude to, the one without a title, the introductory eight lines of *Notes toward a Supreme Fiction*, that tells a richer (if elliptically condensed) tale of the interior lover. This tale covertly acknowledges Stevens' own devastation over the failure of his human love as the circumstance of his courting of the interior lover, and the failure of what money could buy to be either adequate recompense for the loss of intimacy or sufficient stimulus for the spiritual highs Stevens required to compensate for the "savage torpor," the deadness that bourgeois routines induced in him (Wordsworth's phrase is psychically definitive for Stevens). Among Stevens' major interpreters, Helen Vendler devotes a whole chapter to *Notes* yet has nothing to say of these lines which Stevens so prominently positioned. Joseph Riddel, who leaves nothing alone in Stevens, argues that the introductory verse of *Notes* expresses the humanist desire of all men to be married in their humanity.[80] And Harold Bloom, who has absorbed both Vendler and Riddel, claims these lines are addressed not to Stevens' friend Henry Church—despite the fact that in *Collected Poems* they quite literally are addressed to Henry Church—or to the interior paramour for that matter: he says he doesn't know who they are addressed to, but for sure Stevens loved Elsie, his daughter Holly, and the family he was born into. Maybe, Bloom concludes, this is a poem expressing but also transcending love of family.[81] What these three responses commonly do is to sublimate the personal either by ignoring it or by dissolving it in a generalizing humanism: "transcendence," as Bloom puts it, "is the tenor of this octave." I'm going to disagree with these representative readings of Stevens not because I think them wrong—they aren't wrong—but because they begin too late in the Stevens narrative. They take no measure of the price of Stevens' idealism. The journey he took to the interior he did not willingly take; he would rather it had been otherwise. In other words, idealism is not a "position" in Stevens, it is a motivation, an effort that equipped him, at a specific and painful personal and social juncture, for living.

So Stevens' critics respond initially to the introductory poem of *Notes* as if they were truly dedicated to Henry Church, a real person. What is this? The fastidious and always proper vice-president of the Hartford Accident and Indemnity is brazenly declaring homoerotic affection? The rumors of Stevens' difficulties with Elsie had been around for a long time—is *that* the reason? The opening critical move, in which the personal is glancingly recognized, is strategic only; it gives way before a sublimating move which (this is always implicit in Bloom and Riddel) is intrinsic to the poem's dynamic, as if the poet himself shared the critic's embarrassment over his unconventionally declared intimacy and so needed to annihilate the personal. But the dedication of these lines to Henry Church is in fact a printer's error which Bloom et al. seem unaware of. Church's name should have been printed above, not below, the title of the poem (as it appears in *Collected Poems*). The printer got it right with *Transport to Summer* (1947), the volume in which *Notes* appeared, thanks to Stevens' strenuously repetitive letter to his editor at Knopf in which he stresses three times in the space of a short paragraph that the eight lines are not dedicated to Church, the whole of *Notes* is; that Church must be dissociated from these lines ("they have nothing to do with Church"); and that this must be gotten right, and maybe he should scrap these lines if the printer can't go along with this, though he wouldn't want to do so because these lines "are by way of an introduction to the poem."[82]

Knowledge of Stevens' textual intention may give some satisfaction to sublimating critics, but I don't believe that such satisfaction can be long-lasting. The misplaced dedication to Henry Church in *Collected Poems* enhances, it does not engender, the intimacy of these lines. It is easy to believe that the lines are dedicated to Church because they sound so personal:

> And for what, except for you, do I feel love?
> Do I press the extremest book of the wisest man
> Close to me, hidden in me day and night?
> In the uncertain light of single, certain truth,
> Equal in living changingness to the light
> In which I meet you, in which we sit at rest,
> For a moment in the central of our being,
> The vivid transparence that you bring is peace.

If these lines are written in the mood of reverential awe as an apostrophe to the muse, or to the imagination as interior paramour, or to the idea of humanity, or to the supreme fiction itself (which they presumably "introduce"), or to a love including but transcending love of family, then their tonality is very odd, particularly in the first three lines. Whoever is being addressed as "you" is not the impersonal power that poets traditionally invoke as the goddess who inspires the gift of expression. "Impersonal" seems exactly the wrong word for this passage. This "you" is being talked to, really, quietly, not *addressed*, in a voice resembling in no way the elevated poetic manner required by writers of the long poem. "You" is spoken to as if "you" were a human lover, who draws from the writer not epic but intimate speech that says in lovers' hyperbole "I love only you" and wants its hyperbolic style to be accepted as a sign of sincerity. This effect of intimacy is produced in part by the strong caesuras setting off the phrase "except for you"; this is not love in its formal, aristocratic, high manner but love in its low, romantic, bourgeois phase—love against the world—love, moreover, in the aftermath of the thunderbolt when it becomes necessary for a man to say to a woman "more than it is possible to say," to cite the words of one of Stevens' lesser-known definitions of imagination which links writing and lovemaking as substitutive or metonymic acts.[83] What is most obscured by this poet's spectacular obscurities are his moments of direct declaration. What is plainly there in Stevens is always hardest to see because there is no rhetorical context of plainness within which to read him:

> Home from Guatemala, back at the Waldorf.
> This arrival in the wild country of the soul
>
> . . . .
> Where the wild poem is a substitute
> For the woman one loves or ought to love,
> One wild rhapsody a fake for another.

The lover appeals, in the introductory lines of *Notes*, as he must, to his worthiness by offering perfection of commitment. A double superlative ("extremest," "wisest"), with respect to books of wisdom, comes to nothing in the context of another superlative, beyond wisdom, which is never stated by Stevens because it is perhaps unstatable—and which gains in textual presence and affective urgency in these lines in direct relation to the absence of its textual signification. This extremity of feeling which he does not confuse with books of wisdom, or with books of anything, or with objects of any sort to which he might attach his feeling in a fetishizing act that characterized his life as a collector of objets d'art, is a feeling for which no language can be adequate. At the point at which Stevens taps an ancient gesture of amatory writing (proving his sincerity by speaking agonizingly of his feeling that he cannot speak), this "you," so personlike, in this rhetorical ambience, this embraced and embraceable you ("I press you, nothing else, close to me")—Stevens' taste for sweets extended beyond his cherished gourmet desserts to the extravagant gestures of courtship—no sooner gains than she loses her personal status, in the middle of the third line. At this very point, Stevens lets us in on the process of interiorization, gives us a view, as it were, of the actual moment of movement to the interior: shows her changing places. In this moment of metonymic substitution, which is also a moment of affective transference, one who seemed outside becomes a phenomenon of the inside; one who might have been of the flesh, to whom one might have addressed protestations of fidelity, is bid farewell. In an elegiac moment that is the basis of his later verse, she is bid farewell at the precise point at which, being pressed close, she does something no womanly (or male) lover can do for him: she is pressed inside him in permanent penetration and residence. She (he, it) enters him and in so entering is taken away from the world and secured from it by a lover who can make this beloved safe as he can make no human safe—"hidden in me day and night"—as he can make safe no feeling intended for a human referent.

What we witness, the withdrawal of feeling from its object, its extraction, really, or "abstraction," to use a key word of *Notes*, is definitive of Stevens' lyric moment: the lyric moment being precisely a moment of writing, a wild rhapsody that fakes a true rhapsody, a writing, then, necessarily aware of itself as substitutive satisfaction, necessarily aware of loss. Stevens' lyricism is the motivated creation of a radical privacy in a sphere, one's self, where one can range without impediment because there is no stultifying constraint there. Or, at least, there isn't supposed to be, and there isn't except for the stultification of interiority itself: the psychic prison house of lyricism which Stevens in his last poems movingly tried to escape. Like Penelope hungering for the touch of Ulysses, Stevens woke at dawn, feeling too pent up in mind, and hearing, or thinking he heard, wanting to hear, a cry from the outside ("He knew that he heard it," "It would have been outside," "The sun was coming from outside"). High-modernist lyricism is the creation of radical privacy in the belief that feeling cannot be entrusted to social context. Lukács in that notorious essay of his almost knew this about modernism except for the fact that he could not sympathetically view lyricism's socially hostile ground as its constant agon, traced everywhere "inside" the "closed" lyric sphere, and could not see, in this movement to the inside, in this key psychic plot of high-modernist bourgeois writing, critical implication.

At the moment of interiorization, when the speaker feels entered, the gender differentiation of speaker and addressee becomes confused at least and perhaps reversed. The introductory lines of *Notes* reenact the sexual scene of "Sunday Morning" and both replay a strange little story that Stevens wrote as an undergraduate: a young man takes a photograph of his sweetheart to be framed; after it is done and he opens the package, he finds a picture of himself.[84] The implied sexual reversal of this early story anticipates Stevens' later response to his culture's debunking feminization of poetry and its concomitant masculinizing of economic activity. Not a phallicizing of his poetic role in the anxious style of his earlier career, but a refusal of the phallic for an image also (to be sure) culturally bestowed but not now received defensively, not now trivialized in macho perspective—an image now empathetically assumed.

Once "she" is inside, "I" becomes "we" not because "I" has

been enhanced and complemented in a relation with another but because "I" has split itself and become a self-sustaining bisexual unit. In this loneliest conversation, wherein "I" becomes "we" and "my being" is verbally covered by "our being" (a lover's phrase of purest wish), "our being" is enveloped in a doubly encircling light which is at once the legitimating context of love (the light of truth, love's outer circle and encirclement) and the context created by the meeting of lovers (the inner circle, the light they make) in what Stevens describes in "Final Soliloquy" in the superlative "intensest rendezvous," love's ultimate meeting. The tonal change in line 4 is stark: from a voice husky and hushed with intimacy to a larger philosophic voice trying to make itself ample, trying for epistemological authority, speaking, or trying to speak, within the light of truth but not quite making it. The insistent iambs of line 4, following the opening anapestic foot, foreground philosophic desire rushing into the face of contradiction—not the confidence of reason coolly in control but the need to say more to himself, and to the beloved he's created within, than it is possible to say ("In the uncertain light of single, certain truth"). The classic epistemological metaphor of the "light of truth" is broached only to be undone; truth certain, fixed, like an anchor, the guarantee of love, becomes uncertain not because truth has become ambiguous or difficult of access but because it has become reconstituted in the first of two difficult metaphors. The first, "living changingness," by its redundancy encourages us to choose with Stevens and his philosophic soul brothers, William James and Henri Bergson, against the central rationalism of the Western philosophic tradition, and to affirm that truth is change and change is life in its most authentic form. Not really change, either, as a quality of things which change, but "changingness"—a palpability of change, a metaphoric conversion of change as quality (or mode that an object may assume) into change as thingy substance, the real referent of Stevens' substantive. Change as all there is: the totality of the being of an object. This lover's desire, which is the desire for the lyrical in its purest and most desperate modernist expression, is to merge the light of truth with the moment of interior mating, to fix "living changingness" in the interior of the interior: "the central of our being"—the fortified citadel within, the proper place of that which cannot be subject to the constraints of place because it is radically temporal. Radical temporality is the medium of love without "place," love in and as the moment: "For a moment in the central of our being." For a moment *where*? No*where*: "the central" names a quality of feeling about "being," while its syntactical position seems about to name a place for "being" qualified by "centrality." The entire line has the effect of suspending Stevens' feeling as a subjective process without location, and it does this rhetorically, creating, as it were, the temporality effect, sheer time as the groundless (placeless) ground of love. That's what this lover and lyricist wants to say and wants to believe: that everything else is irrelevant and the lyric moment all-sufficient. These introductory lines of *Notes* may be most about the effect of truth so transvalued, an effect not cognitive but affective. The pleasure Stevens names "peace," and which he equates with his interior lover, is "vivid transparence," the second of his two difficult metaphors. The lover, in other words, as the gift of love, and the gift as the medium and possibility of vision: nothing seen, but a freshness of the eye which is akin to the life principle (vividness).

The final image of the introductory lines of *Notes* is final in more senses than one and makes all long-poem writing rooted in action, even meditative action, impossible. The quest is for the end of quest—the intransitive moment of attention when without appetite, will, without trying, while sitting quietly at rest, we are touched by an unprovoked sensation: touched and utterly satisfied. We discover: we do not impose. In that moment we are teased out of ourselves, we feel discovered. This is the lyric moment, of plotlessness itself, before or beyond all conspiracies of intention and design, a moment captured by intensity of love, then remembered in desire which wants to recapture, live it again:

> It was at that time, that the silence was largest
> And longest, the night was roundest,
> The fragrance of the autumn warmest,
> Closest and strongest.

Those lines of heaped up superlatives are a kind of incantation, as if by force of the superlative alone a perfection of intimacy could be recaptured. That was how Stevens voiced his longing in "On the Road Home," one of his few open poems of human lovers. Here is how he does it in *Notes* where, without nostalgia for human presence, desire has been purified of all reference. The superlative is now proleptic of a future deliberately unspecified:

> The difficultest rigor is forthwith,
> On the image of what we see, to catch from that
> Irrational moment its unreason.

"To catch"—desire itself desired, satisfaction imagined as an unraveling of intellect, an irrational moment; the unconjugated, timeless form of the verb as signifier of a gift of pleasure hard won from the life of reason, a kind of transcendence. The three subheadings of *Notes* tell us that a supreme fiction "must be abstract," "must change," "must give pleasure." What Stevens most loves is that in himself, replacing all human loves, most resembling supreme fictions—a consciousness which he calls "vivid transparence," vision washed clean of all that has been said, a freeing from history. Consciousness as vivid transparence is original relation to things, face to face, unmediated by tradition. Vivid transparence would give access to living changingness, it would be the medium of escape from granite monotony, from the enforced repetitions of what has been said, from the condition that literary historicists, after Bloom, must call intertextuality. Vivid transparence is both medium and substance of authentic literariness: perpetual avant-garde of perception and perpetual ground of the new as the ground of peace, and perfect lover of living changingness.

The desire for original relation, face to face, unmediated by tradition—my allusion is to the revolutionary desire for an

American origin announced in the opening sentences of Emerson's "Nature" essay of 1836—is the hope for rupture with Europe in the cultural as well as in the political realm: revolutionary hope become a way of being in the world, down to and maybe most essentially including that revolutionary freshness of perception enabled by what Emerson called "the transparent eyeball." Freshness of perception is phenomenological rupture in the wake of political rupture; it is the medium of a revolutionary everyday life. The transparent-eyeball passage in Emerson is father to the moment of vivid transparency in Stevens, but between Emerson and Stevens falls not so much the struggle of fathers and sons—this is not their chief difference—as a thorough commodification of everyday life. The appetite for American newness, in Emerson transcendental, antihistorical, nature-oriented—become like the rose outside your window, he urges, they are wholly themselves, they make no reference to past or future roses, they are above time—that sort of desire for freshness of natural encounter, already doubtful in Emerson (that is why he urges it), is thoroughly translated by later Stevens into hope for the freshness of commodity consumption. Stevens' encounter with the commodity is motivated not by the need to consume its use value but by the need to consume its signifying properties: his disdain for the mass-produced (the generic in literature or in capitalist economy) is matched by his tireless search for the rare in literature and in the economy of consumable objects. In the same paragraph of a letter I've already cited, in which he says, "There is no music because the only music tolerated is modern music. There is no painting because the only painting permitted is painting derived from Picasso or Matisse," he also says, "When I go into a fruit store nowadays and find there nothing but the fruits du jour: apples, pears, oranges, I feel like throwing them at the Greek. I expect, and you expect, sapodillas and South Shore bananas and pine-apples a foot high with spines fit to stick in the helmet of a wild chieftain." Consumption in Stevens, literary or gastronomical, is always to be understood under the sign of the gastronomical: eating as the gastronomical equivalent of lyric interiorization; eating original signs. The appetite for newness, so politically adventurous in Emerson, in Stevens sustains an economy whose continuing vitality depends on the production and consumption not of use and exchange values (as in Marx's outline of classic capitalism) but of original signs. Need for the new becomes the perpetual ground of production of the "new," in a capitalism therefore become pure, released from the referential grounds of sustenance values; capitalism become like a self-sustaining and self-perpetuating discourse without end because without ends; capitalism become a machine for the production of new signifiers whose content is irrelevant. By consuming original signs—the route to autonomous pleasure, privately indulged—the capitalist subject of pleasure ensures its own political indifference. It is in this economic context that Stevens' classic modernist aphorism ("Originality is an escape from repetition") deserves to be read. Originality—in the English romantics a category of social opposition—becomes, in the later capitalist phase in which Stevens lived and wrote, something close to hegemonic value.[85]

Stevens' idea of the long poem in the post-*Harmonium* period involved precisely the invention of a loose form in which he could feel love in moments of vivid transparency without agenda, which occur just as they occur—yet not a form so loose as not to demand a discipline of exploration in which, in the spaces between moments of transparency, he could reflect upon transparency, and in so reflecting work himself up to the edge ("It is possible, possible, possible . . ."). The long poem would be a collection of moments whose strongest value would be not in things collected (images quarried) but in the pure experience of newness without object. In other words, in the anticipation of newness, just before actual possession, which he knew stultified feelings of newness, just before purchase: a capitalism of mind, the foreplay of consumption without commodity that could and did become easily enough a life of consumption in the ordinary sense, what nine-to-five success made wonderfully possible, and what he fell back on as a substitute for the life of imagination. Capitalism and poetry are not opposites but symbiotic complements, the basis in Stevens of an integrated life, a unified sensibility quite unlike anything dreamt of in the utopian imagination.

"When I get up at 6 o'clock in the morning," he wrote to Henry Church, "(a time when you are first closing your novel, pulling the chain on the lamp at your bedside) the thing"—the idea of a supreme fiction—"crawls all over me; it is in my hair when I shave and I think of it in the bathtub. Then I come down here to the office and, except for an occasional letter like this, have to put it to one side. After all, I like Rhine wine, blue grapes, good cheese, endive and lots of books, etc., etc., etc., as much as I like supreme fiction."[86] Dawn—the time of the supreme fiction, Penelope's hour, the onset of a savage presence that "awakens the world in which she dwells." To feel the supreme fiction is to feel an awakening of consciousness, excitement without climax, excitement not distinguishable from the very pulse of life, as essential as the beat of the heart:

> But was it Ulysses? Or was it only the warmth of the sun
> On her pillow? The thought kept beating in her like her
>   heart.
> The two kept beating together. It was only day.

The beat of the heart, literally the pulse of life, is also a figure of thought, this thought: that life is only life at the brink. Dawn is also the critical temporal setting of the last poem printed in *Collected Poems*, "Not Ideas about the Thing but the Thing Itself":

> The sun was rising at six,
> No longer a battered panache above snow . . .
> It would have been outside.
>
> It was not from the vast ventriloquism
> Of sleep's faded papier-mâché . . .
> The sun was coming from outside.

Those ellipses are cunningly expressive: not of words left out but of the impossibility and irrelevance of verbal presence, and of a place outside words, a moment in consciousness of stunning impact, the breakthrough of presence *through* language, when one feels broken into, entered: "you," Ulysses, "the sun," my love—the thing itself grasped in vivid transparence. Not quite: ellipses work here as a subtle form of representation, figuring the slippage of language, not really its absence. One is about to be entered.

But dawn is also the time when, having consumed the night away in fiction, Henry Church—who is really rich, who buys what he wants, reads when he wants, all night if he likes—can go to sleep. Henry Church doesn't have to report to the office. He doesn't work. Unlike Stevens, he doesn't have to wish for a life "somewhere where I don't live now." Dawn, for Stevens, is an intersected moment: the awakening to the possibility of supreme fiction and the transition period when supreme fictions must be deferred as soon as they are contemplated, not in order to forget them but in order to do what he must do to lay up their representations, the substitutes for supreme fiction that money can buy—good cheese, blue grapes, lots of books, and etcetera, especially, perhaps, etcetera. The endless substitutes that money can buy, the specialty market of supreme fictions, he loves almost as much as the truly real thing, that is to say, the imaginative thing of poetry for which so-called real things, like Rhine wine, substitute. The deferral of imaginative supreme fictions is nothing but the production of desire for that which money can buy. Work, after all, is the site of his writing to Henry Church; work not only enables the purchase of substitutive satisfactions, it enables reflection on the difference between real and substitute supreme fictions; it enables metareflection, as well, on why he has to be concerned with that difference, why he must work, and on what the difference between being Wallace Stevens and being Henry Church actually consists of. Work might have enabled reflection on his difference from

Henry Church as a class difference—work might have been the site of an embryonic class-consciousness—but I see no evidence that Stevens ever quite got to that point, though maybe mentioning to Henry Church that *he* can put out the lights when others, like himself, are turning them on is the gentler form of class-consciousness with all hostility either utterly absent or civilly repressed. *Notes toward a Supreme Fiction* is dedicated to Church, and why not? In another time he would have been the patron of Wallace Stevens. In this time—the poem was published in 1942—the dedication to Church functions doubly: first, to refer to a person living everyday life as Stevens dreamed of living it, as an aesthetic totality; second, to signal the difference between a European aristocrat of leisure (a traditional recipient of poetic dedication) and an American (an untraditional writer of poems) whose economic status and literary ambition created contradictions that Church would never experience. The dedication to Church is an idealization, a little self-ironic, a little (how could it not be?) hostile.

Or consider this even more complicated reflection in a letter to Barbara Church, one of Stevens' favorite correspondents after her husband, Henry, died—who sustained the life of aesthetic vitality that he had imagined for Henry. Consider this meditation on the necessity of perpetual revolution and the staleness of all revolutions except those now in process: "Hélas, what dreary things yesterday's revolutionaries were, particularly the conversational, letter-writing ones." And let's consider his pleasure in avant-garde art not as pleasure in "art in itself" (Stevens rarely reified even in his extreme moments of consumerism) but as pleasure in what he thought must be the radical individual behind avant-garde art, the avant-garde self, the pleasure of his company as the pleasure of fresh perspective: "More and more, one wants the voices of one's contemporaries—*today's* music, painting, poetry, thinking. . . . When I was able to sit in a room full of the paintings of Raoul Dufy: not ambitious nor pretentious things, my chief pleasure was in the companionship of Dufy himself. It was possible really to see things as he sees them." And let's consider his weariness with routines at the office ("the rock pile," as he calls it) and his need to transform everydayness, in one's house, one's apartment, the domestic grooves of boredom, into a pleasure garden of perpetual aesthetic revolution: avant-garde art translated at the site of burgherdom into a perpetual revolution of interior decorating—a desire which Barbara Church can indulge but he can't: "If I could afford it I should throw away everything I have, each autumn, but particularly this one, and start all over with all the latest inventions: radiant heat c-inclus, fresh walls, new pictures. . . . I think you must feel this way, too, because your apartment is always a bit different and better: more comfortable, more genial." Different, new, *therefore* better.[87]

4

Sometime in the middle 1920s Stevens augmented his two careers as surety-bonds expert and avant-garde lyricist with a third career in collecting and gourmandizing—for him there was no difference. This activity he characterized ironically, but sincerely, as his vocation as "spiritual epicure."[88] Collecting and gourmandizing were not just another project in an already heavily projected life, but a mediation of his first two careers, the perfect fusion of aesthetic Stevens and economic Stevens—a fusion, moreover, enabled by his economic prowess, though this latter was a fact he wanted to defend himself from (forget, really) and did defend himself from in some of the stranger passages of his correspondence.

A full theme in his letters after about 1922, collecting was already in evidence in his Harvard days, in his journal-keeping activity, where moments of metareflection, even as early as 1899, at twenty years old, seem in the trajectory of the self-conscious ("mature") writer he would become: "Diaries are very futile. It is quite impossible for me to express any of the beauty I feel to half the degree I feel it, and yet it is a great pleasure to seize an impression and lock it up in words: you feel as if you had it safe forever."[89] The psychic plot of his poetics, at best nascent here, and never easy to discern in his life as a writer, is fully overt in his life as a collector. Stevens' life of collecting involves seizing an object and making it safe for his consumption by withdrawing it from the social network in which it was embedded and which, embedded or withdrawn, it covertly signifies, just as his quintessential lyricizing act of poetic composition requires the disinvolvement of impressions from their material grounds, a making interior. Collecting was poetry made easy of access because Stevens commanded the necessary monetary wherewithal and the proper contacts with people in the right places: money and contacts, the insurance of aesthetic satisfaction and the guarantee, like poetic discourse, of transcendence (making "safe forever").

The question Stevens did not ask himself in 1899—make it safe from *what?*—he answered with subtle candor in an essay published forty-four years later. The ostensible subject of this essay is poetry in general; its true subject is the poetry Stevens wrote, or wanted to write, and the poetry he bought in the form of the things he collected. An artist, he says in "The Noble Rider and the Sound of Words," must "extract" the work of art from the real world when he does not compose it entirely. And since "everything like a firm grasp of reality is eliminated from the aesthetic field," it is not possible to condemn "escapism" because "psychologically" the poetic process is fundamentally escapist.[90] Stevens in his essays is almost always vague and ambiguous: the traditional philosophic mind (Paul Weiss's, for example) finds him incoherent.[91] I would say that Stevens is importantly vague and importantly ambiguous in his essays. By "reality" he means, in the passage I've alluded to, "social reality." By "work of art" he means a thing entirely fabricated or a thing (like a handcrafted commodity, the work of an artisan) entirely found, a valuable thing, something like a natural resource which (in a word that echoes the coded language of corporative noncolonial imperialism) must be "extracted." And by "escapism" he means two things: first, the removal of the artist's consciousness from the social field, its withdrawal into an interior which works to protect consciousness from an outside perceived as hostile; and, second, the removal of the found object, *its* extraction from the social field, the "escape" of the found object from the place where it was produced. Weiss, if he could comment on this second sense of "escape," would surely have found it imprecise and forced. And it is, but that very imprecision is the key to its political resonance. This second sense suggests what is not the case—that an object can have intention: in this instance, to move itself. Escape in this strategically imprecise sense covers the human intention which extracts and makes it harder for us to see that the object, the objet d'art—generally of third-world origin in Stevens—is constituted as a commodity in an imperial field of intention, that the object is torn rudely by the roots, as it were, from the cultural context where it was organic, and brought within an alien first-world context where, as a fragment from a repressed totality, it can function nonfunctionally, as aesthetic sustenance, a work of art which expresses nothing but itself, and therefore may be consumed for itself alone.

The usually impossible question of origins pertains here, too, to Stevens as collector—when did he begin? Evidence from his early journals encourages us to think that his beginning as a collector coincided with his beginning as a writer: writing as a form of collecting, the recording of impressions and reflections a kind of hunting, the quarrying and capturing of trophies by an aesthetic imperialist. Here is an entry for 14 October 1900: "In the morning I called on Frank—Lieutenant Mohr. His den was filled with Filipino weapons, hats, etc—a great variety of Oriental odds and ends. Frank is a first-class fellow & may come to N.Y. His trip took him around the world."[92] There are four other entries for the same day, all of them in the self-conscious style of youthful antiliterary literary play—comparisons of *Paradise Lost*, a heavenly thing, to the shaft of sunlight in which he sat as Milton was read to him by a friend ("The sun was better than the poetry"); a rueful comparison of modern man to the "old fellows," whose thought was so much more "vigorous" (but not that rueful: the young fellow who says "old fellows" isn't feeling all that much anxiety over the masters of the past); drunken apostrophes to starlight and moonlight, "a treasure house" of impressions profaned by the language he must use to invoke them ("Bah—mere words"); and last a telling little literary game played at the expense of unknowing bartenders and Keats: "Livy and I thought it rather good fun to ask them about Mike Angelo, Butch Petrarch, Sammy Dante. We asked one fellow whether he had heard that John Keats had been run over, by a trolley car at Stoney Creek in the morning. He said that he had not—he did not know Keats—but that he had heard of the family. Spirit of Adonais!" These various entries for 14 October 1900 figure varieties of aesthetic experience and the effect of their sheer listing is ʳeductive: they are radically equivalent. All become stored objects—in forms of notation, forms of pleasure—and the Filipino "odds and ends" are a political instance of the phenomenology of odds and ends, not a unique instance. Journal writing for Stevens was not only a form of collecting, a severing of odds and ends from wholes: it was the ur-form of the poetic and a crucial step on the way to the lyrical discourse of an interiority that would be free.

It is beside the point to make a point of the snobby game, played by spoiled rich kids, at the bartender's expense. It is not beside the point to remember our foreign policy at the end of the nineteenth century, our incursion into the Philippines and Cuba, our need to "open the door" to China, and the relationship of this noncolonial imperialism to the needs of an economy whose production, especially in the 1890s, outstripped its domestic market's ability to consume. It is not beside the point to retrieve that memory because by doing so we mark the political moment of Stevens' journal entry—it simply could not have been written five years earlier. In so marking that moment have we thereby marked, in Fredric Jameson's penetrating phrase, "the political unconscious" of Stevens' writing? [93] There is not a ripple of discomfort, embarrassment, guilt, contradiction, nor any telltale verbal anomaly, of any sort, in the passage on Filipino "odds and ends." Third-world handicrafts, the contexts of their production, the medium of Stevens' access to that line of handicraft, the specific human costs in producing them in the first place and getting them into the United States in the second place—in other words, the complex political signification of third-world objects at the point of their entry, or possibility of their entry, into first-world aesthetic reflection and writing—none of this touches the discernible intention of the entry (clearly), and none of it touches the tone of the entry. The entry is politically thoughtless as perhaps only a twenty-year-old can be politically thoughtless. The very status of the entry as itself an "odd and end" among other "odds and ends" depends on such thoughtlessness. There is, maybe I should say, a political *context* to the entry on Filipino odds and ends, but no repressed reservoir of political *content*; we are not dealing, at this point in Stevens' life as a writer, with the phenomenon of repression at all; there is no trace of awareness that he is involved as a writer in an *action of severing* parts from whole, an act which would be, at the same time, a banishing of the repressed social whole to a place we can call the unconscious. The entry in question on Filipino odds and ends is not, for him, a haunted house, though it might be for us.

But if Stevens at twenty is politically thoughtless in the sense that he has no political thought, then Stevens at forty-three is willfully so, because needfully so. In 1922 Harriet Monroe introduced him to her sister, Lucy Monroe Calhoun, the widow of William Calhoun, who had been U.S. minister to China. Through Harriet, his double agent, Stevens arranged to have various items sent to him from Peking. The variety of these items and others sent to him by a friend in Paris, like the variety of entries in his journal for 14 October 1900, is belied by similarity of function. Jasmine tea from China is like candy sent from the place de l'Opéra, is like a book of Parisian photographs: the metonymic shape of these items is generated from their ability to give their recipient the pleasure of release from the office—"a desk that sees so much trouble," as he puts it in crisp allusion to the economic and legal issues that it was his job to manage profitably on behalf of the company, "is blessed by such reversions to innocence."[94]

The aesthetic leavening of everyday life at the office is good, but even better was the leavening of something else. At the time when he made his contact with Lucy Calhoun, Stevens was collecting something else, his own poems for his first volume, and was finding them bad. The carved wooden figure of an old god, a small jade screen, two black crystal lions, a small jade figure, but especially the old god in wood, he tells Harriet Monroe, have a consoling effect. This old god says to Stevens "not to mind one's bad poems," nor to mind his status as an after-hours writer, but, in effect, to bide his time and to let his objets d'art supply, for the time being, the poetry that was not being written. The blessed reversion to innocence at forty-three is at once the blessing of forgetting where you work and what you've written and the blessing of hope that you can begin again. It was a much-needed blessing in a period when life at the office and life as a husband and father seemed to be all the life there might be.[95]

Stevens went to extraordinary lengths to will the innocence of his efforts as a collector and to conceal from himself the intentional character of his activity; here the term "repression" seems appropriate to the activity that desperately wills its political purity. He wonders, in a letter written in 1935, again to Harriet Monroe, whether her sister might wish to do some shopping for him. He doesn't have sufficient cash, now; he needs to pay off some income tax first and "another substantial item," which he doesn't specify. But soon, he says, "I shall have some money I can call my own": free money with which to "buy, say, a pound of Mandarin tea, a wooden carving, a piece of porcelain or one piece of tinqueire, one small landscape painting, and so on and so on": as if the series might be extended indefinitely; as if the things desired, however desirable in themselves, were not, in themselves, so desirable; as if the things in the series—and what is the principle of a series that includes Mandarin tea and a landscape painting?—stood in for something else, were representations of a special sort, effigy-like, containing the innocence that he needed to revert to: pleasures bought and brought home. But he would not send the money directly to Mrs. Calhoun; no direct economic contact between himself and the agent of his pleasures. He insists upon this: Harriet would be sent the money and *she* would pass it on to Mrs. Calhoun.[96]

The point of his semideluded self-conscious exercise in self-delusion was to so mediate the process of procurement of pleasure that he could experience the arrival in Hartford of oriental handicrafts as the purest gift, out of the blue. And poetic composition had to have the same feeling: writing not as intention but as surprise, expression as a gift of spontaneity, from some unknown benefactor. What he once said of his writing— "I almost always dislike anything that I do that doesn't fly in the window"—describes the phenomenology of his collecting habits.[97] The stuff that might be sent him, he explained to Harriet Monroe, like a "small landscape by a scholarly painter," would do him "good" (that's the word: good), but only if "picked up by chance." He'd lose the good, he implies, if he asked for something "specifically." Feel free, he tells Leonard Van Geyzel, his man in Ceylon, "to send whatever you like"; "You are not to trouble about telling me how the money was spent" on these (same phrase from the journal thirty-seven years earlier) "odds and ends." In this exercise in motivated innocence there is, of course, both intention and an end in view: the procurement of that which is not procurable in the "general market." Original, one of a kind, non-mass-produced, unstandardized, uncommodified—those are the values, and their subject (tea, wooden carvings, poems) is virtually irrelevant. Writing and collecting become twin expressions of Stevens' intention to live outside intention, because all intention is contaminated by a capitalist ethos to commodify for a general market which it brings into being. Never mind that he pays his income tax first; never mind the conditions of "opening up" the Orient to his innocent consumption.[98]

A few months later Stevens writes to Van Geyzel, again, to thank him for the goods (in both senses now) that had arrived just in time for the Christmas holidays and to express hope that when summer comes around maybe this "sort" of thing could be done again, "interesting odds and ends" could be found perhaps in some other place—"say, Java or Hong Kong or Siam." "Say" works a lot like "and so on and so on"—"say" because these places are not so much what they are, specific places, but metaphorical names, examples, really, of an exotic geography whose social and political conditions have been bracketed and that Stevens would like to possess. "I selected as my own," he says to Van Geyzel of the things sent for Christmas, "the Buddha which is so simple and explicit that I like to have it in my room." Of course, Van Geyzel cannot visit all those places on Stevens' behalf, but maybe he knows people who could be enlisted, "people of taste . . . who are really interested in doing this sort of thing as part of the interest of living." Above all: no tourist's junk and "feel free to incur any reasonable expense." If, in 1900, he seemed genuinely not to know, then in 1937, when he was telling Van Geyzel to feel free within limits, he does know. The finely fashioned Buddha in his room is therapy, he tells Van Geyzel, for what is being done to his nerves by Hitler and Mussolini—and even Buddha, in these times, he admits, is "hard to get around to."[99]

So consumption in Stevens, whether of gourmet foods or of art objects, is radical metaphor for nourishing empty interior spaces—a taking into the home, "my room," the mind, spirit, heart. Consumption is a sustaining of the soul, and the extraordinary in Stevens is the fare of basic psychic sustenance, the very "bread of life," as he put it, in this, his privileged life; the source of rare visions; a rich, but not so rich, and not so comfortable, man's necessity:

Dear Daughtry:

Many thanks for the persimmons. These meant more to me than you can imagine. I have far more things to eat and far more things to drink than are good for me. I indulge in abstemious spells merely to keep my balance.

Wild persimmons make one feel like a hungry man in the woods. As I ate them, I thought of opossums and birds, and the antique Japanese prints in black and white, in which monkeys are eating persimmons in bare trees. There is nothing more desolate than a persimmon tree, with the old ripe fruit hanging on it. As you see, there is such a thing as being a spiritual epicure.[100]

5

Very late in his life in a poem called "The World as Meditation" Wallace Stevens returned to the figure of the poet not as virile youth (a figure, for him, of the persistent anxiety he felt for his masculinity) but as woman, Homer's Penelope as himself, without a trace of the self-consciousness that accompanied his earlier, ladylike poses as the versifier of the trivial. The world as field of action belongs to Ulysses; the world as meditation is Penelope's creation. Penelope's poetry is her special kind of writing, her active passivity; she is his final representation of desire as a capacity for reception, rather than an agitated seeking of desirable objects, a traditional female image with which he identifies completely in the last printed poem in his *Collected Poems*, without the safe distancing effect that the character of Penelope provides in "The World as Meditation." It was what, as writer and collector, he wanted all along; it was the position, poetical and sexual, that he courted all along; it was his way of saying "no" to the life he felt forced to lead.

If Ulysses is the male principle expressed as the epic genre of action, then Penelope is the female principle expressed as the lyric genre of contemplation. Ulysses is quickly and tellingly reduced as "The interminable wanderer": a comedic sort of epithet which has a very different, undercutting kind of effect in the context of the heroic style that is being recollected. This is not Homer's man skilled in all the ways of contending; this

Ulysses is closer to Bill Bailey, whom Pearl of the same sur-
name importunes, in a low musical genre of domestic relations,
"Won't you come home?" Penelope is drawn into the poem's
center of consciousness: Stevens' *Odyssey* is not the great later
books of adventure but wholly its beginning, in the perspective
of Penelope who imagines maximum distance, absence, and uncertain return: a radical reduction of the *Odyssey* to domestic
anecdote. (Will he ever return?) Ulysses is an exterior figure,
quite literally, outside the room which is the universe of her
waiting, just as the sun, with whom Ulysses is strategically
confused, is outside. The division of the genders (and genres)
is starkly projected in the "fire" and "cretonnes," antithetical
figures of male energy and female enclosure:

> Someone is moving
>
> On the horizon and lifting himself up above it.
> A form of fire approaches the cretonnes of Penelope,
> Whose mere savage presence awakens the world in which
> she dwells.

The "savage presence" in this poem of his last years retrieves by self-quotation the self-conscious, primitive moment
of forced phallic music from "Sunday Morning" 7. This "savage presence" implicitly grants, without anxiety, what Stevens
anxiously desired in his youth to grant himself, as poet and
economic actor—autonomy of the male principle figured as the
energy of a system, the sun itself (in appropriate pre-Copernican
vision) like a self-sufficient hero "lifting himself above" the
horizon. (Stevens' father might have liked that phrase: it came
so close to his kind of cliché, like lifting yourself up by your
own bootstraps.) Stevens grants to Ulysses what males have
typically claimed for themselves but which he does not wish to
claim for himself (now) and in the same act grants to canonical
Homer an authority of epic mastery for which he no longer
yearns through the disguises of sexual self-irony and his self-
styled minority.

It is the sun (or the thought of Ulysses) which stirs Penelope's consciousness from sleep to vision; she depends upon it (him), it (he) motivates her meditation. The sun lifts itself over the horizon, Ulysses approaches (maybe), Penelope both dwells in and creates a dwelling place. Her power, located literally within the domestic dwelling place, is the power of lyric meditation, whose actual domestic site is a figure for a site and dwelling which she makes and which is impervious to male presence: it needs no real Ulysses to fill her desire, for there, in the dwelling she makes, she is the composer of selves, the single artificer of the world in which she dwells, the principle of high formalist imagination so revered by modernist writers now (unlike its earlier canonical evocation in "The Idea of Order at Key West") unequivocally rendered and accepted as a female principle, the autonomous goddess of radical creativity whose function is much more than formal. She composes selves—his as well as hers—and she places them in a sheltering beyond violation. She creates them—in that sense she composes them. She consoles them—in that sense also does she compose them: gives them poise in the face of unassuaged grief. She gives deeply founded stability—not a "shelter," but a "sheltering"; not a place but a process of mind, in never-ending meditation, whose security is inviolable; perfection of lyric internalization, Penelope's poetry:

> She has composed, so long, a self with which to
>   welcome him,
> Companion to his self for her, which she imagined,
> Two in a deep-founded sheltering. . . .

Her meditative process is "so long" because its object is absent—and though in the end, in Homer's story, Ulysses is brought home, in Stevens' version he is kept away; in Stevens' version there is no plot, no culmination of touch. Erotic fulfillment is imagined ("His arms would be her necklace / And her belt"), and imagined as an alternative to the worldly booty he might bring but which she doesn't want ("She wanted no fetchings" because "His arms" would be "the final fortune of their desire"). Note: not *"her* desire," which might seem logical, but *"their* desire" which is correct because the world as meditation is wholly hers. Ulysses has no say in it; there, she is the arbiter of all desire; what she wants is what he wants. In Stevens' lyricizing of Homer's narrative, in his draining of plot and draining of time, Penelope is placed in the suspension of an interminable imagining because knowledge of the end is denied her: no narrative climax, no sexual climax.

The trajectory of the long poem Stevens compared to the trajectory of love: prolonged attention to a single subject is like prolonged attention to a forbidden woman, and success in the longer forms is like success in love—if, that is, one can write/love like an Italian. Both trajectories were denied Stevens, and he likewise denies them to Penelope. Lyric longing is no more a choice than erotic longing; they are impositions, that's how it felt to him, and he so imposes them on Penelope who accommodates (we need the pun) her circumstances, what she does not choose, with a tenacity and force that answer Ulysses' savage presence and absence with her own "barbarous strength" which "would never fail." Stevens' Penelope is a strong revision of Whitman's agonized voyeur ("Song of Myself," section 11), whose desire to be male, painfully described in her fantasy of assuming the classic male sexual posture, only underscores what she really is: a proper and properly repressed lady. Stevens' Penelope refuses all male posture, but she is no "lady"—her sexual and poetic identity is "within her," it is not imposed by a male superego, it's primitive. Savage to savage. Penelope's meditation sustains her life; Stevens is of no mind to designate it "trifling poesy."

But Penelope, though the poem's center of meditation, is not the poem's voice: this Stevens reserves for himself, as a kind of frame meditator and would-be storyteller, reduced to telling and brooding over one moment of the *Odyssey*. With all narrative action denied him, the long poem that he attempted repeatedly in the thirties and forties now frankly beyond his possibilities, Stevens pens his farewell in "The World as Meditation" to the

Homeric text which he can in no way rewrite in the epic spirit but can appropriate in his lyric mode, converting Ulysses' world as field of action, male arena, into Penelope's world as interior moment of reflection: the world not as object of meditation but the world *as* meditation—victory over the canonical principle of epic bought at the heavy cost of idealization. Poetry at the interior, lovers at the interior, both set by the frame meditator into a natural context large and inhuman ("an inhuman meditation, larger than her own") which he insists is itself a creative process of meditation, yet so figured as to render the inhuman domestic, a process of Penelope's mind: the grand natural cycles a reflection of household work, mending and washing ("The trees are mended. / That winter is washed away"), as if Penelope herself were what she never was, a dutiful bourgeois wife. And then, having adopted Penelope's metaphors as his own, he reduces his lovers to greeting-card sentiment: "friend and dear friend." Here, at last, is a Homer for the little things, the small tasks and pleasures of the sort of house that Stevens knew so well because he lived in it. Stevens, who was never confident of his ability to stand with "your man-poets," here, in this poem of 1952, has made over the canonical of canonical poets into an image of himself: the frame meditator becomes Penelope.

If Penelope's isolation is terrible, that is because her idealization fails to compensate perfectly for her exclusion from her husband's world. Hers is an incantatory poetry, dependent on its absent male object of focus: "She would talk a little to herself as she combed her hair / Repeating his name with its patient syllables" (Ulysses, Ulysses). Ulysses is at home in the Greek universe, taken care of by such as Aeolus, even recognized by his dog after all those years. Penelope does not belong: "No winds like dogs watched over her at night." What she has, in the end, is what is left over when all "fetchings" have been refused: purified lyric longing. And what a miracle of a creation "fetchings" is, even for this poet who performed them as second nature. *Fetch:* to reach by sailing, especially against the wind or tide; to go or come after and bring or take back. *Fetching:* attractive, pleasing. Thus *fetchings:* attractive or pleasing things, which bring a price, as the price a commodity will *fetch*, brought back over water, defined as commodities by the act of fetching which brought them home, valued as fetchings in the homeland of the actor who fetches: an etymology of imperialism. She wanted none of that.

Notes   Index

Notes

Anatomy of a Jar

1. Kenneth Burke, *A Grammar of Motives* (1945; Berkeley, Los Angeles, London: University of California Press, 1969), pp. 59–61, 323–325.

2. *The Collected Poems of Wallace Stevens* (New York: Alfred A. Knopf, 1954), pp. 203, 198, 380–381. All citations of Stevens' poems are to this volume.

3. Josiah Royce, *The Problem of Christianity*, with a new introduction by John E. Smith (Chicago: University of Chicago Press, 1968), pp. 244–245, 253, 273–295. George Santayana, *Interpretations of Poetry and Religion* (New York: Harper and Row, 1957), pp. 166–216.

4. Stevens, *Collected Poems*, pp. 193–194.

5. Ibid., p. 151.

6. *The Complete Poetical Works of Percy Bysshe Shelley*, ed. Thomas Hutchinson (London: Oxford University Press, 1965), p. 238 (*Prometheus Unbound*, 2. 4. 116).

7. Shelley, "A Defense of Poetry," in Hazard Adams, ed., *Critical Theory since Plato* (New York: Harcourt, Brace, Jovanovich, 1971), p. 512.

8. T. E. Hulme, "Bergson's Theory of Art," in *Critical Theory since Plato*, p. 779.

9. *Literary Essays of Ezra Pound*, ed. with an introduction by T. S. Eliot (New York: New Directions, 1968), p. 3.

10. Wordsworth, Preface to Second Edition of "Lyrical Ballads," in *Critical Theory since Plato*, pp. 439, 440.

11. Shelley, "Defense of Poetry," p. 503.

12. *Letters of Wallace Stevens*, selected and edited by Holly Stevens (New York: Alfred A. Knopf, 1966), p. 198.

13. Michael Herr, *Dispatches* (New York: Avon Books, 1978), pp. 260, 107.

14. F. O. Matthiessen, *The James Family: A Group Biography* (New York: Alfred A. Knopf, 1961), p. 626.

15. See Fredric Jameson's suggestive essay "Wallace Stevens," in *New Orleans Review* 11 (Spring 1984), 10–19, and his methodological meditation in *The Political Unconscious: Narrative as a Socially Symbolic Act* (Ithaca: Cornell University Press, 1981), pp. 74–102, for a powerful historicist approach both different from and sometimes opposed to mine. On Sartre's defeat in contemporary theory, see Perry Anderson, *In the Tracks of Historical Materialism* (Chicago: University of Chicago Press, 1984), chap. 2.

16. Don De Lillo, *Ratner's Star* (New York: Alfred A. Knopf, 1976), pp. 306–307, 340–351.

17. Herr, *Dispatches*, pp. 92–93.

18. Matthiessen, *James Family*, pp. 633–634.

19. Ibid., p. 633.

20. Michel Foucault, *The Archaeology of Knowledge*, trans. from the French by A. M. Sheridan Smith (New York: Harper and Row, 1976), p. 17.

21. Matthiessen, *James Family*, p. 633.

22. Stevens, *Collected Poems*, pp. 250–251, 334–335.

23. Ibid., p. 406.

Chapter 1. Michel Foucault's Fantasy for Humanists

1. Michel Foucault, *Language, Counter-Memory, Practice*, ed. with an introduction by Donald F. Bouchard; trans. from the French by Donald F. Bouchard and Sherry Simon (Ithaca: Cornell University Press, 1977), pp. 131–132.

2. Michel Foucault, *The Archaeology of Knowledge*, trans. from the French by A. M. Sheridan Smith (New York: Harper and Row, 1976), pp. 126–127.

3. Michel Foucault, *Discipline and Punish: The Birth of the Prison*, trans. from the French by Alan Sheridan (New York: Pantheon Books, 1977), pp. 7, 29.

4. Foucault, *Discipline and Punish*, pp. 10, 30.

5. Ibid., p. 9.

6. Ibid., p. 73.

7. Ibid., pp. 24–25.

8. Ibid., pp. 25–26.

9. Ibid., pp. 26–27.

10. Ibid., p. 27.

11. Ibid.

12. Ibid.

13. Ibid., p. 43.

14. Ibid., p. 46.

15. Ibid.
16. Ibid., p. 47.
17. Ibid., p. 57.
18. Ibid., pp. 48–49.
19. Ibid., pp. 58, 59, 60.
20. Ibid., p. 63.
21. Ibid.
22. Ibid., p. 67.
23. Ibid., pp. 68, 69.
24. Ibid., p. 73.
25. Ibid., pp. 77, 79, 80.
26. Ibid., pp. 82–89 passim.
27. Ibid., pp. 87, 90.
28. Ibid., p. 94.
29. Ibid., pp. 94–95.
30. Ibid., p. 102.
31. Ibid., pp. 95, 101.
32. Ibid., pp. 104, 105, 110.
33. Ibid., p. 113.
34. Ibid.
35. Ibid., pp. 115–116.
36. Ibid., p. 125.
37. Ibid., pp. 126, 128–129.
38. Ibid., pp. 130–131.
39. Ibid., pp. 135–136.
40. Ibid., p. 137.
41. Ibid., p. 138.
42. Ibid., p. 139–140.
43. Ibid., p. 140.
44. Ibid., p. 142.
45. Ibid., p. 143.
46. Ibid., pp. 143–144.
47. Ibid., p. 145.
48. Ibid., p. 148.
49. Ibid., p. 149.
50. Kenneth Burke, *Attitudes toward History* (Boston: Beacon Press, 1961), p. 94.
51. Foucault, *Discipline and Punish*, p. 154.
52. Georg Lukács, *History and Class Consciousness*, trans. Rodney Livingstone (Cambridge: MIT Press, 1971), p. 90.
53. Harry Braverman, *Labor and Monopoly Capital: The Degradation of Work in the Twentieth Century* (New York: Monthly Review Press, 1974), pp. 87, 90, 92, and chap. 4 passim.
54. Ibid., p. 119.
55. Foucault, *Discipline and Punish*, pp. 176–177.
56. Ibid., p. 177.

57. Ibid.

58. Ibid.

59. Antonio Gramsci, *Selections from the Prison Notebooks*, ed. and trans. Quintin Hoare and Geoffrey Nowell Smith (New York: International Publishers, 1971), pp. 309–310.

60. Karl Marx, *Capital*, Vol. 1, introduced by Ernest Mandel, trans. Ben Fowkes (New York: Vintage Books, 1977), 439–454 passim.

61. Foucault, *Discipline and Punish*, p. 135.

62. Ibid., pp. 170–171.

63. Ibid., pp. 185, 184.

64. Ibid., pp. 184, 186.

65. Ibid., p. 191.

66. Ibid., p. 197.

67. Ibid., p. 198.

68. Ibid., pp. 198, 199.

69. Ibid., p. 200.

70. Ibid., pp. 200, 201.

71. Ibid., p. 204.

72. Ibid., p. 219.

73. Ibid., p. 221.

74. Ibid., pp. 238, 255, 303.

75. Ibid., pp. 243, 257–292 passim.

76. Ibid., p. 276.

77. Hippolyte Taine, Introduction to *History of English Literature*, in Hazard Adams, ed., *Critical Theory since Plato* (New York: Harcourt, Brace, Jovanovich, 1971), p. 602.

78. Raymond Williams, *Marxism and Literature* (Oxford: Oxford University Press, 1977), p. 83.

79. Taine, Introduction to *History of English Literature*, p. 603.

80. Ibid., p. 604.

81. Ibid., pp. 613–614.

82. Stephen Greenblatt, *Renaissance Self-Fashioning* (Chicago: University of Chicago Press, 1980), p. 6. For important accounts of the issues and players of new historicism see the essays by Louis Montrose and Jean E. Howard in *English Literary Renaissance* 16 (Winter 1986).

83. Stephen Greenblatt, Introduction to *The Forms of Power and the Power of Forms in the Renaissance*, *Genre* 15 (1982), 3–6 passim.

84. Though Foucault inhabits *Renaissance Self-Fashioning* mainly in Greenblatt's notes, my point is that Foucault's key obsessions and terms shape Greenblatt's argument, particularly in its "Marxist" moments, more than does the work of Clifford Geertz which appears to be more central to Greenblatt than it is. In any event, Geertz's descriptive and apolitical account of culture enhances Greenblatt's Foucauldian legacy of "political grid-lock" (a phrase I steal from a conversation with Lee Patterson, who invented it).

85. Greenblatt, *Renaissance Self-Fashioning*, p. 6.

86. Greenblatt's dissertation was partly on Orwell.

87. Stephen Greenblatt, "Loudun and London," *Critical Inquiry* 12 (Winter 1986), 343.

88. Ibid., pp. 341, 342.

89. Ibid., pp. 341, 343.

90. Greenblatt, *Renaissance Self-Fashioning*, pp. 5, 6.

91. Ibid., p. 256.

92. Ibid., pp. 203, 204, 205, 206, 207, 208.

93. Ibid., pp. 209–210.

94. Ibid., pp. 214, 220.

Chapter 2. The Return of William James

1. *Selected Critical Writings of George Santayana*, ed. Norman Henfrey (Cambridge: Cambridge University Press, 1968), 1: 149–150.

2. William James, *"Pragmatism" and "The Meaning of Truth,"* introduction by A. J. Ayer (Cambridge: Harvard University Press, 1975), pp. 28–29.

3. Ibid., p. 98.

4. Stanley Fish, "Consequences," *Critical Inquiry* 11 (March 1985), 435.

5. James, *Pragmatism*, pp. 122–123.

6. C. S. Peirce, *Selected Writings*, ed. Philip P. Weiner (New York: Dover Publications, 1966), p. 103.

7. James, *Pragmatism*, p. 126.

8. Ibid., p. 71.

9. Ibid.

10. Ibid., p. 124.

11. See, for example, ibid., pp. 31, 40, 125, and F. O. Matthiessen, *The James Family: A Group Biography* (New York: Alfred A. Knopf, 1961), p. 633.

12. Michael Herr, *Dispatches* (New York: Avon Books, 1978), p. 92.

13. James, *Pragmatism*, pp. 17–18.

14. Ibid., p. 18.

15. Ibid.

16. Matthiessen, *James Family*, p. 626.

17. Ibid., p. 622.

18. Quoted in Cleanth Brooks, R. W. B. Lewis, and Robert Penn Warren, eds., *American Literature: The Makers and the Making* (New York: St. Martin's Press, 1973), 1: 10n.

19. *The Selected Writings of Ralph Waldo Emerson*, ed. Brooks Atkinson, foreword by Tremaine MacDowell (New York: Random House, 1968), pp. 430–431.

20. Ibid., p. 427.

21. Ibid., p. 123.

22. Ibid., pp. 5–6.

23. Ibid., p. 148.

24. Ibid.

25. Herbert Marcuse, *Negations: Essays in Critical Theory*, trans. Jeremy J. Shapiro (Boston: Beacon Press, 1968); see the essay "The Affirmative Character of Culture."

26. Emerson, *Selected Writings*, p. 26.

27. Ibid., p. 263.

28. William James, *The Principles of Psychology* (New York: Dover Publications, 1950), 1: 226.

29. Ibid., p. 291.

30. Ibid., pp. 297–98, 299–305.

31. Matthiessen, *James Family*, pp. 624, 626, 633.

32. Ibid., pp. 633, 635.

33. Ibid., p. 398.

34. The relevant documents are collected in W. J. T. Mitchell, ed., *Against Theory: Literary Studies and the New Pragmatism* (Chicago: University of Chicago Press, 1985). For my critique of Richard Rorty's relationship to neopragmatism see *Criticism and Social Change* (Chicago: University of Chicago Press, 1983), pp. 15–19.

35. James, *Pragmatism*, p. 18.

36. Steven Knapp and Walter Benn Michaels, "Against Theory," *Critical Inquiry* 8 (Summer 1982), 723, 742.

37. For pragmatism as a woman see James, *Pragmatism*, pp. 43–44; on rationalism as an Old World gentleman, see pp. 38, 40. The metaphor of pragmatism as a woman is infrequent in James; rationalism as a "gentleman" is common.

38. I allude to the classic treatment of intellectuals in *The German Ideology*.

39. Fish, "Consequences," p. 444.

Chapter 3. Writing after Hours

1. Shere Hite, *The Hite Report on Male Sexuality* (New York: Ballantine Books, 1982), p. 74.

2. *Letters of Wallace Stevens*, selected and edited by Holly Stevens (New York: Alfred A. Knopf, 1966), p. 180.

3. Cheryl Walker, *The Nightingale's Burden: Women Poets and American Culture before 1900* (Bloomington: Indiana University Press, 1982), p. 23: "Twain's allusions may be obscure now but they would not have been so in their day. His humor depends partly upon their accessibility." See Ann Douglas, *The Feminization of American Culture* (New York: Alfred A. Knopf, 1977), for a major and (to me) persuasive account of the subject of her title.

4. Quoted in Holly Stevens, *Souvenirs and Prophecies: The Young Wallace Stevens* (New York: Alfred A. Knopf, 1977), p. 71.

5. Wallace Stevens, *Letters*, pp. 52–53.

6. Quoted in Milton J. Bates, *Wallace Stevens: A Mythology of Self*

(Berkeley: University of California Press, 1985), p. 4. Bates's book is generally useful as is Glen MacLeod's *Wallace Stevens and Company: The Harmonium Years, 1913–1923* (Ann Arbor: UMI Research Press, 1983).

7. Quoted in Holly Stevens, *Souvenirs and Prophecies*, pp. 82–83.

8. Quoted in ibid., p. 111.

9. Quoted in ibid., p. 78.

10. Quoted in ibid., p. 114. I would have been technically indebted to a few points in Joan Richardson's fine biographical essay on Stevens in *Raritan* 4 (Winter 1985) had her essay not appeared after my own work was drafted.

11. Harold Bloom, *Wallace Stevens: The Poems of Our Climate* (Ithaca: Cornell University Press, 1977), p. 27.

12. Quoted in Holly Stevens, *Souvenirs and Prophecies*, p. 72.

13. Quoted in ibid., p. 73.

14. Ibid.

15. Ibid.

16. Ibid.

17. Quoted in ibid., p. 48.

18. Wallace Stevens, *Letters*, p. 96.

19. Quoted in Holly Stevens, *Souvenirs and Prophecies*, p. 80.

20. Quoted in ibid., p. 71.

21. See the excellent account by Willard Thorp in Robert Spiller et al., eds., *Literary History of the United States* (New York: Macmillan, 1960), pp. 809–826.

22. Quoted in Holly Stevens, *Souvenirs and Prophecies*, p. 40.

23. E. C. Stedman, *Genius and Other Essays* (New York: Moffat Yard, 1911), pp. 82, 85. Originally in *Century Magazine*, February 1884, pp. 599–603.

24. *Letters of Richard Watson Gilder*, ed. Rosemund Gilder (Boston: Houghton Mifflin, 1916), p. 414.

25. Stedman, *Genius and Other Essays*, p. 87.

26. Henry Van Dyke, "The Influence of Keats," *Century Magazine*, October 1895, pp. 911, 912.

27. Helen Vendler, *On Extended Wings: Wallace Stevens' Longer Poems* (Cambridge: Harvard University Press, 1969), p. 49.

28. Quoted in Bates, *Wallace Stevens*, p. 29.

29. Quoted in Holly Stevens, *Souvenirs and Prophecies*, p. 38.

30. Raymond Williams, *Culture and Society, 1780–1950* (New York: Columbia University Press, 1958).

31. Wallace Stevens, *Letters*, pp. 110–111.

32. Ibid., p. 171.

33. Ibid., p. 237.

34. "The Well Dressed Man with a Beard."

35. Quoted in Joan Richardson, "Wallace Stevens: Toward a Biography," *Raritan* 4 (Winter 1985), 42.

36. Quoted in ibid., pp. 45, 48, 54.

37. Quoted in ibid., p. 42.

38. Quoted in Holly Stevens, *Souvenirs and Prophecies*, pp. 81–82.

39. Toril Moi, *Sexual/Textual Politics: Feminist Literary Theory* (London: Methuen, 1985), p. 65. Also see Gayle Greene and Coppelia Kahn, eds., *Making a Difference: Feminist Literary Criticism* (London: Methuen, 1985) for a number of pieces which work outside the essentialist mode.

40. Sandra M. Gilbert, "What Do Feminist Critics Want?" in Elaine Showalter, ed., *The New Feminist Criticism: Essays on Women, Literature, and Theory* (New York: Pantheon Books, 1985), p. 41.

41. Ibid., p. 44.

42. Sandra M. Gilbert and Susan Gubar, *The Madwoman in the Attic: The Woman Writer and the Nineteenth-Century Literary Imagination* (New Haven: Yale University Press, 1979), pp. 17, 89.

43. Ibid., pp. 16, 27, 46, 48.

44. Ibid., pp. 21, 24, 25, 28, 42.

45. Ibid., pp. 86–87.

46. Ibid., p. xi.

47. Ibid.

48. Ibid., p. 71.

49. Ibid., pp. 545, 558.

50. Gilbert, "What Do Feminist Critics Want?" pp. 33, 34.

51. Sandra M. Gilbert, "The American Sexual Poetics of Walt Whitman and Emily Dickinson," in Sacvan Bercovitch, ed., *Reconstructing American Literary History* (Cambridge: Harvard University Press, 1986), pp. 128, 133, 134–135, 138–139.

52. Ibid., pp. 130–131, 140, 142, 144–145, 152. See Gilbert and Gubar, *Madwoman in the Attic*, p. 67: "Most Western literary genres are, after all, essentially male. . . ."

53. Gilbert, "What Do Feminist Critics Want?" pp. 33–34.

54. Wallace Stevens, *Letters*, p. 333.

55. Ibid., p. 669.

56. Ibid., p. 171.

57. Ibid., p. 790.

58. Ibid., pp. 122–123.

59. Ibid., p. 42.

60. Ibid., p. 505.

61. Ibid., p. 604.

62. Helen Vendler, *Wallace Stevens: Words Chosen out of Desire* (Knoxville: University of Tennessee Press, 1984), p. 41.

63. Wallace Stevens, *Letters*, p. 603.

64. Ibid., pp. 621–622.

65. Ibid., p. 79.

66. Ibid., pp. 740–741.

67. Ibid., pp. 237, 831.

68. Ibid., p. 446.

69. Ibid., pp. 231, 232, 237.

70. Ibid., p. 639.

71. Ibid.

72. Ibid., p. 230.

73. Ibid., p. 245.

74. Ibid., p. 301.

75. *New Masses* 217 (October 1, 1935), 41–42.

76. Wallace Stevens, *Letters*, p. 286.

77. Wallace Stevens, *The Necessary Angel* (New York: Alfred A. Knopf, 1951), p. 30.

78. Karl Marx and Frederick Engels, *The German Ideology: Part One*, ed. with an introduction by C. J. Arthur (New York: International Publishers, 1978), pp. 42, 49.

79. Wallace Stevens, *Letters*, pp. 241, 244, 245, 246, 247; Peter Brazeau, *Parts of a World: Wallace Stevens Remembered* (New York: Random House, 1983), p. 245.

80. Joseph Riddel, *The Clairvoyant Eye: The Poetry and Poetics of Wallace Stevens* (Baton Rouge: Louisiana State University Press, 1965), p. 165.

81. Bloom, *Wallace Stevens*, p. 167

82. Wallace Stevens, *Letters*, p. 538.

83. Wallace Stevens, *Necessary Angel*, p. 62.

84. Quoted in Holly Stevens, *Souvenirs and Prophecies*, p. 60.

85. Wallace Stevens, *Opus Posthumous*, ed. with an introduction by Samuel French Morse (London: Faber and Faber, 1957), p. 177.

86. Wallace Stevens, *Letters*, p. 431.

87. Ibid., p. 659.

88. Ibid., pp. 393–394.

89. Quoted in Holly Stevens, *Souvenirs and Prophecies*, p. 48.

90. Wallace Stevens, *Necessary Angel*, p. 30.

91. Brazeau, *Parts of a World*, pp. 184–187, 212–214.

92. Quoted in Holly Stevens, *Souvenirs and Prophecies*, p. 87.

93. Fredric Jameson, *The Political Unconscious: Narrative as a Socially Symbolic Act* (Ithaca: Cornell University Press, 1981).

94. Wallace Stevens, *Letters*, pp. 229–230.

95. Ibid., pp. 230–231.

96. Ibid., pp. 278, 280.

97. Ibid., p. 505.

98. Ibid., pp. 323–324.

99. Ibid., pp. 324, 333, 337.

100. Ibid., pp. 393–394.

Index

Rusche, G., 36

Santayana, George, 13, 104–5
Sartre, Jean-Paul, 23
Savage, Philip Henry, 142–43
Schiller, Friedrich von, 217
Shakespeare, William, 6, 91, 158,
 169–70
Shelley, Percy Bysshe, 17, 19–20,
 185
Showalter, Elaine, 159
Sigourney, Lydia, 160
Smith, Adam, 121
Stedman, E. C., 160, 162, 163, 167,
 168
Stevens, Elsie Moll, 138–40, 169,
 171–72, 208–9, 218
Stevens, Garrett, 140–42, 143,
 146–47
Stevens, Holly, 216, 218
Stevens, Wallace, 3–27, 112–13,
 114, 115, 135–244
Stoddard, R. H., 160

Taine, Hippolyte, 86–90, 93, 94,
 96
Taylor, Frederick (and Taylorism),
 61, 65–66, 70–71

Tennyson, Alfred, Lord, 158, 183,
 186–87
Twain, Mark, 139, 186

Van Dyke, Henry, 160, 162–63
Van Geyzel, Leonard, 237–38
Vendler, Helen, 159, 166–67,
 204–5, 218
Vermeil, F. M., 55
Virgil, 211

Walker, Alice, 189
Washington, George, 3, 5
Weiss, Paul, 232–33
Wendell, Barrett, 143
Whitman, Walt, 13, 139, 158, 165,
 180, 186–87, 190–93, 242
Williams, Raymond, 87, 168
Winthrop, John, 114–15
Wittgenstein, Ludwig, 105
Woodberry, G. E., 160, 162
Woolf, Virginia, 190
Wordsworth, William, 17–20, 64,
 183, 218

Yeats, W. B., 17, 160, 185